Old Stories Retold

Old Stories Retold

Narrative and Vanishing Pasts in Modern China

G. Andrew Stuckey

LEXINGTON BOOKS
A division of
ROWMAN & LITTLEFIELD PUBLISHERS, INC.
Lanham • Boulder • New York • Toronto • Plymouth, UK

Published by Lexington Books
A division of Rowman & Littlefield Publishers, Inc.
A wholly owned subsidiary of The Rowman & Littlefield Publishing Group, Inc.
4501 Forbes Boulevard, Suite 200, Lanham, Maryland 20706
http://www.lexingtonbooks.com

Estover Road, Plymouth PL6 7PY, United Kingdom

British Library Cataloguing in Publication Information Available

Library of Congress Cataloging-in-Publication Data
Stuckey, G. Andrew, 1974–
  Old stories retold : narrative and vanishing past in modern China / G. Andrew Stuckey.
     p. cm.
  Includes bibliographical references and index.
  ISBN: 978-0-7391-2362-1
  1. Chinese literature—20th century—History and criticism. 2. Chinese literature—Taiwan—20th century—History and criticism. 3. Intertextuality. I. Title.
  PL2303.S78 2010
  895.1'09112—dc22   2010002748

Printed in the United States of America

For Jennifer

Contents

Acknowledgments

I owe intellectual and personal debts to many friends and colleagues, teachers and mentors. While I cannot hope to ever repay them, nor are they in any way to blame for the faults that remain, I do wish to acknowledge them in this space. First and foremost, I want to thank Ted Huters who has been my first and best reader. Ted has seen this project at all of its stages and has offered insightful and frustratingly critical comments all along the way. Eileen Cheng, too, has read portions of this study and made helpful suggestions for its improvement. Others also due my gratitude include Henry Cohen, Madeline Chu, Rose Bundy, Kirk Denton, Nick Kaldis, Richard King, Hu Ying, Yomi Braester, Luo Liang, Zhang Enhua, Matt Johnson, Makiko Mori, and Shu-mei Shih.

Portions of Chapter One are updated from "Memory or Fantasy? *Hong-gaoliang*'s Narrator," *Modern Chinese Literature and Culture* 18.2 (Fall 2006): 131-162. My thanks to the editor of that journal, Kirk Denton, for allowing the use of this material.

Finally, my family has provided unstinting support for me. My parents, George and Millie Stuckey, always had faith in my abilities, and I am eternally grateful. But it is my beautiful son, Matthew, and my equally beautiful wife, Jennifer, who put up with me day in and day out. I rely on their love and encouragement.

Chapter 1
Introduction: History, Memory, and Phantasmal Pasts

—In the continual trauma that is "modernity," the question that returns to haunt the Chinese intellectual is that of the continuity and (re)production of culture. This is a question about pedagogy. What can be taught to the younger generation? How is culture—in ruins—to be passed on, by whom, and with what means?
Rey Chow, "Pedagogy, Trust, Chinese Intellectuals in the 1990s: Fragments of a Post-Catastrophic Discourse"

—[The historian] grasps the constellation which his own era has formed with a definite earlier one. Thus he establishes a conception of the present as the "time of the now" which is shot through with chips of Messianic time.
Walter Benjamin, "Theses on the Philosophy of History"

In February of 1917, Chen Duxiu, as a response to and elaboration of Hu Shi's "Wenxue gailiang chuyi" (A Modest Proposal for the Reform of Literature) published just the month before, printed his "Wenxue geminglun" (On Literary Revolution) in which he proclaimed his three tenets for literary revolution:

> 1. Topple the ornate and fawning aristocratic literature and establish a plain and expressive people's literature; 2. topple the decrepit and extravagant classical literature and establish a fresh and truthful realistic literature; 3. topple the pedantic and obscure hermit literature and establish a clear and popular social literature.[1]

It is no surprise that it should be Chen who, in one fell swoop, would denounce what amounts to the whole of Chinese literature and call for a revolution which would erect a literature able to correct the "fault" at the core of Chinese letters, namely that it was "utterly incapable of standing shoulder to shoulder with European [literature]."[2] The literary revolution inaugurated here and elsewhere in the pages of *Xin qingnian* (New Youth) gave birth to a new vernacular literature which, Chen and other likeminded thinkers hoped, would supplant traditional

1

literature. The struggle to escape the influence of traditional literature was, as we might suspect, an unevenly successful endeavor. Indeed, as Ban Wang so eloquently says, "the past is not something one can throw out the window on the morning of enlightenment."[3]

What are we to make of Chen's explicit desire to be rid of the dead weight of all previous Chinese literature when it is precisely (and only) that which had led up to this moment? The logical extension of the argument, and one which was quickly arrived at, was complete westernization; that is, the denial of Chinese identity or specificity. Beyond being an impossibility because of the sheer mass of the Chinese population and weight of tradition, this denial explicitly undermines the ultimate goal that Chen laid out for literary revolution, namely, Chinese parity with the Europeans, not for the Chinese to be newly recreated in the European image.

Chen's article appeared in the context of the so-called "Eastern/Western culture debate" which, as early as 1916 with the establishment of *New Youth*,[4] was largely monopolized by a group of young radicals not least of whom was Chen Duxiu, the magazine's editor. Both sides of this debate principally shared the same terms: a series of (mutually interchangeable depending on the context) dichotomies including East (or China)/West, old/new, traditional/modern, calm/active, spiritual/material, and intuitive/rational to name only the most common. These dichotomies "essentializ[e] cultural difference between China and the West and then giv[e] that difference a temporal value."[5] In the life or death struggle (evolutionary terms also borrowed from the West) in which the Chinese found themselves the only tools which seemed to allow a competitive edge were those associated with the second term in each of the dichotomies, and given the mutually exclusive nature of the terms, choosing the West, the modern, and the new meant rejecting the East, the traditional, and the old. A key effect of valorizing the new and modern at the expense of the old and traditional was the creation of a sharp disjuncture between the future and the past where the present, in accordance with a modern teleology, looks to the future for validation.[6]

What I have been describing here is one embodiment of what Yü-sheng Lin has called a crisis of Chinese consciousness and its concomitant totalistic anti-traditionalism.[7] However, there is an internal paradox involved in this process which Lin does not acknowledge. In a slightly different context, Theodore Huters has insightfully and concisely described this paradox at the heart of the reorientation towards the future and the anxiety created by the association of the modern with the West. It is worth quoting him at some length to indicate the inescapable contradiction of this move.

> This vision [of how the future was to be understood]—which could never quite separate itself from the need to somehow reconcile the demands of continuity with those of the break with the past, as signified by the modern—kept asserting itself largely through its persistent capacity to push alternative possibilities ever farther towards the margins. But in this process, the perception of the legacy of the past invariably turned up as a negative, and anything that became associated with the old came to be regarded as that which had to be left behind. The need to assert continuity was, however, so thoroughly imbedded in the dis-

courses of the modern—mainly nationalism—that a central paradox became lodged in the process of reform itself, in which reform needed to present itself as an internally generated imperative even as it insisted upon rejecting the legitimacy of any possible content to anything marked with the stigma of the past.[8]

The simultaneous pull in opposite directions—the need to assert Chinese strength in the face of Western aggression and the need to deny Chinese tradition as a means to that end—that Huters describes here and the impossibility of its transcendence is what doomed cultural reform of the early twentieth century to ever-increasing radical responses and the ever-increasing recognition of roadblocks obstructing a fundamental transformation of Chinese society which helped to fuel the cycle.

The studies that follow are fundamentally an attempt to explore how narrative literature worked through the tensions created by this paradox in different periods of the twentieth century. Nonetheless, we cannot forget that the Chinese preoccupation with ridding themselves of the past and tradition stems from the political conviction that self preservation required economic, technological, military, and cultural strength that would put them on a par with the global Euro-American and Japanese powers. Thus, while the overarching principle that guides the progress of this study is an examination of the ways the past resurfaces, through invocation or denial, and is redeployed in modern Chinese fiction, we find ourselves coming back again and again to issues of politics. Even if the desire, in a sense masochistic, active in the early twentieth century to deny tradition's impact on the present, as the example of Chen Duxiu above illustrates, seems to have found its apotheosis and solution in a Communist movement bent on achieving a millennial utopia through revolution, we will see that the issue continues to be relevant in fiction from Nationalist Taiwan as well as the post-socialist period in the mainland. In Taiwan, Nationalist cultivation of a cultural foundation facilitating cohesiveness in the state contrasts sharply with Communist attempts to erase tradition and start anew. Thus traditional cultural forms play an intricate role in Taiwanese literary efforts to support the Nationalist government's claim to represent authentic China. On the other hand, thirty years after the founding of the People's Republic of China, the earlier disavowal of the past and tradition came to be inversely mirrored by Roots (*xungen*) writers of the 1980s who, as the name of the movement suggests, sought out links to the past and bridges to tradition which had been denied over decades of political turmoil. As we will see, though, their stories illustrate the ultimate impossibility of recovering an untarnished past even as they recuperate certain aspects of that past.

Modernity and Tradition

The words *tradition* in English and *chuantong* in Chinese are intricately bound up with the question of transmission. The first character in the Chinese binomial *chuantong*[9] is a specific reference to the action of passing on tradition. Anxieties over transmission, of pure and comprehensive transmission or, in historical moments of modernization, of the pernicious influence of continued transmission, reveal themselves as vital concerns in discussions of tradition. However, Raymond Williams has noted in his examination of the term in English, that

> When we look at the detailed processes of any of these traditions, indeed when we realize that there are traditions (real plural, as distinct from the 'plural singular' present also in *values* and *standards*), and that only some of them or parts of them have been selected for our respect and duty, we can see how difficult Tradition really is, in an abstract or exhortatory or, as so often, ratifying use.[10]

The recognition of a multiplicity of traditions in the face of its totalistic and totalizing usage is "difficult" indeed. On the other hand, in many ways, it was precisely the slippage between an always already incomplete, ruptured, and fragmentary tradition and its totalizing presentation that enabled reformers in the early twentieth century to cite certain traditions, the classical language for example, and synecdochically make those aspects stand for the entirety, while all along claiming other traditions—claimed precisely for their putative non-traditional, progressive characteristics—vernacular fiction for example, as precedents and points of continuity with a *Chinese* past that could be cited as examples of Chinese strength in the face of Western cultural and political imperialism.

This making of *tradition* into a pejorative is not uncommon in discourses of modernity and modernization.[11] The rupture with the past and adoption of a linear and teleological temporality, with its resulting valorization of the future is a key component of modernity. But, if there are multiple traditions, then there are likewise multiple pasts that are also sifted, selected, and ignored or redeployed for constructive or destructive goals, as the case may warrant. This, indeed, is the distinction between traditional historiography, in which, in Ban Wang's words, "the classics and history were identical as the repertoire of ancient wisdom and statecraft,"[12] and modern history, which organizes the past into a coherent and progressive sequence reflecting the interests of the nation and its place in global relations.[13]

The adoption of a modern teleology necessarily requires a temporal reorientation towards a valorized future in which the *telos* may be achieved. Thus, as I have been arguing, the modern temporal sense orients itself toward the future while it simultaneously produces history from the past—history mobilized for the achievement of nation-building goals. Such a history systematizes the past for modern understanding, but for this very reason also fossilizes the past as something dead and inactive in the present moment.

Such a repressed past, however, makes its return in the eruptions of memory in lived experience. In a study of two of the foremost practitioners of literary modernity in the West, Elissa Marder demonstrates how the works of Baudelaire and Flaubert pile image upon image of the erasure of experience and involuntary forgetting (a negative figure of Proustian involuntary memory) as artistic protest against the personal psychological trauma inflicted by modernity. Private memory, as an alternate mode of encompassing the past, is denied by modern history precisely because it forsakes collective appropriation of the past and facilitates linking to the past on a personal and individual level. We see an example of involuntary forgetting in *Madame Bovary*, when Emma's lover, Rodolphe, goes through a collection of mementos from their affair, none of which recall Emma's visage to his mind. *Sentimental Education* is perhaps even more clear, for here the possessions of Frédéric's great love, Mme Arnaux, that have the capacity to evoke his experiences in her home are auctioned off and dispersed into the homes and shops of various Parisians, including his current mistress, Mme Dambreuse. The commodification of these items drains the emotional charge they previously had for Frédéric. The dramatization of the erasure of memory in modernist literature, as in these examples from Flaubert, serves to bring to consciousness modernity's rejection of memory.[14]

In China, the political necessity of erecting and maintaining a viable nation-state that could stand as one among equals on a global stage made the achievement of modernity imperative. We see this most clearly in May Fourth and, later, Communist—especially Maoist—literary practices. Nonetheless, even in classic May Fourth texts, such as Lu Xun's stories, a clear tension between memory and history, tradition and modernity can be discerned. Ban Wang, in fact, has argued for an analysis that starts precisely from a recognition of this tension, that demonstrates what he calls "critical historical consciousness":

> Historical consciousness is the ever-intensified self-conscious discourse that criticizes the "natural," embodied, inherited practice based on memory. Premised on the rupture with the past, history is forward-looking and change-driven. The modern "teleological" narratives, be they revolutionary, capitalist, or neoliberal, fit this category. Yet memory, although subjected to historical critique, can also offer a countercritique. . . . Thus we have a critical historical consciousness, which, caught in modern acceleration, is also capable of self-critique from the vantage point of its "other" and past: the milieu of memory.[15]

Although this understanding, which suggests that memory, as a counterbalance to modern historical discourses, operates by drawing attention to that which is forgotten and erased by modern historical discourses, is quite useful for our consideration, I would push Wang's notion a step further. To state the issue more precisely, memory functions by drawing attention to that which is *in the process of being* forgotten and erased. Memory is the phantasmal rearticulation of the vanishing.[16]

Let me give an illustration to begin to explain what is entailed in the notion of memories that are in the process of being forgotten. In his *"Nahan zixu"* (Preface to *Call to Arms*), Lu Xun begins

> When I was young I, too, had many dreams. Most of them came to be forgotten, but I see nothing in this to regret. For although recalling the past may make you happy, it may sometimes also make you lonely, and there is no point in clinging in spirit to lonely bygone days. However, my trouble is that I cannot forget completely, and these stories have resulted from what I have been unable to erase from my memory.[17]

The focus here on what Nicholas Kaldis has alternatively translated as "incomplete amnesia"[18] corresponds to the involuntary forgetting Marder describes in Flaubert and Baudelaire discussed above. Unlike his European counterparts, though, Lu Xun desires to forget and bemoans the inability to fully forget, for the memories are painful in their recollection. However, since he cannot put the memories out of his mind, he uses these incompletely forgotten memories as the basis for his fictional works.

There are two aspects of Lu's particular approach to this problem that are important for our consideration here. First, in China as in the West, the experience of modernity can be conceptualized as a form of trauma. The difference is that, as Kaldis argues, the return to these painful memories marks an ethical stand of the Chinese artist, and perhaps especially Lu Xun, to confront "the passivity and placidity of the ego"[19] which otherwise prefers to avoid and repress the pain associated with forgotten dreams. In Kaldis' argument, this repeated and compulsive return, though it carries no guarantee of success, in effect marks the space that "hope" fills in Lu Xun's creative practice and points to a kind of fundamental optimism that may at first glance seem contrary to Lu's hard-nosed, satirical descriptions of his contemporary Chinese society.

The second point that deserves note is that this construction indicates a conception of memory which, whether pleasant or painful, is precisely in-between remembering and forgetting. Lu Xun has forgotten most of his youthful dreams, but some of those dreams or some portions of them resist erasure. Memory for Lu Xun, here, and for the ways memory is used in this study, is neither replete nor dissipated; it can never return us to the past, but it nevertheless marks the traces of the past that are inscribed in our hearts. I return to this issue again below in my discussion of vanishing pasts.

In my consideration of the tension between memory and history or between tradition(s) and modernity, I am guided by Walter Benjamin's notion of history, especially as refined by Tejaswini Niranjana. Niranjana links Benjamin's well known "The Task of the Translator" with Benjamin's later essay "Theses on the Philosophy of History" to show how in each Benjamin is concerned with describing the afterlife of language/the past. In other words, the arranging of the constellation of "now-time" (Benjamin's *Jetztzeit*) and the piecing together of fragments of language, which are, respectively, the essence of Benjamin's notions of historical work and of translation, are speaking to analogous activities. However, as Niranjana puts it, "This is not to say that the past can, simply, be made whole again. As Benjamin suggests in his ammetaphor [sic] of the amphora [a broken vessel that is reassembled in translation], the fragments that are pieced together in translation were fragments to begin with."[20] It should not be difficult to see how this notion of the reassembly of a fractured past corresponds to Lu Xun's "incomplete" memories. As with language in the process of translation, fragments of the past are subjected to a kind of transformation as they are arranged into new constellations. Translation and history both piece together these fragments of language/the past into new configurations (Benjamin's "constellation") the better to serve present needs. Thus, Niranjana asserts that these activities can and should be "deliberately interventionist and strategic."[21] That is to say, the articulation of the past into new historical configurations disrupts accepted understandings of the past, and as such, can be intentionally pitted against modernist historical knowledge to resist the modernist ends which that knowledge is mobilized to achieve.

It follows from this that Benjamin's sense of history is at odds with the achieved history—achieved in the sense of an active organization, systemization, and construction of history out of the past—of modernist discourse, which I describe above. In fact, the "Theses on the Philosophy of History" is full of statements that explicitly mark Benjamin's concept of history as diametrically opposed to modernist history: "The concept of the historical progress of mankind cannot be sundered from the concept of its progression through a homogenous, empty time. A critique of the concept of such a progression must be the basis of any criticism of the concept of progress itself."[22] It comes as no surprise that Benjamin's famous statement that history is based on "time filled by the presence of the now [*Jetztzeit*]" follows immediately upon these lines. One hardly need add that Benjamin's description of the angel of history, which depicts the angel forced backwards into the future ever gazing upon the past in ruins, is the iconic image of an anti-modernist and anti-progressivist sentiment.[23]

Instead of the constant forward progress of modernist history, Benjamin's conception of history and translation intends to rearticulate fragments of the past/language and infuse them with resonance and relevance for the present moment. In this way Benjamin's history is analogous to the action we have attributed to memory above: to recall a past divorced from a *telos* and pregnant with personal meaning. Indeed, for Benjamin, the work of history is precisely the act of yoking the memories of a specific past era or eras to each other as well as to the present in order to bring them into a new relationship with each other. Therefore, as a clarification, I will use *Benjaminian history* and *memory* to signify this sense of (partial) connection to the past; I will use *modernist* or *nationalist* or *official history* to signify a future-oriented history of rupture with the past.

It needs to be said, though, that by employing this framework of competing historical modes because it is useful in helping us to conceptualize the uses to which various pasts are put, I am not therefore claiming that we can somehow neatly categorize historical work into these two types. Modernist history also selectively "remembers" and arranges certain pasts, and even incorporates alternative voices such as oral histories, into its modernist discourse. The slippage between the deployment of different traditions—classical and vernacular literature—by May Fourth modernizers mentioned above is merely one example of this. As the editors of a recent book on collective memories say, "rather than positing memory in opposition to history, [we] have found that memory is often constructed in an ambivalent relation to—rather than being autonomous from— elite historical discourses."[24] Likewise, the object of my study is the dynamic tension created between the urge to create a modern China and the psychological imperative to remain fundamentally *Chinese*, to move forward without cutting off roots. The chapters that follow, then, from one perspective can be seen as attempts to show the range of possibilities in rearticulating specific pasts in narrative which are opened up by different authors and texts under the influence of different historical moments. Chapter Four, "Interlude," in fact, discusses the ways that even nationalist historical projects from both sides of the Taiwan Strait engage their own pasts and vanishing memories in staking their respective claims to be the one legitimate voice of the Chinese people.

Case Study: *Red Sorghum* and Narrative Order

Mo Yan's family saga *Honggaoliang jiazu* (Red sorghum clan, 1987)[25] presents us with an exquisite example of how memory invokes and re-presents the past. The novel is narrated by a man whose grandparents led a grass roots resistance against the Japanese during the Anti-Japanese War. The story is primarily that of his grandparents, their love story and their war story, but it is their grandson, born long after the events of the story, who tells their story based on what he has unearthed through the memories of those still alive who participated in or witnessed the events. What is especially striking, though, is that the narrator tells the story as if he were physically present, as if the story were drawn from his own memories; that is, he appropriates the memories of others (principally his father and grandfather) as his own, connecting himself to a past that cannot be directly available to him.

There is a wealth of critical literature devoted to *Red Sorghum*. The novel is frequently cited as a representative text of the *xungen* (searching for roots) movement and equally often as a reworking of the historical novel genre.[26] At the same time, other critics highlight the novel's similarities with Magical Realism—similarities that exist irrespective of direct influence; Mo Yan has claimed that he did not read García Márquez's *One Hundred Years of Solitude* until after he had written *Red Sorghum*—and they treat it as an example of experimental fiction.[27] Although "searching for roots" and Magical Realism are not necessarily mutually exclusive, they are seldom invoked together by critics. These varying theoretical frameworks reveal much about the critics who employ them, but perhaps, more important, they point to a complex novel that evades narrow categorizations and exceeds any particular meaning attributed to it.

An integral part of *Red Sorghum*'s narrator's attempt to reconnect with his personal past and family history is the reconstruction through memory of his ancestors' lives that leads him to the conclusion that the race has degenerated (*zhong de tuihua*).[28] The narrator's conviction of the degeneration of the race, as evidenced in the novel, then, is frequently taken as a critique of the Communist and especially Maoist practices which governed life in China after Liberation which, according to this criticism, not only has failed to benefit the Chinese but has actually led to their decline. Although translating *zhong* as "race" is certainly appropriate and, as an important theme in the novel, degeneration of the race may certainly speak to Chinese culture or society as a whole, in a very real way, it is the narrator's sense of his own personal inadequacy vis-à-vis his own ancestral line that leads to his concern with this question. And in this sense we may think of *zhong* as "seed" and, thus, *zhong de tuihua* as the decline of the narrator himself from the former glory of his forbearers. Therefore, although the sequence of events starting from the search for family roots and leading to the realization of his degeneration seems natural, in truth, the narrator begins with a sense of inadequacy that spurs him to seek out his heritage. That is, rather than revealing degeneration, the narrator's personal crisis of identity—"For the first time since I had fled my birthplace ten years ago, bearing the contamination of the emptiness and falsehoods of witty high society, bearing the stench of filthy city life that had steeped into every pore of my body, I stood in front of my Second Grandma's grave"[29]—is what spurs him in the first place to return home in search of something more fundamental, more vital. Memory is the narrator's point of access onto this something more fundamental and vital that has been corrupted because of his removal to the city. In this scene, the ghost of his Second Grandma urges him to bathe in the local river for three days to "wash clean your body and soul, then you will have returned to your own world."[30] The turn from displacing modern discourses to an embodied memory, as represented by this baptism, which is intended to wash away the sins of modern corruption, is what enables the narrator to connect with a past resonant with personal meaning.

The narrator's search for his family's roots confirms a sense of the greatness of his forebears, whom he recalls and re-presents to us, his audience, through memory. As I mentioned above, the narrator is conspicuous in his arrogation of others' memories for his own use, as he does, for example, in this passage from Chapter 1, Section 1, which depicts the narrator's father making his way to the site of a planned ambush of Japanese soldiers:

> After leaving the village, the militia men advanced along a narrow dirt road. The sound of the men's footsteps mingled with the *xisuo* rustling of the grass beside the road. The fog was surprisingly thick and shifting. Countless tiny dots of water crowded together on my father's face and solidified into a large pearl of water. Whenever he touched his hair it would paste itself to his scalp. From the sorghum on both sides of the road floated a faint scent of mint and the bitter but slightly sweet smell of ripe sorghum. My father had early on become accustomed [to this smell], neither new nor interesting. But marching in the fog, my father smelled something novel, a scent between yellow and red, both offensive and pleasant. The smell came out obscurely from the mixture of mint and sorghum and called up a certain extremely distant memory in the deep place of Father's heart.[31]

I must first note the attention to detail exhibited here. In this passage alone we hear footsteps and rustling grass, we feel the moist fog and damp hair plastered onto the narrator's father's head, we smell the sorghum (which permeates the entire novel), and even in a scene which is visually obscured by thick fog, the narrator employs visual synaesthesia to describe the odors in terms of color. As I argue in Chapter Five, the lyrical reliance on figural language, as in onomatopoeia and synaesthesia, is a principal means by which to retrieve and re-present a lost past in narrative. Further, the anti-realist tendency of lyrical language, such as that in this passage, is one of the primary means employed by Roots authors like Mo Yan to resist and propose alternatives to the Maoist discourse that had dominated the cultural scene for at least the two decades prior to the publication of the novel. In this way, Roots texts attempt to reconnect to a pre-communist moment. Specifically for *Red Sorghum*'s narrator, the return to an originary pre-communist past is coterminous with a return to family roots that he can then tap to revitalize his own depleted self.[32]

At the same time, though, it is precisely this degree of vividness achieved through lyrical detail that confirms the reality of the story he is telling. This verisimilitude is possible only with his father's memory, now claimed as the narrator's inheritance. To be sure, it is no accident that the passage cited above ends with the invocation "a certain extremely distant *memory* in the deep place of Father's heart." This memory is invoked and asserted as further proof of the authenticity of the narrator's story. That is, although we are never told precisely which memory (in fact, the next line is a digression about the events of seven days after the ambush), we may speculate that it is a reference to Father's conception, which occurred there in the sorghum fields, and thus would constitute a kind of genetic memory to which the narrator too would have access.

On the other hand, by constantly referring to "my father" or "Father," the narrator both reconfirms the secondhand nature of his information (in a sense, citing his sources and thus further validating its authenticity) and disclaims any responsibility for it; he simultaneously asserts the truth of his tale and forestalls suspicions that he should not have access to these memories. This is perhaps more clearly shown in the narrator's appropriation of his grandmother's voice as she lies dying in the sorghum field:

> Grandma felt exhausted. That slippery handle on the present, that handle on the human world was about to slip through her hands. Is this death? Am I about to die? Never again to see this sky, this earth, this sorghum, this son, this lover who is in the midst of battle? The sound of guns is so far away, everything is blocked out by a thick layer of smoke. Douguan [the narrator's father]! Douguan! My son, come give your mother a hand, hold on tight to me, I don't want to die. Heaven! Heaven . . . Heaven granted me a lover, Heaven granted me a son, Heaven granted me wealth, Heaven granted me thirty years of life as fruitful as the red sorghum. Heaven, since you gave [all this] to me, don't take it back! Forgive me, let me go! Heaven, have I sinned in your eyes? Should I have laid my head on the same pillow with a leper, given birth to a brood of devils with rotting flesh, and pollute this beautiful world? Heaven, what is chastity? What is morality? What is virtue? What is evil? You never told me; all I could do was follow my own feelings. I love good fortune, I love strength, I love beauty. My body is my own, I am my own mistress. I don't fear sin, I don't fear punishment, I don't fear your eighteen-level hell. I've done everything I had to do, I don't fear anything. But I don't want to die, I want to live, I want to see more of this world, my Heaven.[33]

By the third sentence of this passage, the narrator has slipped from recounting his grandmother's death to completely assuming his grandmother's voice as she lies dying of a gunshot wound. I suggest that it is the narrator who has wrested control of Grandma's voice, rather than her voice rising up and overpowering the narrator, because the content of what is related in this passage serves the narrator's ends—namely, showing how great his ancestors were—much better than it serves any possible purpose of Grandma's. That is to say, while it is perhaps unlikely that Grandma's dying thoughts are an existential justification of her life and (over)zealous defense of her morality, this defense of her morality is precisely what the narrator needs to show how much he has degenerated by comparison. And it is precisely because of this degeneration that he needs to reestablish a connection to his ancestors and to his past through the deployment of these memories. There is a trade-off, though, for in the process, Grandma has—as indeed have all the other characters—long since ceased to be herself and has become one of many spokespersons for the narrator.[34] Likewise, the memories which are evoked and invoked over the course of the narrative disassociate themselves from the characters to whom they are attributed and fully become the narrator's own. Nevertheless, it is only in this way, that is by subjecting them to transformation, that the memories of the past can truly resonate with the narrator on a personal and Benjaminian level and become active in the present moment and for the present needs of the narrator himself.

One might object that any character in any narrative is always already the mouthpiece of the narrator, but to my mind this objection is wrongly put. Any character in any narrative is always already the mouthpiece of his author; to the narrator (whether implied or one of the characters himself) is delegated the task of presenting the characters created by the author. The narrator of *Red Sorghum*, in addition to his role of presenting the characters has also claimed for himself the privilege of being the sole voice of the narrative.[35] What I am arguing here is that this arrogation of others' memories as his own is a necessary means for the narrator to establish a historical constellation which resonates for him and serves to counteract the debilitating effects modern life (here signified by his time in the city) has had on his psychology. He needs these memories so that they will not be forgotten; he needs to preserve them before they are completely erased.

Equally as important as the adoption of others' memories as his own to the successful creation of a historical constellation is the narrator's skillful deployment of narrative order to make one coherent whole. In his groundbreaking book, *Narrative Discourse*, Gérard Genette divides narrative "tense" into three constituent parts: (1) order, or the "connections between the temporal *order* of succession of the events in the story and the pseudo-temporal order of their arrangement in the narrative"; (2) duration, or the "connections between the variable *duration* of these events or story sections and the pseudo-duration (in fact, length of text) of their telling in the narrative—connections, thus, of *speed*"; and (3) frequency, or the "relations between the repetitive capacities of the story and those of the narrative."[36]

The question of duration in *Red Sorghum* is an important one. Speed of narration, as measured through the length of text devoted to any given event of the story, in comparison to juxtaposed events becomes, in effect, a study of the rhythmic ebbs and flows of the narrative. A consideration of frequency in the narrative, on the other hand, would note that there is very little repetition, with one significant exception: the execution of Luohan Daye.[37] His execution is first recounted on page 8 (Ch. 1, Section 1) in less than two lines of text in which the barest description of his flayed corpse is given. The second time the story is told (Ch. 1, Section 2, 14–5), little more than three lines quoted by the narrator from the local gazetteer (*xianzhi*) describes Luohan's death, stripping the event of all color and substituting official history for the event itself. Only in the third telling (15–27, 39–46) which spans two sections including the whole of Chapter 1, Section 3 and a large portion of Section 4, does the story blossom into a full recounting of Luohan's death in which every aspect—from Luohan's conscription by the Japanese, to his escape, capture, and skinning alive, to the miraculous disappearance of his corpse in an overnight rain storm—is recalled in the minutest detail. If we compare the third telling with the other two, the contrast between modernist history and Benjaminian history becomes powerful: in the third telling, true links are forged with the past through the fullness of memory; in the second telling, that fullness is denied by modernist history, which appropriates Luohan's death merely as a step toward the revolutionary future of the nation, while the first telling is simply a decontextualized description of Luohan's lifeless and amorphous body, which cannot, then, be made meaningful by articulation into a historical constellation.

Examinations of duration or frequency, however, do not quite reveal the full ramifications of the aspect of the novel that I want to highlight here—namely, memory. For that I must turn to a consideration of order, modifying somewhat what Genette meant by the concept. In the most basic terms, the study of narrative order constitutes a comparison between a chronological telling of a story from beginning to end and various "anachronies" in which that chronological order is disrupted. From the very first pages of *Red Sorghum*, it is quite clear that Mo Yan's narrator is intertwining his temporalities together, binding the present to various pasts. The novel begins in this way:

> In 1939, on the ninth day of the eighth month by the old calendar, my father, the seed of bandits, was little more than fourteen years old. He went with the troop of Commander Yu Zhan'ao, whose heroic name would later spread across the heavens, to lie in ambush at the Jiaoping highway for a Japanese motorized company.[38]

Even in these first two sentences we see references to what was and is no longer (the old calendar) and what will be (Yu's fame), not to mention a specific reference to the narrator's heritage (the seed of bandits). This is followed in the next two pages by a quick relating of (probably) the narrator as a small child at his father's grave many years later (it is unclear, really, when Father dies: this scene likely takes place in the late 1950s, but the text later mentions Father being present at the time of Grandpa's death in 1976), a paragraph-long disquisition on the qualities of Gaomi county, a return to the day his father went to ambush the Japanese,[39] and finally another paragraph on the events of seven days after the ambush (the fifteenth of the eighth month, or Mid-Autumn Festival).

Already we can see the basic division of anachronies into leaps toward the past and leaps toward the future, or "analepsis" and "prolepsis," as Genette terms them, respectively. In my analysis of the novel, I divide the narrative into three basic temporalities: (1) the story, that is the events of the ninth of the eighth month, 1939 and what follows; (2) analepses, which relate events prior to that date; and (3) prolepses, which relate events after that date (if the story has not already reached that point in the narrative). To these three, I add a fourth category, which I call "Asides." Asides are a combination of two of the five functions Genette attributes to the narrator, the testimonial and ideological,[40] in which the narrator discusses various thoughts, feelings, philosophies, and analyses that do not further the plot and therefore constitute a temporal degree zero of the narrative.

I have tabulated, by chapter and section, those portions of the text that fall into each of the four categories. Genette speaks of lines of text as a unit of measurement, but it seems clear to me that in a language like Chinese, in which each character takes up an equal amount of space on the page, the natural unit is certainly the character. When put in numerical form, this approach to narrative order is revealing. First, the temporal schemes of analepsis and story are clearly the most prevalent throughout the novel (overall over half of the narrative is presented as analepsis, while story takes up more than a third—for a total of over 85%). When we compare chapters, we find that Chapter 1 integrates the various temporal schemes much more closely than the other four chapters. Only Section 3 (the first part of Luohan's death) of Chapter 1 is narrated entirely in one temporal scheme (analepsis); whereas, in the other chapters it is quite common for an entire section to be narrated in one temporal scheme. In addition, even when more than one temporal scheme is employed in the narrative, it is very common in the four later chapters to under-employ one or more temporal schemes, while in Chapter 1 about half of the narrative is narrated in a combination of all four of the narrative modes, the time of the story, analepsis, prolepsis, and the temporal degree zero of the narrator's own voice. Nevertheless, to the extent that the later chapters also intertwine the various temporalities, they also make a significant contribution to a complex and carefully deployed narrative order. This is especially true when we consider the fact that Chapters 2 through 5 use analepsis within analepsis or prolepsis within prolepsis as further complications of narrative order much more frequently than Chapter 1.

What, we may ask, does narrative order have to do with memory? To begin to answer this question I may first note that Genette's book is in fact an extended study of a novel obsessed with memory, Proust's *A la recherche du temps perdu*, and therefore comprises methods of understanding (at least in part) the function of memory in the novel. Second, therefore, just as much as in Proust's novel and as I have already begun to argue, memory drives the formation of *Red Sorghum*. On the structural level, analepses in *Red Sorghum*, the most prevalent temporality, are as often as not explicitly presented as memories, usually those of Father. These are almost always introduced with the phrase "Father thought . . ." (*fuqin xiang*) or "Father recalled . . ." (*fuqin xiangqi*). The act of remembering by characters in the novel and the content of those memories, thus, are both important thematic and plot devices. Even more than this, these acts of remembering recall the past (or at least a specter of the past) and re-present it to the character (and through the narrative to its audience). And it is this remembering on the part of characters in the novel that figures the ultimate act of remembering, the novel itself as the narrator relates it to his audience.

Third, the ways all of these modes, not just analepsis, are intertwined and arranged is clearly an act (or perhaps acts) of re-membering and re-articulating different strands of the past into a Benjaminian constellation of history. The explicit suturing of fragmented sections and chapters into one whole narrative, in addition to the seamless weaving of temporalities within sections, enacts the Benjaminian rearticulation of a past in ruins into a historical constellation. Such a constellation is replete with personal significance for the narrator himself and as such is opposed to attempts to absorb his narrative into an official narrative of national triumph over Japan.

In addition, because it keeps the audience off balance and unsure as to where and to what time the narrative will suddenly shift, this intertwining of temporalities also facilitates the narrator's appropriation of all memories in the novel as his own—without calling attention to that fact—and thus enables the assertion of his personal connection to the past. This is true on all levels in the narrative. Above I have discussed the interweaving of temporalities between and within chapters and sections; this interweaving, though, exists on other levels as well. The following passage is but one example of how the various temporalities can be interwoven within a single paragraph. In the following, plain text represents story, underlined text represents prolepsis, italicized text represents analepsis, and bold text represents aside.

> Quickly, the troop turned [off the road] into the red sorghum fields. My father instinctively felt that the troop was moving forward in a south-easterly direction. The country road that they had just taken, which went straight along the Moshui [ink] River, was the only road leaving the village. This narrow country road was a pale white in the daytime. The road was originally made from black, oily earth, but from the passage of many feet the black had worn down to its bottom layer. The impressions of so many flower petal hoof-prints of oxen and goats, the half-circle hoof-prints of horses, donkeys, and mules; horse, mule, and donkey droppings like withered apples, oxen droppings like worm eaten flat cakes, and goat droppings like pattering black beans shaken off the vine were layered on the road. Father often walked this road; <u>later when he was suffering at the Japanese charcoal kiln, this road often flashed before his eyes.</u> *Father didn't know what kind of romantic lead my grandma had played on this road,* **but I know.** *Father also didn't know that Grandma's shining white jade-like flesh had lain on the black earth hidden by the shade of the sorghum.* **But this too I know.**[41]

It could be argued that there is another analepsis beginning with "The road was originally . . ." but I feel that these lines serve more as description of the road rather than as an analeptic leap. In any case, the various temporalities, the story-line item concerning the path the troop takes, quick glimpses of what will come to pass (Father's capture) and what has been (Father's conception in the sorghum fields) are related in a way that serves the narrator's goal of piecing together a historical constellation.[42] It is the narrator's short declarations of his own knowledge (and therefore intentionality), however, that should draw our attention. Here, the narrator claims sole authority over the positioning of a crucial event (Grandpa's seduction/rape of Grandma and Father's conception) in his

Benjaminian historical constellation. He establishes a loose link to Father's conception by obliquely referring to this event, but he also delays a full recounting until he is ready to fix the event in his own personal historical constellation. Thus, we can see that the analeptic references to Grandma are also proleptic in the sense that the narrative has yet to relate those events. That is to say, Father did not know the details of his conception (although the assertion of "a certain extremely distant memory in the deep place of father's heart" just two pages prior to this passage might suggest that on some level Father did know), but even more to the point is that the narrator's audience does not yet know either. Of course, the narrator knows, and he will manipulate this information in a way that constructs the most appropriate (or in Niranjana's terms "deliberately interventionist and strategic") constellation that meets his historical needs and connects him to his heritage.

We should add, though, that this is not merely an exercise for the narrator himself. As extradiegetic recipients of this narrative, we are also able to gain a purchase and a perspective on the historical constellation created therein. And as a result, it has the opportunity to personally and profoundly affect us. It is here, I believe, that we can see how truly at odds a Benjaminian history grounded in the conscious deployment of memory is with modern histories. That is to say, when the historical constellation is revealed to others, it creates a group experience of contact with a fragmented past (in re-articulated form) but does not, therefore, unlike, say, nationalist visions of history, bind those individuals into a unitary, cohesive collective. Thus not only does Benjaminian history tend to subvert progressive histories that seek to produce, not unlike factory assemblage, citizens (or consumers) all from the same mold out of its audience, but it also enables an alternative means of interrelating and collective experience without simultaneously suppressing individuality.

Vanishing Pasts

Certainly, one of the conclusions we may draw is that the narrator's appropriation of other characters' memories in *Red Sorghum* ultimately falsifies his narration.[43] In the end, though, the past is inalienably past, which of course is why Benjamin's angel of history gazes upon ruins, and why, as Niranjana points out, historical work in the Benjaminian sense involves the reassembling of fragments which never belonged to a whole in the first place. Therefore, rather than simply castigate *Red Sorghum* (or the narrator) for failing to erect a "true" Benjaminian constellation linking some primal, "originary" past with the present, I want to argue for a more nuanced reading which takes the fragmentary nature of the past into consideration. The notion of phantasm, which Marilyn Ivy has defined as "an epistemological object whose presence or absence cannot be definitively located," should prove quite useful in this regard.[44] Additionally, if we recall our earlier discussion of memory in Lu Xun, it should not be hard to see how memory which is neither fully forgotten nor fully remembered corresponds to this notion of the phantasmal. Ivy argues that "originary" events can only ever be approached through phantasmal discourses of displacement and deferral. Memory, as a phantasm of a vanishing past, allows *Red Sorghum*'s narrator to construct his Benjaminian historical constellation out of fragments of a past even as it evades complete capture within his narrative. Memory as phantasm, then, cannot be either natural or embodied in the way Ban Wang suggests when he places memory in opposition to modernist history. Memory, however, has not lost its efficacy as an oppositional discourse—it needs only to be understood differently. That is to say, memory, as a "countercritique," points to the vanishing of the past as opposed to modernist history, which seeks to fossilize the past as history. Perhaps we can say that memory also slows the speed with which the past vanishes. Hence, as *Red Sorghum*'s narrator constructs his history out of memories, his own and those of others, he enacts the process of shaping vanishing pasts into a meaningful and personalized relationship with what has gone before. As a phantasm of a deferred and displaced past, memory not only reveals the ruins upon which Benjamin's angel of history gazes, but also reauthorizes both past and present to mutually illuminate each other. Furthermore, as recipients of this historical work, we the audience join Benjamin's angel as witnesses to the wreckage of the past and thus are also included in the collective illumination of past and present.

In a slightly different context, David Wang has reminded us that the *Erya* defines "ghost" (*gui*) as "that which returns" (*gui*).[45] The etymological relation between ghosts and returning (specifically *gui* means to return home) matches a cognitive connection which is possibly obvious only in hindsight. Ghosts certainly are returnees, but they are more (or perhaps I should say less) than that too. Ghosts return differently; they return transformed; they return as phantasmal fragments of their former selves. Ghosts are dead, but they gain a certain reanimation in their return through their interaction with the locales and people of their former life.

Take, for instance, the ghost of *Red Sorghum*'s narrator's Second Grandma. In her incomplete, fragmentary, and spectral return at the narrator's invocation she gains a second life, one which, even in its insubstantiality, augments the sum total of her former life in the relationship she (re)creates with her step grandson. This relationship, of course, works in both directions, for the narrator is likewise transformed (renewed) in the baptism his Second Grandma prescribes to cure his ailments. This is precisely the reactivation of the past in the present *and* the present in the past that Benjaminian history enables. But it hinges on the messianic and liberatory transformation that is based precisely on the fragmentary, phantasmal, vanishing nature of a past in ruins.

The following studies, then, explore the ways modern Chinese fiction has illuminated and is illuminated by certain pasts or traditions even as they vanish away. For all of the individual studies in the project, the citation and circulation of traditional or historical resources are taken as analogous to Benjaminian historical constellations and so are examined with an eye to the alternative historical sensibilities they enable, or in a few cases, fail to enable. Principally, as the title of this book, *Old Stories Retold*, indicates, my focus is on the modern redeployment of previous literature. As I have been arguing above, however, there is no unified Past that these texts seek to tap. As will quickly become clear in the individual studies below, each author and each text establishes its own bond with specific fragmentary pasts, some real and some imagined, to reconstitute a (new) relationship between itself, those pasts, and its readers. Each text goes about this process of constructing Benjaminian constellations in different ways according to its own needs. A main goal for this study, then, is to elucidate how and why each text reaches out to those particular pasts or traditions and the effects created therein. Thus, I hope that the individual studies, taken together, will reveal a range of possibilities available to narrative literature in Twentieth Century China for creating these resonances with various pasts and traditions.

In Part One, this examination takes the direct form of tracing intertextual connections between twentieth century texts and specific earlier, predecessor texts which are parodied by their modern "copies." My use of the term parody differs from its standard usage in English in that the texts I examine do not ridicule their predecessors through exaggerated mimicry; rather, they attempt to supplement the original with a new interpretation and thereby establish their own superiority. Thus, in this section, I am concerned with the connections drawn between text and text and the uses for which those connections are deployed. Chapter Two explores Lu Xun's largely understudied *Old Stories Retold*, specifically its earliest story, "Mending Heaven," as a parody of, in this case, the Chinese origin myth of Nü Wa who creates mankind and repairs a broken heaven. In his new version, Lu Xun puts a distinctly May Fourth interpretation on his traditional sources, but simultaneously reanimates them and reconfirms their inherent force even in the modern age. Chapter Two also takes up the story "Shi Xiu" by Shi Zhecun, one of the principal Shanghai modernists of the 1930s. "Shi Xiu" retells one episode from the classic Chinese novel, *Water Margin*, which relates the events leading to Shi Xiu and his sworn brother, Yang Xiong, joining the bandits gathered in the marshes. Shi Zhecun, in his retelling, opens Shi Xiu's thoughts to Freudian psychoanalytical interpretation as a way of diagnosing the pathology of Chinese tradition, but, in my reading, the traditional text proves to be more than an inert subject and displays an inherent resistance to Shi Zhecun's program.

The last study in Part One, Chapter Three, looks at two late twentieth century examples of parody, both written by Han Shaogong. There are two principal differences between these two parodies and the previous two examples. First, while the parodied texts are clear in each case, Han does not actually tell the same stories; rather, Han's parodies conform to the narrative structure of their respective predecessor texts while inserting new characters and settings. Second, Han Shaogong's revisions of earlier texts, Zhuangzi's famous butterfly dream in "The Homecoming" and Lu Xun's "The True Story of Ah Q" in "Dad Dad Dad," re-enunciate and extend the originals rather than deconstructing them. What is especially interesting is that in the second case, a modern May Fourth text is already traditional by the mid 1980s.

Dividing Parts One and Two is a brief Interlude. The Communist revolution at mid-century led to divergent literary and cultural evolutions in the mainland and Taiwan (this statement is, of course, further complicated by the fact that their preceding literary and cultural evolutions were never the same given Taiwan's fifty years of colonization under Japan). This chapter discusses the major points of divergence in terms of the relationship with Chinese traditional culture, using texts from both locales produced between the 1940s and the 1970s as examples. I also point to aspects of convergence in Taiwanese and Mainland literature of the 1980s and 1990s.

In Part Two, on the other hand, I complicate the structure of connections probed under the rubric of parody in Part One by multiplying the source texts referenced in later texts, by exploring the recycling of modes, styles and themes in addition to specific texts, and by contrasting the ways these techniques develop in the mainland with the ways they develop in Taiwan. Chapter Five explores Shen Congwen's redeployment of a certain Chinese poetic lyricism and the question of temporality in narrative. I compare a similar intent of the 1980s "Roots" authors' adoption of lyricism and examine why the literary temporality created thereby changes in these later texts.

Chapter Six deals with Bai Xianyong's collection of short stories, *Taipei People* which describes the lives of mainlanders in Taipei and their nostalgia for a lost homeland. For example, there is the story "Roaming the Garden, Waking from Dream." The title of the story refers to one of the most popular scenes from the famous Ming Dynasty opera, *Peony Pavilion*, which the main character is known to have performed exceptionally well when she was a singer and courtesan before retreat to Taiwan. The intersection of nostalgia for earlier (happier) times on the mainland, the performance of arias from this scene, the perpetuation of an elite culture that that entails, and the parallel plots of the original play and the short story constitutes a nexus of past and present, tradition and modernity, history and politics that I tease apart in this chapter.

Chapter Seven looks at Wang Anyi's popular novel from the mid 1990s, *Song of Everlasting Sorrow*. The novel tells the story of a modern, urban beauty pageant finalist and her several love affairs. At the same time, the title is, of course, taken from Bo Juyi's ballad about the love between the Tang Emperor Xuanzong and his favorite concubine Yang Guifei and the political turmoil to which it gave rise. Bo's poem and this story went on to influence the Qing dynasty drama *Palace of Everlasting Life* by Hong Sheng. I examine the intertextual resonances and historical sensibility that Wang Anyi's novel creates as it plays with this heritage even as it tells a different story.

Finally, Chapter Eight focuses on Zhu Tianxin's novella *The Ancient Capital*. *The Ancient Capital* is an extended musing on the transformations Taipei has undergone from colonial Japanese rule to the mid 1990s. The novella's narratee (the story is a second person narrative), who frequently travels back and forth between Kyoto and Taipei, takes an impromptu tour of Taipei following the directions of a colonial-era Japanese guidebook. As she tours the city, she contrasts what she actually sees with her own adolescent memories of the Martial Law period cityscape as well as with the descriptions of the various locales in the guidebook. At the same time, the novel establishes multiple intertextual resonances with, most prominently but not exclusively, the Nobel prize winner Kawabata Yasunari's novel *The Ancient Capital* (the same Chinese characters as

Zhu's novel) by quoting from Kawabata's novel on many occasions. These resonances construct an implicit comparison between Kawabata's heroine (and her relationship with her sister) and Zhu's heroine (and her relationship with her daughter and her friend A). I focus on the novella in this chapter, then, as a palimpsest of "the ancient capital" superimposing Taipei of the Japanese colonial era, Kyoto, Martial Law era Taipei, and contemporary Taipei on one another through memory, architecture, intertextual connections, and a guidebook.

Part I
Parody: Traditional Narrative Revamped

Chapter 2
Tradition Redux: Parody and Pathology

I will begin with an examination of what is commonly called historical fiction but which I will, instead, consider as examples of parody. As with so much in modern Chinese literature, I will start with Lu Xun, specifically his short story "Butian" (Mending Heaven, 1922). In addition I will also look at Shi Zhecun's short story "Shi Xiu" (1931). There are several aspects of these stories which make them especially interesting for the study of the uses of the past in modern Chinese literature. First, both stories are set in China's past. In this alone they stake a claim for the continued relevance of the past in their own modern society (even if only a negative relevance). Second, while both stories were eventually published in collections of historical fiction often treating more properly "historical" people and events, in the case of at least these two stories, both the original and their modern revisions are purely literary, which is to say mediated solely by the written word. And these intertextual relationships will be the focus of this chapter and model the kinds of analyses I will pursue in later chapters. Finally, both stories perform their respective parodies not through mimicry and ridicule, as the usual understanding of the term *parody* in English might lead one to believe; rather, each attempts to update its original by supplementing a modern, and as it happens, Freudian perspective to the original story. I will return to these issues again below, but before turning to the stories themselves, I would first like to explore parody as a framework in which we can then place the two stories for examination.

Parody

Definitions of parody frequently trace the word back to the Greek *parodia* which is alternatively glossed as a song sung in opposition or an imitative song.[1] While claims that appeals to a word's origins reveal the "true" meaning of the term are open to debate, it is interesting to note the ambiguity that such a definition creates. A song sung in opposition implicitly offers a critique of the thing opposed whereas an imitative song very easily could be adulatory (imitation is, after all, the finest form of flattery). At the same time, the potential for imitation to hold its object up for ridicule (what we could say is the common understanding of *parody* today) is by no means ruled out by such ambiguity. What is, at least, certain is that a parody is a work of art that is spurred into being by another precursor work of art.

At the same time, satire, a word which is imbricated with and in many contexts interchangeable with parody, works on more or less the same terms. The etymology of Satire traces the word back to the Latin *satura* which is generally accepted to signify a particular type of food made from a wide variety of ingredients. Its use to designate a genre of writing, then, is seen as a metaphor for a diverse, eclectic and rich literary form, but which also could be taken, as Gay Sibley has suggested, as "a mixture of ingredients that were blended in such a way that only those with 'discriminating palates' could come close to knowing what it was they were tasting."[2] Again we run into an ambiguous and potentially self-contradictory definition: that is, a vibrant and inclusive form versus an esoteric form intended for the initiated.

To complicate matters, both satire and parody rely heavily on irony. Following Linda Hutcheon, at its most basic level, irony is nothing more than "the opposition between an intended and a stated meaning or, simply, . . . a marking of contrast" but she also goes on to add that, in a pragmatic sense, irony also judges.[3] Thus ironic texts (including both parody and satire) highlight difference and implicitly assign values to either side. This, of course, is the source of criticism found in ironic texts: the flow of relative values from one side of the divide to the other. Furthermore, we now realize we should understand irony, satire and parody each as a mode (or in Hutcheon's terms, an ethos) that transcends genre. Indeed, we could add other modes, such as travesty, pastiche, and burlesque among others, which interrelate with irony, satire, and parody and each other in such close and complex ways that precise distinctions become increasingly impossible.[4]

Nevertheless, we should be wary of applying Western terms like *satire* and *parody* wholesale to Chinese texts. On the one hand, satire has long played a role in Chinese literature—from the Warring States period philosophical polemics (some passages of Zhuangzi in reference to Confucius come to mind) to the seventeenth century novel *Rulin waishi* (*The Scholars*), which was so influential to May Fourth writers—and as such its continued pertinence seems assured. The history of parody, on the other hand, as a category of classification, is much hazier, if it exists at all. This fact notwithstanding, I feel that, for at least the twentieth-century stories like "Mending Heaven" and "Shi Xiu" that update older tales, the Chinese saying *jiuping zhuang xinjiu*, which literally means pouring new wine into an old bottle, may provide us with an indigenous view of parody. Certainly in the 1920s and 1930s, the import of Western concepts and styles was actively pursued and attempts were made to synchronize these Western imports with Chinese society analogously to pouring new wine into an old bottle. Freudian analysis, which both Lu Xun and Shi Zhecun employed in their revisions "Mending Heaven" and "Shi Xiu," is one example of such an import. Additionally, it must also be admitted that the phrase "pouring new wine into old bottles" in effect describes the essential action that parody takes, for parody takes new content and pours it into the old form of a previous text. This metaphor also preserves parody's dual action that we discussed above, namely imitate (here in preserving the shape of the original bottle) and oppose (here the new taste contained in that vessel). I suggest that we keep both understandings of "pouring new wine into old bottles" in mind as we consider not only the infusion of foreign theories (Freudian psychology) but also the use of a new (or at least unremarked) literary technique, namely parody.

Parody, however, for it to work at all, requires both imitation and variation, both proximity to and separation from the parodied text which it uses to produce an ironic difference between the two texts. Thus "one has to have a certain knowledge of the pre-text (even if it stems only from the parody itself) and to use it to perceive the alterations of the parodied text in the parody."[5] Otherwise the parody fails as a parody. Furthermore, Andreas Böhn distinguishes between parody as genre and parody as technique. The latter is employed along with other literary modes and techniques to achieve an effect, such as might be found in more contemporary texts, for example Wang Shuo's *Wan'rde jiushi xintiao* (*Playing for Thrills*, 1989). The former however, which Böhn defines as "nearly identical repetition of the form of the pre-text with change to the content,"[6] seems to describe both "Mending Heaven" and "Shi Xiu" fairly well.

Before coming to the texts themselves, I would like to take a closer look at irony and especially its role as contrasting agent. Fredric Bogel has suggested that, "satire is not a response to a prior difference but an effort to *make* a difference, to create distance."[7] Bogel's point is equally pertinent to our subject here. Irony, then, as it is used in satire or parody adds something extra to the topic at hand, generally in an attempt to exaggerate. Motives notwithstanding, the end result is that irony supplements a given scenario. *Supplement*, as Derrida reminds us, is an ambiguous word also with two meanings: to supply something which is lacking and to supply something additional.[8] We will see that "Shi Xiu," and "Mending Heaven" in fact do nothing more nor less than supplement the original on which they are based. And it is this extra something, which simultaneously fills a gap and is utterly superfluous, that marks the separation between the original and its parody, that differentiates, that makes them into two distinct, yet comparable, entities which when viewed in relation to each other (either directly or by implication) reveal value.

These stories, as I hope to show, could not have been written without such a technique of differentiation. This technique, furthermore, recalls another multivalent term which Derrida employs: *différance*. *Différance* again means two things, to differ and to defer. It is that which enables thought, and yet is itself unthinkable. As Derrida himself says, "*Différance* is not only irreducible to any ontological or theological—ontotheological—reappropriation, but as the very opening of the space in which ontotheology—philosophy—produces its system and its history, it includes ontotheology, inscribing it and exceeding it without return."[9] This is because language and philosophy, to name only two, are systems based on mutual exclusion; one word in a language or one philosophical term means exactly what no other word or term in that language or philosophy means.

> Thus one could reconsider all the pairs of opposites on which philosophy is constructed and on which our discourse lives, not in order to see opposition erase itself but to see what indicates that each of the terms must appear as the *différance* of the other, as the other different and deferred in the economy of the same . . . And on the basis of this unfolding of the same as *différance*, we see announced the sameness of *différance* and repetition in the eternal return.[10]

Here is the rub; we are faced with the paradoxical conclusion that differentiation is (only) a deferred sameness. I would like to make one final note before turning to the texts themselves. Margaret Rose has called parody's action an "ambivalent renewal."[11] Admittedly, I have taken this phrase out of context, but I think that her description is suggestive and appropriate to what my readings will reveal about "Mending Heaven" and "Shi Xiu."

We should note, in addition, that this notion of an ambivalent renewal also resonates with the notion of Benjaminian history and vanishing pasts that we discussed in Chapter One and which inform this entire study. If, as we have discussed, for Benjamin, history emerges from the interplay of a fragmented past with present concerns, and that each is activated in the other, then parody similarly redeploys a past text for the purpose of achieving present goals. As we will see, though, as with Benjaminian history, not only are those present goals pursued, but the memory of the past text is also reanimated and comes to exert its own influence over the parody.

It will become apparent that since my examples are drawn from two authors and two texts which were actively participating in the modernizing project of early twentieth century China, the energies of parodied text and parody are directed in opposite directions and serve to undermine each other. Put in other words, the examinations of these two stories that follow reveal what we discussed as Lu Xun's incomplete amnesia in the previous chapter. These unforgotten memories of past literature assert themselves within the boundaries of modernizing narratives designed to overturn and denounce the traditional culture for which those past texts are made to stand.

Lu Xun and Chinese Origins in "Mending Heaven"

Lu Xun, of course, was the writer who, with the publication of "Kuangren riji" (Madman's Diary, 1918), first translated the iconoclasm and radical anti-traditionalism of *New Youth* into an artistically achieved short story. He continued this process in creative reworkings of the intellectual and cultural issues most important to the youth-centered New Culture or May Fourth Movement in the stories collected into *Nahan* (*Outcry* or *Call to Arms*, 1923) and *Panghuang* (*Hesitation* or *Wandering*, 1926). Early on Lu Xun had shown an understanding of the critical uses of parody. Most famously, the first chapter of "Ah Q zhengzhuan" (The True Story of Ah Q, 1921) serves up a brilliant parody (as technique in Böhn's terms) of traditional Chinese biographies.

However, after the publication of *Hestation*, Lu Xun channeled his writing into various essay forms, all but giving up fiction altogether. In November and December, 1935, though, Lu Xun wrote four short stories, which he then collected together with four other stories (one written in 1934, the other three from his earlier period of fiction writing 1922-1926) and published as *Gushi xinbian* (*Old Tales Retold*) in January 1936, just months before his death.[12]

Old Tales Retold, as the title suggests, is a collection of updated versions of various legends and myths as well as stories about several of the most important early Chinese philosophers including Zhuangzi, Mozi, Laozi and Confucius. It has been difficult for many critics to place *Old Tales Retold* in Lu Xun's *oeuvre* because of the subject matter and because of the literary techniques Lu Xun employed in their narration, many of which do not fall in line with the mainstream May Fourth realist approach to literature.[13] In attempts to fit the collection in with other realist modes, most have categorized the stories as either historical fiction or political satire and highlighted aspects of the stories which support each position.[14] Neither of these classifications, though, is completely satisfactory, and more recently scholars have dropped them in favor of other more ad hoc terms.[15] In any case, very few seem to consider the book a success, with the possible exception of Marston Anderson who comes a long way in appreciating the complexities of the stories. Unlike these other critics, though, my analysis will focus on the intertextual relationship between "Mending Heaven" and the traditional sources for the story, with special emphasis on the supplement Lu Xun brings to the story.

The general opinion of the book's failure, in no small part, can be traced back to Lu Xun, himself, who in the preface to the collection bemoaned his frequent resort to facetiousness (*youhua*).[16] Marston Anderson directly links this facetiousness to Lu Xun's use of anachrony which "shock[s] the reader into recognizing both the deep penetration of the past into the present and the modern world's perpetual reinterpretation of the past in the light of its own concerns."[17] This mutual connection between past and present is, of course, a major concern of this study, and as such, I will briefly outline Anderson's point. Anderson notes the incongruity of language and social institutions when twentieth century terms and phenomena intrude on stories set in an ancient and in some cases mythic past. For example, the pedantic scholars in "Lishui" (Curbing the Flood, 1935), which retells the story of the sage king Yu who is said to have controlled the flooding of China's rivers, who greet each other in pidgin English "'Gumaolin (good morning)!' 'Haodu youtu (how do you do)!'"[18] even as they debate the likelihood of Yu's success or failure dealing with the floods based on theories of "evolution" or alternatively, the etymology of Yu's name. The absurdities and illogic of the sorts of traditional argumentation which are parodied here are highlighted by the "shock," to use Anderson's (or perhaps Benjamin's) word, created by the contrast of such modern phenomena in ancient contexts and thus reveal the judgment of the parody. Thus anachrony—specifically the irony (facetiousness) established thereby—reveals itself as one of the major components enabling parody in these stories.

The first story in *Old Tales Retold*, "Mending Heaven," was also the first one written. It was finished in 1922 and included in the first edition of *Call to Arms* under the title "Buzhoushan" (Broken Mount). However, because that story was singled out for praise by the Creation Society critic Cheng Fangwu, while the other stories in the collection were disparaged, Lu Xun removed it from all later editions of *Call to Arms.*[19] "Mending Heaven" tells the story of Nü Wa, the mythical creator of mankind as well as the one who repaired heaven with multi-colored stones when its supports were destroyed. The *locus classicus* for the Nü Wa story appears to be in chapter 6 (Lanmingxun, Peering into the Obscure) of the Han era *Huainanzi*. The relevant passage tells how Nü Wa repaired heaven after it split by fusing stones of the five colors and using the feet of a giant turtle as pillars to support heaven. For the story of how she created humans, the earliest source is the *Fengsu tongyi* (Penetrating Customs). Here, Nü Wa is said to have molded men from yellow earth.[20]

Lu Xun takes these fragmentary episodes and combines them into one narrative. This action is not only reminiscent of Nü Wa's fusing of the heavens into one piece, but more important, is also precisely what we mean by the creation of a Benjaminian constellation. Lu Xun, as an important player in the May Fourth modernization project, does this with an activist agenda, namely to reveal the corruption of traditional Chinese culture (here embodied in the origin myth of Nü Wa) and thereby to promote the discarding of tradition in favor of new and modern cultural forms. As we have learned from Benjamin, though, each node of the historical constellation is authorized in its own right and asserts its own perspective. As such, as we will see, the traditional stories of Nü Wa resist serving as tools of their own destruction.

In the first section of Lu Xun's retelling, Nü Wa simply "wakes suddenly" in a, one assumes, newly formed world. She feels "a lack, but also a surfeit of some kind,"[21] which leads her to form men out of the mud almost without intending to do so. As soon as they are created, though, the humans become alienated from their creator and begin to speak in a language Nü Wa finds unintelligible. In the second section, which makes up the bulk of the story, humans wage war upon one another, the fierceness of which punches a hole through heaven. Nü Wa, feeling responsible for her creations' actions, fills the crack in heaven with stones of many colors which she then fuses to heaven with fire from Mount Kunlun. After this she dies from exhaustion. In the third and final section, Nü Wa's story is passed on and warped in the memory of her creations, men.

The irony (facetiousness) of Lu Xun's version is expressed in many ways, but the most prominent is certainly in the juxtaposition of different registers of language, especially in conversations between Nü Wa and men. The following is one representative example.

> She glimpsed one of them staring at her stupidly with white eyes; it was mostly wrapped in strips of iron and it wore an expression of seeming hopelessness and fear.
> "What's going on?" she casually asked.

"Alas, Heaven has collapsed and brought ruin," it said miserably and pitiful-ly. "Duan Xiang was without virtue and rebelled against my lord [Kang Hui]. My lord personally saw to his righteous suppression and [they] battled in the wilderness. But Heaven does not support the virtuous, and verily my master fled . . . "

"What?" She was very surprised because she had never heard anything like this before.[22]

Nü Wa then turns to another human to see if she can get a clear answer, but is again disappointed by the following response:

"No longer are the hearts of men like the ancients. Kang Hui verily had the heart of a swine, and held the heavenly throne through villainy. My lord [Duan Xiang] personally saw to his righteous suppression and [they] battled in the wilderness. Forsooth, Heaven supports the virtuous. My master's martial prow-ess is without equal and he put Kang Hui to the sword at Broken Mount."[23]

Unfortunately, my translations can only approximate the absurdities of these exchanges. Nü Wa's speech and the descriptions given in the narrative (which we take as Nü Wa's perceptions for the most part) are consistently given in a lucid modern vernacular (*baihua*); whereas, the dialogue of the humans she creates is, if not pure gibberish such as "Nga! Nga!" and "Akon, Agon!"[24] are delivered in tortured classical Chinese made even more difficult by the use of archaic and seldom used expressions. In a classic May Fourth maneuver the classical language is, in these exchanges, linked both to sheer nonsense as well as the senseless and brutal violence of human relations. In this way, the case to dismantle (Chinese) tradition and replace it with a civilized, modern society is buttressed.[25]

To further exacerbate the difference marked here by linguistic register, we see that, in contrast to Nü Wa who to the best of her ability consistently (in her modern, realist, and ostensibly transparent vernacular) speaks what she truly wants to say and perceives and describes things as they truly appear to her, her human interlocutors mostly dissemble and rationalize. The examples above demonstrate this fact, both in the differing spins the two warring factions put on the same events, but also most explicitly when using the exact same words, as in "My lord personally saw to his righteous suppression and [they] battled in the wilderness" (*wohou gongxing tiantao, zhan yu jiao*). Or there is the following phrase which is the same except the negative in one is changed to an affirmative in the other "But Heaven does not support the virtuous" and "Forsooth, Heaven supports the virtuous" (*tian bu you de* and *tian shi you de*). The duplicity of the uses to which humans put language is here made explicit.

Clearly, the narrative is structured in such a way as to encourage us the readers to identify with Nü Wa (and Lu Xun) and shake our head in disgust if not actually despise the buffoonery of these men and their self-righteousness. And this conclusion is no surprise when we remember that this story was first penned in 1922 when Lu Xun was at the height of his anti-traditional short story writing career. Nevertheless, a second consideration reveals that the process whereby Lu Xun created this story, taking the several episodes from traditional

sources and changing emphases or details while leaving enough so that it is recognizable as the same story—that is to say, parody—and all of this for politi-
cal/polemical reasons, nicely mirrors the tasks the self-righteous buffoons set for
their answers to perform on their behalf. In other words, the parody of the Nü
Wa myth as performed in this account, is but one spin on the story. Admittedly,
this spin is one that levels a devastating critique against Chinese society, which
here is held responsible for the destruction of heaven, and in the final section of
the story is shown to be incapable of understanding Nü Wa's sacrifice on their
behalf, instead indulging in superstitions as well as continuing their warlike
ways. Nevertheless, Lu Xun's parody, by repeating the ancient story for different purposes, proves to be as equally self serving as the apologists for war had
been.

Let us return for a moment to the beginning of the story where Nü Wa is
said to feel "a lack, but also a surfeit of some kind." This, of course, is exactly
the definition of *supplement* as we have been using it. And this supplement, a
need for something more which arises at the same time as that extra comes into
existence itself, leads to the creation of humans. The creative act is described in
highly sexualized terms (note the Freudian influence) as in the passage below.

> "Ai, Ai. I've never been so bored before," she thought. Abruptly, she stood
> up, raised her arms which were full and round and brimming with vitality, and
> stretched and yawned towards heaven. Thereupon, heaven suddenly lost its
> color and took on a miraculous flesh red. For a moment, she could not tell
> where she was.
> She walked to the seaside under this flesh red sky. The lines and curves of
> her entire body dissolved in a rosy sea. It was only at her midriff that the water
> coalesced into a pure white. The waves marvelously undulated in rhythm,
> sprinkling her body. The pure white shadow fluttered in the water, as if scatter-
> ing in all directions. But she herself did not notice; instead, unconsciously she
> knelt on one leg, reached out her hands, grasped the soft earth still dripping wa-
> ter, and rolled it about several times. Then there was a little something not un-
> like herself in her two hands.[26]

Marston Anderson notes that the addition of Freudian theory marks Nü Wa as
foreign: "Not wishing to bestow further prestige on a tradition he condemned as
'cannibalistic,' Lu Xun seems intent on reinventing traditional images as he borrows them."[27] Nevertheless, the dual action of parody, which allows Lu Xun to
point to the foreign and its representative in the story, Nü Wa, as an alternative
to Chinese civilization, simultaneously points back to Chinese civilization itself.
That is, the story cannot represent a complete escape; at best the escape is partial
for the old bottle of our metaphor cannot be done away with without destroying
its contents. Thus, as in our examination of the linguistic irony performed in the
story, we see again the ambiguous renewal of the original in its différance from
the modern parody.

As we see, Lu Xun cannot avoid "ambiguous renewal" in his parody of the
traditional source. However, this does not necessarily render his critique of tradition invalid. Instead, if we see the intertextual relationships established in the
parody in the light of a Benjaminian historical constellation, even an antagonis-

tic approach of the modern to the traditional (re)kindles an afterlife for the traditional story, from which vantage tradition is able to reflect back upon (or reveal hidden within) the modern parody the very same faults which were leveled against tradition in the first place. Again, this is not to say that traditional Chinese culture was not backwards, superstitious, mendacious, or self-serving. Rather, it is to say that it is only from the perspective of this modern moment that such a claim could ever be made. Additionally, it is to say that making such a claim does not preclude tradition from holding a mirror up to the modern era to reveal its own faults.

Here we see an example of the stubborn power of the past, of a memory of a past text, to resist simply being used as part of the modernizing project and then discarded. The reassembly of the fragmented original story into a new coherent narrative is, as I have said, emblematic of the construction of a Benjaminian historical constellation. As such, it is deployed to achieve certain ends: in this case, the display of the fundamental (and original) faults which form the basis of the entirety of Chinese civilization. In this sense, although ridicule is not its principal mode, this function seems particularly suited to the ways we generally think literary parodies operate. At the same time, the memory of the past text is thereby reanimated and escapes complete control by the narrative intention. Instead, it erupts through the narrative to reveal the narrative's complicity with the very same fundamental and original faults it had thought to denounce. In the same way, we can see this also in the frame of *différance* in which the different— the modern parody—is shown to be merely a deferred version of the original.

From this perspective, it seems quite clear that one would do best to simply let the past vanish at its own pace if modernization is one's goal. But, as we discussed in the previous chapter, Lu Xun bemoans precisely the fact of the past's lingering in memory, of its resistance to complete erasure. For one who wishes to forget, these incomplete memories, as with the Nü Wa myth, mark the complicity and continuity of the modern moment with the past it rejects.

Tradition in Therapy: "Shi Xiu" and the Freudianization of *Water Margin*

The "ambiguous renewal" of a parody's traditional source can be seen even more clearly in "Shi Xiu." "Shi Xiu" was first published in the February, 1931 number of *Short Story Monthly* and then collected with three other stories of the historical fiction genre in *Jiangjun di tou (The General's Head*, 1932).[28] In the early thirties, Shi Zhecun was still at the beginning of his most productive period, which lasted only until 1937 and the outbreak of the Anti-Japanese war. The disruptions of war and the new political dictates of Communist China created an environment hostile to Shi's writing, and so he turned to scholarship (Shi Zhecun was a renowned scholar of Tang poetry).[29] In the years just before and after the publication of "Shi Xiu," though, Shi was editor of several literary magazines culminating in his editorship of *Xiandai (Les Contemporains*, 1932-1935). Also at the same time, Shi, along with friends and colleagues such as Liu Na'ou, Mu Shiying, and Dai Wangshu, was writing and translating more properly modernist fiction and poetry.[30] Thus, in this same period when Shi Zhecun was writ-ing "Shi Xiu" and the other stories in *The General's Head*, he was also writing his (perhaps) better known modernist stories such as "Modao" (Devil's Way, 1931), "Zai Bali da xiyuan" (In the Paris Theater, 1931), and "Meiyu zhixi" (One Rainy Evening, 1929).

I have briefly summarized this, by now, well known account of Shi's career in the early 1930s to begin to show that, despite its typical classification as his-torical fiction, "Shi Xiu" is a modernist story reflecting concerns comparable to those found in "Devil's Way" or "In the Paris Theater." That is to say that dis-cussions of Shi's modernism tend not to examine "Shi Xiu" or the other stories in *The General's Head*; likewise scholarly examinations of "Shi Xiu" generally treat it alone.[31] And yet the close temporal proximity of the composition of these stories certainly indicates a closer connection than is often allowed.

Similarly, all of these stories reflect a concern with male sexuality in vary-ing degrees of (Freudian diagnosed) disfunction. For the male protagonists of these stories, women, as objects of desire, are enticing, but women, as desiring subjects, simultaneously pose dire threats to the protagonists' senses of their own masculinity. For these narratives, the modern discourse of Freudian psy-choanalysis reveals the controlling influence of the libido on human action. If, as Shu-mei Shih has argued, the adoption of modernism as a literary mode by Shi and other writers centered in Shanghai in this period involved a mental sidestep-ping of the implications of Western imperialism in order to embrace a cosmopo-litan outlook, then the implementation of a Freudian psychological framework to present these protagonists, likewise, shows the universality of human nature irrespective of society or culture.[32] In "Shi Xiu," since the story is set long be-fore the Chinese encounter with Western nations, the use of this Freudian struc-ture to "explain" the protagonist removes the possibility of the contingent or accidental exposure to Western culture as the absent cause of the protagonist's psychology. Instead, "Shi Xiu" indicates the universality of human na-ture/psychology which is indigenous to all societies.[33]

At the same time, "Shi Xiu" displays the most clearly pathological and ex-treme version of the male sexual disfunction which is also a main focus of the other modernist stories. This, it seems to me, is no accident. For even if the Shanghai modernists like Shi were not keen on (ostentatiously) overthrowing traditional culture in the same way as Lu Xun, Chen Duxiu, or other May Fourth modernizers were, embracing a modernist outlook necessarily entails a sense of rupture and discontinuity with the past/tradition. While in the West, as in the examples from Flaubert mentioned in the previous chapter, this rupture is expe-rienced negatively, for those Shanghai modernists who, in Shu-mei Shih's words, "flaunted" modernity there can only be a sense of relief at (finally) having got-ten rid of the dead weight of traditional culture.[34] In this way, Shi and his fellow modernist writers were not so different from their May Fourth contemporaries.

As "Mending Heaven" was a retelling of the Nü Wa story, "Shi Xiu" is a retelling of an episode (chapters 43-45) of the classic Chinese novel *Shuihu-zhuan* (*Water Margin*, ca. fourteenth century). Here again we see the reuse of a fragmented text taken from its original context and reformed, akin to Benjamin's constellation, into a modern narrative. The basic plot elements shared by both "Shi Xiu" and its predecessor are that Shi Xiu and Yang Xiong meet, become sworn brothers, and Shi Xiu begins to work in Yang Xiong's family butcher shop; Pan Qiaoyun has an affair with the Buddhist monk Pei Ruhai, which Shi Xiu discovers; after telling Yang Xiong of his wife's betrayal, Shi Xiu devises a plan to catch the lovers with their pants down; although Shi Xiu had warned him not to say anything to Pan Qiaoyun, Yang Xiong begins to berate his wife for her treachery, she then claims that Shi Xiu fabricated the story of her adultery because she had refused his advances; Yang Xiong and Shi Xiu have a falling out, but Shi Xiu understands that Pan Qiaoyun is behind it all and so holds no grudge; Shi Xiu kills Pei Ruhai outside of Yang Xiong's home early one morning as he was leaving an assignation with Pan Qiaoyun and takes his clothes as proof; with this evidence, he and Yang Xiong are reconciled; Yang Xiong takes Pan Qiaoyun and Yinger (her maid who aided and abetted the affair) to Cuibing-shan, a deserted mountain, and with Shi Xiu's help exacts a brutal revenge for his damaged honor; the two then run off to join the group of bandits at Liang-shan.

The modern version of the story makes two significant changes to the narration: first it limits the point of view to Shi Xiu himself, and second it adds the suggestion of romantic love between Shi Xiu and Pan Qiaoyun. Traditional Chinese narrative techniques tend to omniscient modes that yet seldom venture into individual character's minds. By focusing on Shi Xiu, Shi Zhecun in one way limits his story (especially as concerns Yang Xiong) but in another opens up a whole new facet to the story, that of Shi Xiu's inner thoughts and development. Not surprisingly, Freudian psychoanalysis can and does play a significant role in this inner development.[35] The conflict in Shi Xiu's heart between his duty to his sworn brother and the passion he conceives for his sworn brother's wife is the fuel that drives Shi Zhecun's story (and implicitly, the narrative would have us think, the original as well).

Shi Xiu, in this version then, encouraged by her, falls in love with Pan Qiaoyun, but represses his desire out of faith to Yang Xiong. As Andrew Jones says, "On a pathological level, Shi Xiu clearly comes to suffer from what Freud terms 'obsessional neurosis.' Shi Xiu's neurosis, of course, is occasioned by his psychical conflict between adherence to the code of brotherhood (Freud's 'ego instincts') and his sexual desires, his libido."[36] Pan then, since her attempts to seduce Shi Xiu come to nought, commences an affair with Pei Ruhai, the monk. Shi Xiu, whose passion, although frustrated, nonetheless burns as fiercely as ever, translates his sexual desire into a sadistic desire for women's blood: ". . . thus the pleasure of sleeping with a woman, in Shi Xiu's mind, absolutely could not compare with killing a woman."[37] In the end, Shi Xiu comes to fulfill both his duty to Yang and his lust for Pan through this act of sublimation.

We would be remiss, however, if we did not examine the history of Shi Xiu's passion and its transformation into sadism. "Shi Xiu" begins almost a quarter of the way into the story (measuring by *Water Margin*, chapter 44) with a long monologue of Shi Xiu's thoughts on his first night living in Yang Xiong's home. His thoughts range from Shi Xiu's chance encounter with Yang Xiong, and refer to the bully who was harassing Yang Xiong and whom Shi Xiu drives off as well as to Shi Xiu's equally chance encounter with two of the Liangshan bandits who invite him to join them in their hideout. I believe it is safe to assume that hardly any Chinese reader would be unfamiliar with *Water Margin*, and so, these references to Liangshan, brief as they are, are nevertheless crucial because they are the first links establishing a parodic relationship between the two texts. From here Shi Xiu's musings progress to his introduction to Pan Qiaoyun and the source of his disquiet (he hardly sleeps at all): his desire for her which is already consciously present in Shi Xiu's mind. Shi Xiu ends his deliberations with a determination to "self control" for "Is it depraved to conceive a foolish love for a woman after just seeing her? Of course not. Yet it definitely is depraved to fall for my sworn brother's beautiful wife. This is because she already belongs to my sworn brother, is his possession, and to be his sworn brother means there is no hope for me."[38]

It is worth noting that this first section, with the exception of a few phrases drawn from *Water Margin* and one or two lines of quoted (here in Shi Xiu's memory) dialogue which are lifted directly from the original, is entirely Shi Zhecun's addition to the story and is written in what Andrew Jones, following Dorrit Cohn, labels "psycho-narration": "the narrator's discourse about a character's consciousness."[39] A notable exception is the opening phrase, *queshuo*, which translates to something like "as we were saying. . . ." *Queshuo* is a standard opening in traditional Chinese narrative and in "Shi Xiu" instantly throws us the readers into the vein of traditional narrative style, even as Shi Zhecun immediately drops this style in favor of the modern psycho-narration. Thus we can already see the parodic relationship developing between these two texts for the connections between the texts are established, and at the same time distinct differences are immediately erected. That is, Shi Zhecun is adding exactly what the original in *Water Margin* lacks, Shi Xiu's thoughts, fears, motivations and above all desires.

"Shi Xiu" then tells of the following morning, before he is employed in the butcher shop. This again is not found in the original in which Shi Xiu and Pan Gong, Yang Xiong's father-in-law, set the shop up directly. As soon as she hears him stirring, Yinger, the maid, comes into Shi Xiu's room to tidy up. Shi Xiu finds Yinger to be also extremely attractive and thinks, as the narrator relates

> Shi Xiu's consciousness was very clear, since he had already thought seriously about Pan Qiaoyun and made up his mind, then of course just the same he could not have any absurd hopes for Pan Qiaoyun's maid, because this also was disrespectful (*buyi*) to Yang Xiong. However, if we were to ask what kind of thoughts were in Shi Xiu's head at that moment, it couldn't be simpler to explain. To say that Shi Xiu, in the moment when he saw this beautiful maid's face, was dazzled is not as precise as to say he was terrified. Although he knew that Pan Qiaoyun was Pan Qiaoyun, and the maid was the maid, clearly two distinct people, with differences both in face and figure, Shi Xiu, still dimly felt that this maid was Pan Qiaoyun herself. Pan Qiaoyun was this maid, this maid was Pan Qiaoyun. No matter if she was this maid or if she was Pan Qiaoyun, in Shi Xiu's warped vision, she was equally seen as a venomous and terrifying element. Usually, people who quote sayings like "as poisonous as a woman's

heart" are men who have already suffered disaster at a woman's hand, but Shi Xiu had hardly ever had any contact with women before and could not have formed an evil opinion of women. Can we say, though, that Shi Xiu saw the villainy in Pan Qiaoyun and this maid's faces? Of course not. The Pan Qiaoyun and maid that Shi Xiu saw are the same Pan Qiaoyun and maid that we see: two attractive women separated in age by eleven years the likes of which are not easy to find in Suzhou. Then how do I explain describing it thus, saying that Shi Xiu was terrified? We should look for the explanation in the two women's beauty. *It seems that Shi Xiu, in that moment, felt that all beauty was a terrifying steel blade flashing like snow, cold light piercing his eyes, this was beautiful, killing a man, blood splashing all around, this was beautiful, but at the same time also terrifying.*[40]

I have quoted at length here to illustrate both Shi Zhecun's use of and indeed reliance on "psycho-narration" as well as the first step that Shi Xiu takes in his transition from embarrassed young man to sadistic killer by describing beauty in terms of violence and blood. Intense repression of desires such as that described here, as any lay psychologist could tell you, will find release in some form or another. This early association of beauty and desire with violence and blood only increases the likelihood that this release will take a violent form.

One final note on this passage, besides showing the beginning of Shi Xiu's psychological evolution, it also explicitly states the *différance*, the sameness deferred as difference, between Yinger and Pan Qiaoyun. Additionally, in so doing, it implicitly differentiates between Shi Xiu and the women. Women are that which supplements men, to be desired for the extra-male aspects they possess and to be feared for the implied lack in men that they fill. Feminists have long argued that "female nature [is] violently repressed and compromised by patriarchal and misogynistic societies that have prevented a woman from fully knowing herself, other women and womankind."[41] Discourses such as Freudian psychoanalysis which defines a woman by the fact that she "lacks" a penis, that is in terms of men, constitute this patriarchal and misogynistic society. The difference between men and women is then extrapolated to create a whole system of differences, or as Julia Kristeva says

castration is, in sum, the imaginary construction of a radical operation which constitutes the symbolic field and all beings inscribed therein. This operation constitutes signs and syntax; that is, language, as a *separation* from a presumed state of nature, of pleasure fused with nature so that the introduction of an articulated network of differences, which refers to objects henceforth and only in this way separated from a subject, may constitute *meaning*.[42]

Women, of course, are the "casualties" of such a language; it is they who are made into different things into other creatures and assigned meaning through this difference.

Shi Xiu, in the passage above, performs just such an operation of differentiation. The logic expressed here is that the beauty of Pan Qiaoyun and of Yinger is so different from that of a man (that is that with which Shi Xiu could be expected to be familiar) that it is exotic and enticing, but at the same time, dangerous, like a mesmerizing cobra. Furthermore this beauty is generalized to the beauty of all women: "No matter if she was this maid or if she was Pan Qiaoyun, in Shi Xiu's warped vision, she was equally seen as a venomous and terrifying element." Despite the fact that the narrative—as I will argue below, for the purpose of denouncing the traditional text—clearly labels Shi Xiu's thoughts negatively as "warped," it nevertheless, here and elsewhere, continues to unquestioningly engage this language of difference, for as we have seen, parody cannot exist without such separation. This is only the first example of symmetry between the story's misogyny and its parodic activities. Here in the early portions, the misogyny of the text is only implied, but by the end it becomes extremely violent and explicit.

Returning to the text, Yang Xiong, before he goes to work, directs his wife to give Shi Xiu a change of clothes (this detail is also found in the original). When she does, the two meet and have a conversation (which is not in the original). The result of this conversation is to display Pan Qiaoyun's obvious flirting with and enticing of Shi Xiu as well as the fact that as far as women are concerned, Shi Xiu is all thumbs. The text reminds us frequently that heretofore, Shi Xiu had had no contact with women. And it shows. He does not know what is proper to say to women nor does he know how to act around women. At the end of this section, Pan asks him if he is married or not, and blushing and with shame in his eyes he answers no. This, of course, only furthers Shi Xiu's sense of threat from (and secret desire for) Pan Qiaoyun and women in general.

In the third section, Shi Xiu discovers that Pan Qiaoyun used to be a prostitute (while the original states that Pan had been married twice, there is no mention that she was a prostitute), and armed with this information he eventually works himself up to attempt a romantic encounter with Pan. Initially he meets with success, since Pan insists on continuing her leg massage (given by Yinger) which exposes some leg for him to see after Shi Xiu comes into the room. But in the end he is wracked by guilt and leaves abruptly, followed by the women's laughter.

In the fourth section of the text, Pan Qiaoyun begins her affair with Pei Ruhai, the monk, which attracts Shi Xiu's attention. He is ashamed that she would have an affair with a monk rather than a young, strong man like himself, ashamed for his sworn brother's cuckoldry (of course without admitting his own—potential—role as adulterer). To ease his broken heart, but also in the hopes that Pan Qiaoyun will find out and be jealous, Shi Xiu goes to a brothel for the first time in his life. There, while peeling a plum, his chosen prostitute cuts her finger:

> On that white, fine, bright and clean skin flowed a thread of beautiful and delicate scarlet blood. The wound was on her left index finger, and the crimson ribbon slowly trickled until it extended about half an inch. As it passed over the fingernail, it was like a transparent ruby, or a shooting star in the summer racing through the sky and then gone. It flashed in the dim lamp's light and dropped to the floor in the table's shadow.[43]

Shi Xiu is transfixed by the sight of her bleeding hand, and indeed this is the turning point of the narrative. Here we see the final step that Shi Xiu takes in his psychological evolution. And just as in the earlier passage quoted above, beauty is again equated with violence and blood, only this time instead of describing beauty in terms of blood, blood is described with these beautiful and fabulous metaphors of a crimson ribbon, a ruby and a shooting star.

That this moment is the turning point in Shi Xiu's career manifests itself in several ways, one of which is Shi Xiu himself. Not only does the night in the brothel mark the beginning of Shi Xiu's fixation on blood, and especially women's blood, but it also marks the end of his awkwardness and indecision and the beginning of a new, self-confident, and sure Shi Xiu. Certainly it is no accident that this change comes at the moment of sexual initiation. Indeed, in this sense, spilled blood marking the loss of virginity (despite the fact that we are talking about Shi Xiu's virginity and not the prostitute's) effectively tags the later scenes of blood as sexual encounters. Moreover, this change in Shi Xiu's character is clearly reflected in the language used to describe Shi Xiu. Over and over the word *dai* (dull, stupid) and others of similar import are used to describe Shi Xiu (for example, *daizuo*, to sit staring into space), or alternatively in conversation with Pan Qiaoyun, the phrase *dabushanglai* (unable to answer, speechless) or some variation is used. After the night in the brothel these linguistic markers attach themselves to Yang Xiong and not Shi Xiu, a point which I will take up again below.

One other important way in which the brothel scene marks a clear division in the story is that in the first four sections, the narrative makes only the slimmest of references to the original text, instead adding a modern and Freudian take on the story. On the other hand, the fifth and final section of the story, which is also the longest, in which Shi Xiu gets concrete proof of the affair and orchestrates the final denouement on Cuibingshan, follows the original text so closely that perhaps as much as half of the section is quoted directly from *Water Margin*. This quoted material, moreover, is primarily dialogue, though not exclusively so. Indeed, the closer to the end the story gets the more of this quoted material finds it way into the story, until by the last several pages the spoken dialogue is, almost in its entirety, taken directly from *Water Margin*, the few exceptions to this being a word or short phrase added (and in a few cases, deleted) to make these sentences slightly clearer to a modern reader. The dialogue, then, is divided by sections of "psycho-narration" which describes Shi Xiu's reaction to the action and dialogue of the text. For example, there is the scene in which Shi Xiu and Yang Xiong are reconciled and plan how to deal with Pan Qiaoyun. In this quotation and the ones following, italic text indicates quotations taken directly from *Water Margin*.

> *"Brother please take no offense, tonight I will destroy this wretch* [Pan Qiaoyun] *and ease my aching heart."*
> Shi Xiu had a hearty laugh to himself that there was such a rash person in the world, simply crying out for me to manage the situation. He laughed to himself for a moment, and when he had decided what to say said,
> *"Elder Brother, if you do as I say, I'll make a man out of you."*

Gullibly, Yang Xiong said,
"Brother, how will you teach me to be a man?". . . .[44]

I believe that such deliberate and sustained quotation from the original on which
"Shi Xiu" is based can only be understood as a clear claim that the modern "Shi
Xiu" is simply fleshing out the original story. In other words, the motivations,
the emotional states described in this story are already present in *Water Margin*;
all it takes to see it there is to read between the lines. I agree with Andrew Jones
that

> The forced insertion of Freudian psychoanalytic theory into a vernacular text
> also serves as an act of pointed cultural and literary critique. The central opera-
> tive principle of *Outlaws of the Marsh* [*Water Margin*] is the strict code of bro-
> therhood [*yi*] to which each of the outlaws must adhere, under penalty of
> death. . . . If *yi* is the primal (and distinctly patriarchal) *totem* of the bandit
> community at Liangshan, sexuality is its attendant *taboo*. As is made abundant-
> ly clear by the culmination of the original "Shi Xiu" episode, the Liangshan
> brotherhood is founded upon the violent repression and sublimation of hetero-
> sexual desire. This interpretation is reinforced by the fact that it is only after the
> brutal removal of the threat posed by Pan Qiaoyun that Shi Xiu and Yang
> Xiong take up residence at Liangshan. The insight becomes even more striking
> when we realize that this kind of violence against women is by no means iso-
> lated to this particular episode within the text as a whole.[45]

This point can only be felt all the more forcefully by the reader who reads the
two texts together and realizes just how much of it is already there in the original. That is, when the story becomes violent, our attention is drawn to the fact
that this is the original (or if you will, the *real*) story, that this is what the story
has displayed from the very beginning. The rest is simply signage pointing the
way, clues left for the reader to come to a clear and true understanding of what
has been there all along: Chinese culture, as exemplified by the classic novel
Water Margin, is depraved, brutal and above all pathological.

It will be said, of course, that after all there really isn't anything out of the
ordinary here, that this kind of critique of Chinese culture was standard fare for
literature by the 1930s. In fact cultural criticism of this sort had begun several
decades before and had led to a debate in which to be progressive meant to be
Western in all things and which brooked not even the slightest defense of traditional Chinese culture.[46] However Shi Zhecun, as Andrew Jones reminds us, by
inserting the new wine of modern, Western, Freudian analysis into *Water Margin*'s old bottle in order to diagnose and expel the demons of tradition "unwit-
tingly recapitulates the violence of China's encounter with the modern West."[47]
Indeed, Andrew Jones' analysis of the violence in "Shi Xiu" nicely reveals several interrelated and yet distinct levels of violence inherent in the text and also in
the reader's reception of the text. However his analysis fails, in my opinion, to
fully emphasize the gendered nature of that violence.

I have already touched on this above, but here I would like to focus on the
violence in "Shi Xiu" especially as it relates to gender. Although it seems to
infuse the entire story, actually there is no violence (physical at least) in "Shi

Xiu" until the final section. Immediately following the brothel scene, however, Shi Xiu begins to fantasize about how he would handle Pan Qiaoyun, always, of course rationalizing his actions as on Yang Xiong's behalf: "he and Yang Xiong, in the end, would not be able to bear this woman's sight. It serves her right. Although it was none of his business, yet for brother Yang Xiong to be betrayed by her hand. Ai! For a warrior, a hero to be less than a Buddhist monk in a woman's eye is shameful;" and "At that time, because I wanted to preserve Yang Xiong's good name, I didn't dare touch that woman. But she went ahead and destroyed Brother Yang Xiong's reputation on her own. This woman cannot be forgiven."[48] Here, of course, we see threats of implied violence to Pan Qiaoyun because of damage she has caused to Yang Xiong and Shi Xiu's sexuality (or more specifically their control over her sexuality). That is, in the castration language of difference, Pan Qiaoyun has taken up the position of subject rather than object, both in actively flirting with Shi Xiu and in her affair with Pei Ruhai. It is this role reversal that frightens (and also entices) Shi Xiu and elicits his violent response.

When it comes time to actually engage in violence, the gender differences only broaden. Shi Xiu, of course, kills the monk, Pei Ruhai, and his assistant before he kills the two women. Although the text does say, "He had no idea the first time killing a man would be this easy, this straightforward"[49] when Shi Xiu kills the assistant, the description of the man's death, beyond saying the man fell over without a sound, is rather bland and to the point. At the same time, although the description of Pei Ruhai's death is somewhat more lively than the earlier one, it is so only insofar as Pei Ruhai is associated with Pan Qiaoyun:

> Shi Xiu suddenly felt a moment's desire. Not long ago, this was together with that beautiful Pan Qiaoyun's body, it was as if it was her own body, and Shi Xiu couldn't bear to *draw the blade at his bent knee* and strike down. But then he thought of Pan Qiaoyun's venom, how she was divided from his own and Yang Xiong's feelings . . . he also thought of her coldness towards him. . . .[50]

Then Shi Xiu stabs him three or four times and comes to the conclusion that "of everything in the world, killing people is absolutely the most pleasurable."[51] But he immediately moves on to fantasies of killing Pan Qiaoyun, rationalized with statements such as "Because I love her, I want to kill her" and "the pleasure of sleeping with a woman, in Shi Xiu's mind, absolutely could not compare with killing a woman."[52] Thus we see here that rhetorically the violence enacted on women (either imagined or by association) is clearly privileged over that of violence enacted on men because it provides greater enjoyment for the perpetrator. And it is more pleasurable because of the sexual connotation spilled blood carries in this text. Moreover, when compared with the linguistic flourishes and vividness with which the murders of Yinger and Pan Qiaoyun are described, which will be discussed below, the gendered nature of this violence seems irrefutable.

As we progress towards the conclusion, the degree to which one feels this gendered separation of violence only increases. In the passage quoted above, in their planning stages Shi Xiu tells Yang Xiong that he will make a man of him (by showing Yang Xiong how to kill Pan Qiaoyun). As I mentioned earlier, the verbal marker *dai* among others at this point becomes associated with Yang Xiong. He becomes the one who does not know how to handle women whereas Shi Xiu, who "recently had come to understand a woman's heart/mind (*xinli*) very well"[53] does know what to do and how. From this point on, although Yang Xiong is the one actually wielding the knife, Shi Xiu is clearly the puppet master directing his actions. From the devising of the plan to its carrying out Yang Xiong (the virgin) continually looks to Shi Xiu (as the one with experience, the one who understands the true situation and how to deal with it) for the next move, so much so in fact that Yang Xiong cannot even tell if they are finished or not without Shi Xiu's verification. In this way, then, we take it that Yang Xiong is initiated into the mysteries of the other sex.

Finally, on Cuibingshan, both Yinger and Pan Qiaoyun are made to confess in turn, and as I said above, although ostensibly their inquisitor is Yang Xiong, in truth he is Shi Xiu. After their confessions are torn from them (analogously, Andrew Jones reminds us, to the way that Shi Xiu's consciousness is bared for us the readers by Shi Zhecun), in words quoted directly from *Water Margin*, Shi Xiu says,

> "*Today we have all explained the situation clearly. Now it is up to Brother to decide what to do.*" Shi Xiu chose his words carefully.
> Yang Xiong fell into a deep silence, finally he ground his teeth and said,
> "*Brother, take this wretch by the head for me and strip her. Then I will come and serve her myself.*"
> Shi Xiu had been hoping for just such an order and immediately stepped forward. . . .[54]

The narrative then describes in detail how Shi Xiu strips her naked, first her hairpins and then her clothes which he is pointedly said to take off gently, lovingly. Then the same for Yinger, who is killed first. "It was just as Shi Xiu had imagined it would be, her brilliant white skin was covered with fresh, red blood, her arms and legs twitching on their own. Shi Xiu trembled slightly, and thereafter felt exceptionally at ease."[55] It should not surprise us that Shi Xiu's reaction is thus described in terms that easily could also refer to orgasm since we have noted the link between sex and blood from the beginning. The description of Pan Qiaoyun's death too is described play-by-play, following the original in every detail: first her tongue is cut out, then she is disemboweled in words taken directly from *Water Margin*, and finally her breasts and her limbs are cut off.

I have limited my direct quotations from the denouement of the text, because like Andrew Jones, I am wary of the reader's complicity in such violence, especially because of its gendered nature. In other words, Shi Zhecun's retelling of the story provides a psychological profile of Shi Xiu that offers a possible explanation of the motives behind his actions, that gives him the author and us the readers a "pleasure [derived] from our mastery of the text, from the reassuring knowledge that we can know the truth of, and thus dominate, the world around us."[56] "Shi Xiu" as a case study, that is, allows an easy and reassuring knowledge and mastery of, a feeling of superiority over, the past/tradition, insanity, and most of all women.

The text tells us that "Shi Xiu recently had come to understand a woman's heart/mind (*xinli*) very well;" "Shi Xiu reckoned he was thoroughly able to comprehend a woman's heart/mind (*xinli*)."[57] Not surprisingly *xinli* is the same word (following the Japanese) used to translate the Western term *psychology* into Chinese. Our own understanding of Shi Xiu's psychology works on exactly the same premises as his understanding of a woman's psychology does. Furthermore, it is Shi Xiu's understanding of women that gives him mastery over their bodies and control of their sexuality, that gives him the power to script their death and dismemberment. I must mention again the standard feminist critiques of Freudian analysis which claim that Freud's "explanation" of women authorizes a certain—unwarranted—control over judgments about what constitutes "normal" or "abnormal" female sexuality; as Hélène Cixous says "beware, my friend, of the signifier that would take you back to the authority of a signified! Beware of diagnoses that would reduce your generative powers."[58]

In the exact same way, it is Shi Zhecun's understanding of the original text that gives him mastery of its body and the power to disembowel it before our eyes and for our pleasure, for the sense of control this scene gives us over the traditional novel (and all that it represents). It need hardly be said that this mastery and power derives from the parodic techniques of supplementing and differentiating the original. Thus the seamless splice in the final section of original text together with its parody reinforces and exaggerates the violence of the text. This interweaving, as with the reconnection of the fragmented Nü Wa story in "Mending Heaven," marks the Benjaminian constellation created between the modern "Shi Xiu" and *Water Margin*. And as we saw in the case of "Mending Heaven," the reanimation of the traditional text in the modern context enables the past to reflect on and reveal the ruptures and discontinuities inherent in the present moment itself. In other words, it seems that in many ways, "Shi Xiu," rather than revealing any truth about its predecessor, tells us much more about the fears and hopes of the modern moment vis-à-vis traditional Chinese society.

Indeed, it is the ironic separation of and at the same time connection between parody and parodied text, new wine and old bottle, that creates a value differential which in turn allows the modern "Shi Xiu" the power to dissect *Water Margin* the way it does. To be done effectively, "Shi Xiu" needs to walk that fine line between proximity and distance which is created by the weaving together of quotation from *Water Margin* and "psycho-narration." And it is this same process of ironic separation, in the sense of the marking of contrast which Julia Kristeva called the language of castration, that allows Shi Xiu power over Pan Qiaoyun. Thus the symmetrical techniques of the narrative methods employed in revising the text of *Water Margin* and the misogyny Shi Xiu practices preclude any effective critique of that misogyny arising from within the text and indeed can only lead to a certain enjoyment of it as Andrew Jones has said. That is, while the motivation lying behind the parody "Shi Xiu" seems clearly to be a song in opposition, the narrative becomes, through the very action of *différance* that enables it in the first place but returns in the end to a sameness which is only deferred, a song of imitation. And from the vantage of Benjaminian history we see this as the capacity of the past to powerfully affect the present. As with the critiques leveled against tradition in "Mending Heaven," the diagnosis that Shi Xiu suffers from an obsessional neurosis can in no way be adduced from *Water Margin*, unless one *supplements* the reading with Freudian psychology. It would be a mistake, though it clearly is what the modern narrative would have us do, to believe that this supplement simply fills a hole left empty by the original. As our reading of "Mending Heaven" indicates, a similar conclusion can be drawn for Lu Xun's revision of Nü Wa's story. New wine, in the end, can't actually change the old bottle, the coloring may shift revealing new facets, but the bottle in itself is the same. That is, the potential for parody to provide new insights about the parodied text exists equally as much as its potential to distort it, and in fact, I would say parody usually does both. Ultimately, "Shi Xiu" and "Mending Heaven" air what very well may be valid critiques of *Water Margin* and China's myth of origin, but at the same time, they manage to recapitulate and give new voice to the mendacity, ignorance, brutality, and above all to the misogyny that they wanted to expose.

The modern disavowal of a totalized "tradition" erects a fetish in its place, just as Shi Xiu's denial of his desire for Pan Qiaoyun leads to his fetish for women's blood. The modern fetish, in this case Freudian theory, compensates for the loss of continuity with the past but also stands in for the denied tradition.[59] This dual action, like the dual actions of the *supplement* and of parody, marks the upsurge of Benjaminian history, which connects to the past, into the modernizing discourse, disrupting the latter's hopes to discipline the past into a teleological process. It is the dynamic tension created between modernity and tradition, rather than the triumph of one over the other, that should draw our attention. This tension reveals the interconnection, even if oppositional, between past and present, between modernity and tradition, between parody and parodied text.

Chapter 3
Return to the Primitive: De-civilized Origins in Han Shaogong's Fiction

In this chapter we will turn our attention to two other parodies. While the processes involved in the creation of these parodies is comparable to those described in Chapter One, there is also a significant difference: these parodies do not retell exactly the same stories as their predecessor texts. Instead, these parodies fully incorporate the narrative structure of the texts they parody, but new characters and settings supplement the original stories. Rather than Freudian psychoanalysis or some other explanatory discouse, then, the new wine that these parodies bring to the parodied texts is precisely a new story which is, nevertheless, through the action of *différance* recognizable as the same story.

If the parodies of the modernizers at the beginning of the twentieth century, which we examined in the previous chapter, aimed at undermining the valence of traditional thought and texts and as a result unintentionally reiterated them in a modern vernacular, the parodies of Han Shaogong we will discuss in this chapter, "Guiqulai" (The Homecoming, 1985) and "Ba ba ba" (Dad Dad Dad, 1985), seem to excessively identify with their originals and thereby explode them. It is perhaps surprising that these stories were written at more or less the same time as Han's influential essay "The Roots of Literature."[1] In this essay, Han argues that strong literature is connected to its roots; the deeper those roots go the stronger literature will be. In a way, Han certainly has reconnected with his literary roots in these parodies, but as our examinations will reveal, he also blows them out of all proportion so that they become grotesque and debilitating. In an almost inverse motion to what we observed in "Mending Heaven" and "Shi Xiu," the songs of imitation that Han produces come round full circle to become songs of opposition, subverting the traditional texts being parodied. The historical constellation established by linking the traditional and modern texts, in this case then, produces a thoroughly radical and non-progressive temporal scheme in which the memory of a vanishing past is constantly refreshed in an incessant oscillation between past and present. As a result, a static temporality of an un-changing present which is also the eternal past is created in these stories.

An Un-Homely Homecoming

In Han Shaogong's "The Homecoming," Huang Zhixian, the protagonist, finds the village he is passing through to be strangely familiar. He says,

> A lot of people have said it before, on occasion when they go to a place the first time, for no apparent reason they feel that place is familiar. Now I have al-so had this experience.
> I was walking. From place to place, the dirt path had been washed away by the mountain springs, leaving clumps of dirt here and rocks exposed there like sinew and bone and dried out organs when a body's skin has been stripped away. There were several rotting stalks of bamboo in the gulley as well as a tat-tered cow lead. They were signs that a village was about to appear. Several dark and motionless shadows leered out of the small ponds on the side of the path. Before I paid them any attention, they seemed to be rocks, but when I looked closely I discovered they were the heads of young water buffalo staring disconcertingly at me. [Despite being merely calves] they were all wrinkled and whiskered, old as soon as they were born, genetically old. Behind the banana grove ahead was a square fort, with the cold, cold eyes of cannon protruding and thoroughly black walls like it had been smoked, like congealed night. I had heard stories that this area was full of bandits that were a scourge on the locals. No wonder each village had a fort, and the homes of the mountain folk clus-tered tightly together, thick and sturdy, scared and hunkered. Windows opened tiny little eyes, high up so the bandits couldn't use them to get in.
> This all looked so familiar to me, and yet also strange, like when you look at a word, the more you look the more it seems like that word, but also the more you look, the more it seems wrong. Damn, have I been here before or not? Let me speculate: when I step onto the stone road up ahead and round the banana grove, just left of the oil press perhaps I will find an old tree behind the fort. A ginko or a camphor struck dead by lightning long ago.
> In just a moment, I found that my speculation was proven correct. Even the emptiness of the hollow tree and the two children playing with fire in front of it seemed to be part of my imagining.[2]

Huang Zhixian begins the narrative with this passage and indeed continues to speculate about what he will see several more times as he progresses, each with the same result. Similarly, the locals welcome Huang as an old friend returned after "more than ten years, eh?"[3] but insist on calling him Glasses Ma (Ma Yan-jing).

The (mis)recognition of this village as well as of Huang/Ma as at once fa-miliar and strange is nearly the textbook definition of the uncanny. Anneleen Masschelein traces Freud's etymology of the German term *unheimlich*:

> In the lengthy display of dictionary entries Freud reproduces, there are several difficulties which have to do with the negativity of the notion. Un-heimlich is the negation of the adjective heimlich, derived from the semantic core of Heim,

home. Except, it turns out that heimlich has two meanings. The first sense is the most literal: domestic, familiar, intimate. The second meaning departs from the positive, literal sense to the more negative metaphorical sense of hidden, secret, clandestine, furtive. One might say that a certain change of perspective has taken place: in the positive sense, heimlich takes the inside-perspective of the intimacy of the home. In the negative sense, by contrast, the walls of the house shield the interior and in the eyes of the outsider, the secludedness of the inner circle is associated with secrecy and conspiracy.

Unheimlich in the sense of strange, unfamiliar, uncanny, eerie, sinister . . . is then clearly the negation of only the first meaning of heimlich and as such, it almost coincides with the second, negative meaning of heimlich. . . . Freud concludes his lexicographic research by stating that the specificity of the sensation of the uncanny lies in the fact that something is frightening, not because it is unfamiliar or new, but because what used to be familiar has somehow become strange. He quotes a phrase by Schelling which formulates precisely this relation: "unheimlich is what ought to have remained hidden, but has nonetheless come to light."[4]

We should note, first, the similarity between this construction of the uncanny and the ghostly notion of something returned but in transformed shape which we discussed in Chapter One. The unease created in both contexts is a result of the strange transformation of a familiar object, or, as in this case, the strange transformed into the familiar. To return to "The Homecoming," Huang/Ma suffers from precisely this sort of displacement since his perspective is simultaneously that of insider and outsider without the benefit of a rational explanation (for example, that he actually is Glasses Ma returned after a long time away). The strength of this disconcerting sensation is produced by what we may call the "double take." The alarming transformations objects undergo when they are reviewed—the rocks which become buffalo heads, the fabricated landscape of the hollow tree which becomes memory when it appears—is a kind of haunting, a visitation of "what ought to have remained hidden." The use of the term *gui* (ghost, devil, strange) is indicative of this process. In the passage quoted above, it appears twice (translated first as "disconcertingly" and second as "damn"), and while the literal sense of "ghost" is not invoked, it is precisely the uncanny sensation of seeing the dead returned which is created by Glasses Ma's return to this village in the guise of Huang Zhixian. And we can understand this, also, in the sense of a ghost as "that which returns," discussed in Chapter One. The transformation a ghost undergoes as it returns is precisely the transformation of the strange made familiar, of the hidden revealed. As the story progresses even though the relationship between Huang and Ma is inverted, the uncanny sensation evoked by their connection remains just as powerful.

Let us probe the memory which appears here for a moment. The past to which this memory is linked has vanished. Like the tree struck dead by lightning, it perished long ago. Instead, as Huang says, "Even the emptiness of the hollow tree and the two children playing with fire in front of it seemed to be part of my imagining." That is, the memory seems to have its origin not in any past but in Huang's imagination. But, uncannily, the memory is nevertheless accurate. All of a sudden, Huang is inhabiting a fiction he has seemed to create himself. This is why this story is not merely one of misrecognition: the villagers' identification of Huang as Ma, rather, comes as corroboration of and further spur to Huang's own prodigal memory.

Huang, for at first he demurs that he is not Ma, eventually comes to inhabit the persona of Glasses Ma, who the locals presume has killed a local bully, Midget Yang. After sharing a meal with the locals, Huang is invited to take a bath, to which he agrees so as not to insult his hosts. It is here in the bath, as in a baptism, that the transformation begins.

> Above, the wild boar oil lamp cast a bluish haze onto the steam, bathing my body in a layer of blue. Before I put my shoes on, I gazed upon this blue me and suddenly had a bizarre feeling, as if this body was a stranger's. There were no coverings here, no other people, no one to pose for, and no conditions; there was only my naked self, my own truth. Hands and feet can produce things; stomach and intestines can eat things; reproductive organs can propagate descendants. For a moment the world was locked outside; having arrived at [this] place had kept me busy, no time to measure or consider these things. Because of the fact that a long time ago a sperm and an egg happened to meet, there was this ancestor of mine. And this ancestor and another ancestor just happened to meet, leading to another fertilized egg, only thus after generations and generations could I come to exist. I too am a blue fertilized egg which exists only because of a series of countless coincidences. Why have I come into the world? What can I do? . . . Like a simpleton, I think too much.
>
> I rubbed an inch-long scar on my leg I got from a cleat playing soccer. But then again it seemed not, rather . . . I got it from the bite of a midget. Was it a misty morning? Was it a narrow mountain path? He was clutching an umbrella, but my gaze scared him so much he trembled. So he knelt down and said he'd never dare to do it again, never again. He also said Er Sao's death had nothing to do with him and that he had not stolen San Agong's buffalo. In the end, he resisted. Eyes nearly popping out, he bit my leg. His two hands gripped the cow lead around his neck but then suddenly sprang away, like two crabs crawling into the mud. After a while, these two crabs slowly stopped and became calm. . .
>
> I didn't dare to think any further, nor could I bear to look at my hands—do they bear the traces of a constricting cow lead or the stench of blood?[5]

Huang's transformation still is not complete. As the last line of the quotation indicates, he is terrified by his thoughts and especially this memory which, on second thought, reaches up and overwhelms his quaint recollection of a soccer accident. And so "At this point I vigorously determined that I had never been here before and never knew Midget Something-or-other."[6] Yet, in the span of just a few lines, he is fully Ma conversing with the ghost of San Agong and later with the sister of a girl who seems to have loved Glasses Ma.

Joseph Lau notes that "The Homecoming" "reads like a *baihua* variant of Zhuangzi's famous Butterfly Dream parable."[7] I fully agree, though Lau's conclusion that "It should be clear that Huang Zhixian is the former schoolteacher [Glasses Ma], whose good deeds in the past are being evoked by the villagers to reactivate his memory"[8] seems much too schematic and logical to fully account for the profoundly disturbing duplication and transformation described in this story. Let us look briefly at Zhuangzi's famous Butterfly Dream:

> Once Zhuang Zhou dreamt he was a butterfly, a butterfly flitting and fluttering around, happy with himself and doing as he pleased. He didn't know he was Zhuang Zhou. Suddenly he woke up and there he was, solid and unmistakable Zhuang Zhou. But he didn't know if he was Zhuang Zhou who had dreamt he was a butterfly, or a butterfly dreaming he was Zhuang Zhou. Between Zhuang Zhou and a butterfly there must be *some* distinction! This is called the Transformation of Things.[9]

Indeed, there must be *some* distinction, but no distinction we try to impose on the two can ever hold up. Who is dreaming whom? We can never say for sure. At best, there is merely a progression from Zhuangzi to butterfly and back again; that is the Transformation of Things. The doubling envisioned in this brief passage and the crossing of categories reflects again the notion of the uncanny as simultaneously homely and not, hidden and revealed. It is also an example of precisely the deferred sameness of *différence* which plays such a crucial role in parody.

If we think of Han Shaogong's recapitulation of Zhuangzi's Butterfly Dream in his story "The Homecoming" in terms of parody which we explored in the previous chapter, we will notice some differences from what we saw in "Mending Heaven" and "Shi Xiu." First, Han is not retelling a story about Zhuangzi dreaming he is a butterfly (or a butterfly dreaming it is Zhuangzi). Rather, Han tells the story of Huang/Ma and their simultaneous occupation of the same body. Second, as a result, the supplement Han inserts into—or perhaps I should say removes from—this uncanny story of (mis)taken identity is not a modern discourse such as psychology but the erasure of the mediation of dream. In this way, Han's parody, rather than a song sung in opposition, as we might label "Mending Heaven" or "Shi Xiu," instead is a song of imitation. This is not to say that Han's imitative parody has somehow tapped the roots of traditional culture or literature and thereby is able to reinvigorate contemporary life, as perhaps we might assume for the author of "The Roots of Literature." No, in its place we find Zhuangzi's lighthearted dream transformed into a pervasive, nightmarish sense of a fundamental confusion of identity from which there is no awakening.

Let us return for a moment to Zhuangzi's dream. It is surely no accident that one of the terms of this oscillation is a butterfly, a creature whose life cycle is defined by a dramatic transformation from caterpillar to chrysalis to butterfly. This silent third (and fourth) term of transformation can allow a vantage on a thoroughly disturbing and uncanny notion that the caterpillar is identical with the butterfly even as we protest there must be *some* distinction. In nature, the transformation requires time and is recognizably a process going from caterpillar to chrysalis to butterfly. And this duration helps to naturalize the transformation and allow a distinction between the several stages of transformation. This fundamental distinction is elided by the nature of dream which can skip the temporal process of transformation and create a notion of relative and immediate equivalence.

If Zhuangzi's dream is already disturbing despite its lighthearted tone, Han Shaogong's narrative gives full reign to the unsettling sensation of two individual identities which claim simultaneous access to the same psyche. This occurs in the bath scene quoted above, which takes on the function of the chrysalis stage whose temporal duration is foreshortened to further enhance the equivalence of each identity and the strangeness of perception. Cut off from the outside world by the cocoon of blue-tinted steam, Huang Zhixian contemplates the sheer contingency of his existence as a series of coincidences, and he emerges as (almost) Glasses Ma.[10]

There is a horror, understated as it is, associated with this transformation, and it is not simply the horror of Huang/Ma realizing he might have committed murder. Instead, this horror stems from the demonic (*gui*) which Freud associated with the uncanny from the beginning. Peter Brooks notes that the demonic arises from "involuntary repetition" or "compulsive recurrence."[11] These two terms, along with ambivalent renewal, certainly are indicative of the actions parodies take in their revisions of traditional texts, including, in this case, Zhuangzi. And surely, in light of the bath scene quoted above, we can see Huang/Ma's transformation as involuntary. And this gives the lie to the notion that somehow Huang was in control of the return of his memories. But even more than this, as a coming home, the uncanny we sense in this story is that home has become unhomely, or as Homi Bhabha says, unhomed.

> To be unhomed is not to be homeless, nor can the 'unhomely' be easily accommodated in that familiar division of social life into private and public spheres. The unhomely moment creeps up on you stealthily as your own shadow and suddenly you find yourself with Henry James's Isabel Archer, in *The Portrait of a Lady*, taking the measure of your dwelling in a state of 'incredulous terror'.[12]

Indeed, in a sense, Huang (as Ma) has found a home here in this mountain village. But the incredulous terror he experiences upon his return (as Huang) causes him to flee back to the district town. There in the inn he falls asleep and dreams that he is walking that mountain road, using the exact same language used in the story's opening, endlessly walking along the road. The narrative lulls us for a moment: Ah ha, we say, this is merely Zhuangzi's dream returned now to its original state of being a dream. We need not fear that Huang is Ma with no distinction, he has simply dreamed it all. Except, the dreamer wakes and makes a phone call to a friend who calls him Huang Zhixian!

> "What did you call me?"
> "Aren't you Huang Zhixian?"
> "Are you calling me Huang Zhixian?"
> "Didn't I call you Huang Zhixian?"
> I am terrified, my mind blank. . . . Is there still someone called Huang Zhixian in the world? And is that person me?
> I am tired. I can never escape the enormity that is me. Mama![13]

Glasses Ma is now confronted with the same unhomely (mis)recognition that Huang faced at the story's beginning. Ma/Huang have equal right to this psyche. The dream does not end upon waking; the transformation is always in process, each completion merely another chrysalis on the way to further transformations. The memories which Ma erased of Huang's former life, as Ma's had been erased earlier in the text, here recur and return in such strength that Ma's consciousness cannot handle the blow. All sense of continuity is lost except for the compulsive oscillation between these two identities.

The Primitive and Unplottable Origins

As homecoming, "The Homecoming" describes the return of Huang/Ma to the place where Glasses Ma spent his rustification as a *zhiqing* (educated youth) during the latter part of the Cultural Revolution. These youth, many of them former Red Guards, were called upon by Mao to "learn from the peasants," and so most of the young urban people left the cities to live in the vast rural stretches of China's countryside. At once a crude political calculation on Mao's part to disperse the increasingly uncontrollable Red Guard factions into the hinterlands, the call was made in explicitly ideological terms of "learning from the peasants." Naturally, in communist logic this is a call to embrace labor on behalf of the masses as remedial to the bourgeois tendencies engendered by the alienation effects of education. That is to say, as elements of the superstructure, the edu-cated are inherently (at least) one step removed from the primary stratum of so-ciety, namely the laboring class. Thus, this ideological justification can be seen to be couched in terms of returning to an original state of naturalness. This ori-gin, in turn, is located in rural areas where the inroads of modern technologies, both productive and ideological, have been minimal.

Many of the youth, rather than a pristine communist utopia of "happy na-tives" whistling while they worked (if I may be allowed a grotesque mixing of metaphors) found ignorance, oppression, and more than anything else back-breaking toil as peasants wrested subsistence from often hostile land. Disillu-sionment was natural in such situations, and in some contexts the rustified youth have been called a "lost generation" because of the missed opportunities a dec-ade spent in the countryside cost them. At the same time, as a foundational expe-rience, many former rustified youth wax nostalgic about their time in the coun-tryside and bemoan the lack of community they found upon their return to the cities, in contrast to what they had known in the countryside.

I rehearse this account of the rustification movement not to make any claims about Han Shaogong's experience.[14] Instead, I want to focus our attention on the fact that the place to which one returns is conceived of as origin. Here, of course, the origin in question is not the communist one of labor, rather it is a cultural origin and perhaps even a literary origin. As I said above, on one level, the story tells of Huang/Ma's return to his place of rustification where, as Glasses Ma, he served as teacher as well as shared in the communal tasks of the village. In a sense, this mountain village is exactly Glasses Ma's origin for the very concept of rustified youth cannot exist without the countryside location of his reeducation. The figure of the rustified youth, like Huang/Ma, is unhomed: he is simultaneously insider and outsider. Symbolically, Ma's glasses, thus, as sign of civilization, both in terms of ophthalmological science and as the typical marker of education, are an indication of his status as an interloper. Nevertheless, the intimate relationships Ma establishes with the local people, from Ai Ba to San Agong to Si meizi and her sister, clearly show that he has been accepted as one of their own—not least because he is presumed to have gotten rid of the hated Midget Yang. In contrast to the phone conversation at the end of the story, these relationships come across as vital and indicative of real human connection, as opposed to the mediated—by telephone and commerce—relationship of his city persona.

But as we see in this analysis, the notion of origin is not simply that of a source; it also carries the connotation of unformed, natural, uncultivated, uncivilized, or primitive. At the most explicit level this primitiveness is indicated by the archaic language the villagers speak. Instead of the modern *wo* (I) the people here use *wu* (I) for the first person pronoun, and instead of the common *kan* (to see) they use *shi* (to see). For baby they say *wazai*; they use terms like *ganrou* (to pursue meat) and *bige shuafang* (to jest) instead of the more modern to hunt and to joke. On still another level, that of surnames, besides being a common family name in China, Ma means horse, and as a horse, an animal, the closer connection of Glasses Ma to the simple and unschooled people of the mountain village is indicated. On the other hand, Huang means the color yellow, which in contrast to horse would indicate civilization, especially since the Yellow River (Huanghe) is generally taken as the cradle of Chinese civilization, and so marks Huang Zhixian as part of modern society.

Additionally, there is a second transformation accompanying that of Huang/Ma in the story. Si meizi says that her sister, who had loved Glasses Ma before his first departure and suffered as a result, has changed into a bird calling for him day after day. Besides again indicating the animalistic closeness of this community and thus its primitivism, there is also a folkloric quality to this part of the story which is quite appropriate for a backwards and backwoods village. Likewise, the parody of this story, as I have argued above, is a way to fully embody Zhuangzi's original and thus constitutes a return to the primitive (but certainly not unsophisticated) Daoist text.

In a different context, Rey Chow has discussed the "primitive passions" of the Fifth Generation filmmakers of the 1980s. Briefly, she argues that the discernable trend of these filmmakers of "returning to nature" can be linked to a reaction to the (in their works often unnamed) Cultural Revolution.[15] The return to nature marks a conscious intent to start over, to experience a new beginning and, for Chow, focuses on "images of landscape, rural life, and women."[16] Chow lays out a series of seven qualities or qualifications which in sum become a definition of "primitive passions," and it is worth quoting her at some length to explore these complexities.

1. The interest in the primitive emerges at a moment of *cultural crisis*—at a time when, to use the terms of this discussion, the predominant sign of tradi-

tional culture, such as the written word, is being dislocated amid vast changes in technologies of signification.

2. As the predominant sign of traditional culture can no longer monopolize signification—that is, as democratization is forced upon it—fantasies of an origin arise. These fantasies are played out through a *generic* realm of associations, typically having to do with the animal, the savage, the countryside, the indigenous, the people, and so forth, which *stand in* for that "original" something that has been lost.

3. This origin is now "democratically" (re)constructed as a common place and a commonplace, a point of common knowledge and reference that was there prior to our present existence. The primitive, as the figure of this irretrievable *common/place*, is thus always an invention after the fact—a fabrication of a *pre* that occurs in the time of the *post*.

4. The primitive defined in these terms provides a way for thinking about the *unthinkable*—as that which is at once basic, universal, and transparent to us all, *and* that which is outside time and language.[17]

The final three items in Chow's list deal with concerns of comparing inter- and intra-cultural analyses, the simultaneous use of *primitive* as both "backward" and "pristine," and her view that film best embodies these qualities. Because they are aimed at the specific concerns of her study, I have not quoted these last three qualifications. Even so, there is much to think about in her first four qualities. In a moment when the universal signifying traditions of communist China had collapsed,[18] writers such as Han Shaogong, no less than the filmmakers Chow discusses, have access to the imaginary notion of "the primitive" which is both self-apparent and requires seeking, which is simultaneously the kernel of self-definition and "no longer" accurate. The primitive is, in fact, thoroughly unhomely for it both is and is not us.

As a striking confirmation of Chow's concern with ethnography and systems of knowledge built upon observation,[19] Huang/Ma, when confronted with the archaic language of the villagers proceeds to interpret or translate it into (comprehensible) modern vernacular.

"Do you still bethink (recognize? remember?) me? We were still repairing the road through Leisi Peak, I'm Ai Ba."

"Ai Ba, I bethink you, I do." I answered despicably . . .

"Do you bethink yourself of the time we went pursuing meat together (pursuing meat might just be hunting)? When I wanted to placate the mountain spirit you spake (said) that was superstition. Afterwhiles, though, I was right, you ran into some *muma* weed and your whole body was covered in spots. . . ."[20]

The parenthetical remarks are, of course, Huang/Ma interpreting for himself (and for us) to try and make sense of what is being told to him. At the same time the parenthetical remarks mark the scientific, classificatory mode of ethnography which implicitly places Huang/Ma in the position of (modern) observer and the local populace in the position of (primitive) observed. The primitive people of this mountain village, then, present a puzzle, indeed a crucial puzzle since solving the puzzle leads to the recognition of Glasses Ma, earthy and savage, as the primitive stage of transformation for this psyche.

As Glasses Ma, Huang/Ma has returned to his primitive origin. It was in this place that, as a savage, he committed murder with his bare hands. This is the place that renewed him. But as a youth undergoing rustification, this origin can only ever be secondary, never primary; that is, he was always already an outsider from the city. And, indeed, on his second return as Huang Zhixian, this origin is further displaced (or replaced?). As he oscillates between Huang and Ma, we come to see each persona as the spectral, vanishing, and deferred reflection of the other, forever each other's past and forever each other's future.

This oscillating relationship between Ma and Huang, then, comes to figure the relationship between parody and parodied text, between "The Homecoming" and Zhuangzi's butterfly dream. That is to say, similar to the continuous transformation between Huang and Ma, we see see Zhuangzi's text transformed in its new incarnation as "The Homecoming." But at the same time, that transformed text, "The Homecoming," continuously points us back to and hopes to explain its primitive origin in Zhuangzi's dream. The chicken-or-egg scenario we can see in this relationship is perhaps the purest version of Benjamin's kind of history that I examine in this study. Here we see the past allowed full access to the present, allowed indeed almost to overpower the present so that typical questions of cause-and-effect no longer apply. The upshot of the parody's full embrace of the parodied text, as for Huang/Ma at the conclusion of "The Homecoming," is the creation of a thoroughly disorienting and even terrifying sensation. Perhaps this is what Benjamin meant by "the messianic" nature of history.

"Dad Dad Dad"

In "Dad Dad Dad," Han Shaogong again returns us to a space of primitive origins. Like "The Homecoming," which as parody returns the primitive original text to us in spades, "Dad Dad Dad" also explodes the original text it parodies into excess and horror. Lau notes that Han is "spiritually closer to Lu Xun than Zhuangzi or Qu Yuan,"[21] and again Lau points us in the right direction. Bing Zai, the focus of the story, is a halfwit who at birth seemed dead—neither eating, drinking, or doing anything at all for three days—and who ultimately learns to speak only two phrases, "F--- your mother" and "Dad."[22] Bing Zai is constantly taunted by the youths in his home, Chicken Head Village, and though he cannot protect himself, clearly expresses his contempt, even without the use of language: "If you glare at him, he understands and will roll his eyes at a point somewhere above your head, showing you the whites, and muttering 'F--- your mother,' he swings his head around and runs off."[23]

Bing Zai himself can only be taken as a grotesquely expanded and updated version of Ah Q, and the story "Dad Dad Dad," then, I will argue, is a parody of Lu Xun's classic "Ah Q zhengzhuan" (The True Story of Ah Q, 1921).[24] Before we explore the parallels between these two texts, though, it is worth briefly noting the ways that "Ah Q" is itself a parody of traditional biographical texts. The very first chapter of the story, titled "Foreword," is a brief essay in the voice of classic Confucian scholarship justifying the taxonomic choices the narrator has made in presenting this story. Of course, this is in line with a venerable tradition of historians explaining their reasons for writing going back at least to Sima Qian and the *Shiji* (Records of the Grand Historian). However, rather than put forward theoretical principles which guided the composition of his text as Sima Qian does in the famous "Biography of Su Qi and Bo Yi," the first chapter of the biography section in the *Records of the Grand Historian*, the narrator of Lu Xun's story describes a series of "difficulties" involved in its composition, each of which is only inadequately resolved. First and foremost is what to call the text. The narrator tries out "Official Biography," "Autobiography," "Unauthorized Biography," "Legend," "Supplementary Biography," "Family History," and "Sketch," but discards each in turn as inaccurate, settling finally, and meekly, on "True Story." Next the narrator considers Ah Q's name, in the vein of traditional biographers, but while Ah Q's surname might have been Zhao, the local landlord family of that name makes it impossible for Ah Q to claim the name Zhao. As for his given name, since the narrator is not sure which of several homophonous characters is used to write Ah Q's name, he is unable to actually write his name. Instead, after a lengthy digression, he opts for the shorthand of using the initial Q which is used in the Romanized spellings of each of those characters. Finally, Ah Q's place of origin, also standard information given at the beginning of traditional biographies, is completely obscure. The one and only thing of which the narrator is sure is the character Ah, a common meaningless character often used in people's given names as a diminutive, in Ah Q's name. Thus, the entire "Foreword" parodies the form of traditional biographies by presenting a biographer who fails in the litmus test of presenting accurate and relevant historical details about his subject.[25]

When we consider "The True Story of Ah Q" as parody of the genre of traditional biography, we will discover that the parody it performs doubles back upon itself. That is to say, Ah Q, not only because of his lowly and obscure origins but even more because of his mean temperament, his provincial views, his limited faculty for rational thought, and most of all his capacity to transform defeat into spiritual victory, is, according to traditional standards, the least appropriate subject for eternal preservation in biographical form. Yet, as a canonical text of the May Fourth period, parodying the traditional biography by choosing to memorialize just such a person simultaneously reveals the debased national character for which Ah Q serves as epitome as well as the inability of the traditional form—and thus of the entire traditional system for which it serves as synecdoche—to continue to signify in a rapidly modernizing society under pressure from foreign encroachments.[26] As negative example, then, Ah Q is precisely the perfect subject for biographical treatment in the modern age since he reveals the cancer at the heart of Chinese society which must be cut out in order to successfully meet the challenges of the Twentieth Century.

Of course, Lu Xun is seldom so simple. The tragedy of "Ah Q" is precisely that while Ah Q is executed—cut out, to use my own terms—his biography is peopled with multiple doppelgangers, from Young D, to Whiskers Wang, to the young men who sometimes beat him or sometimes laugh and encourage him in his harassment of a Buddhist nun, to the average townspeople who generally scorn Ah Q but welcome him to their homes in order to purchase his stolen goods when the opportunity arises, and so on. So we see that sacrificing Ah Q— for a crime he did not commit no less—could never have been adequate to meet the challenge facing a modernizing China. Indeed, in his one moment of lucidity, Ah Q recognizes the eyes of a wolf, "fierce yet cowardly, flashing with demon fire, as if piercing his body from a distance . . . biting into his soul,"[27] in the crowd which gathers to witness the execution. In a society like this which hungers for his death, rather than reforming the society, his death serves only to maintain the society in its comfortable status quo.

Like Ah Q, Bing Zai is the debased spirit of his times who implicates the entire society in his sin. Direct parallels between the two texts, however, are quite meager. Both of their names are empty signifiers: "Everyone needs a name to go on wedding announcements or a gravestone. So he became 'Bing Zai [Number Three].'"[28] The choice of this name is natural, since if we make Bing Zai's first phrase, "Dad," a subject and his second phrase, "F--- your mother," a predicate, the result is "and baby makes three." Even more so, the extreme indifference with which his name is chosen, "Everyone needs a name. . . " further indicates that the name does not matter, it is a convention and a convenience to facilitate discussion, and that is all.

Still, on a more fundamental level the kinship is clear, and in each instance Bing Zai's case is more severe. Where Ah Q suffers at the hands of those of higher social status and torments those below him, Bing Zai can only endure the cruelty of the other village lads. Where Ah Q can rationalize a spiritual victory out of any defeat, Bing Zai can only roll his eyes and cry. Where Ah Q displays no ability to understand the mechanisms of society which act upon him and ultimately lead to his downfall, Bing Zai's mental state, in Rong Cai's words, is "an abyss where no light of self-consciousness ever penetrates."[29]

Additionally, like Ah Q, Bing Zai is not the only example of (moral) degeneracy. To be sure, as Rong Cai argues, Bing Zai, the fatherless child, is the responsibility of the society which produces him. "A child of all, Bing Zai is a faithful replica of his cultivators and their world. The tragic irony is that the villagers fail to recognize that they are looking at a duplication of themselves when they tease and abuse him."[30] This duplication spirals outwards, as well. The people of Chicken Tail Village, with whom Bing Zai's Chicken Head Village feuds over the geomantic influence of Chicken Head Peak, are just as mired in superstition, the only difference being that Chicken Tail Village happens to be victorious in their battles.

The most important duplicate, however, is certainly Bing Zai's cousin, Renbao.

Shi Ren, whose nickname was Renbao, was one of the older young men who was not yet married. He frequently snuck out to the woods to spy on the girls laughing and splashing as they bathed in the stream. He ached with the pleasure created by those white forms. But his eyes were no good; it was all hazy. So to make up for it, he would watch young girls pee or examine certain body parts of female dogs or water buffalo.[31]

In addition to being a myopic peeping Tom, Renbao also (just as Ah Q did) leaves the village to go traveling about. He always brings newfangled things back with him: "a glass bottle, a broken kerosene lantern, an elastic band, a scrap of old newspaper, or a photo of who knows whom. He wore a pair of leather shoes that didn't fit but on a paved road would slap the pavement with a *jiji gege*, which gave him even more the air of being on the cutting edge."[32] Renbao cultivates this air by speaking in Mandarin with all the tradesmen or anyone else who passes through and using words, such as "conservative," which he has picked up on his journeys and which are incomprehensible to his fellow villagers. But as we can see from the list of objects above, what Renbao gains from these trips are of no real use to him or anyone else except for the purposes of self aggrandizement. Even in his attempts to update the language of the villagers' letter to the authorities gets muddled. He suggests they use "report (*baogao*)" instead of "memorial (*bintie*)," but the villagers feel "report" seems too crass. All the same, since Renbao has seen something of the world, they compromise with "re-orial (*baotie*)."[33]

As in "The True Story of Ah Q," these multiple reiterations of Bing Zai's degeneracy serve to indicate the extent to which this corruption has permeated society.[34] However, as in "The Homecoming," Han Shaogong pushes the original text to its limits in his parody. That is to say, if the dilemma posed by Ah Q and his society is dire, it nonetheless has a solution, namely the May Fourth prescription of social and cultural revolution based on Western models. For Chicken Head Village, however, there is no escape from the blighted darkness of Bing Zai's existence. This is indicated in several ways. First Bing Zai's entire story is thoroughly arbitrary. Bing Zai merely is: "When he was born, with eyes closed, he slept for two days and two nights without eating or drinking, like a corpse. It scared his parents witless. Not until the third day did he make one cry, *wa*."[35] There is no reason for Bing Zai's deficiency, and this is only highlighted by the fanciful rationale devised by the villagers to "explain" Bing Zai:

> . . . once many years ago when [his mother] was getting firewood from the kitchen, she accidentally killed a spider. The spider had green eyes and a red body, was the size of a jar, and its web was like cloth. When she burned it, the stench filled the entire mountain and did not dissipate for three days. Clearly, that was a spider spirit who has taken retribution in this life. What's surprising about that?[36]

Likewise, the villagers' treatment of Bing Zai is equally arbitrary. He is reviled and abused until one day someone notices that his two utterances are positive and negative, just like *yin* and *yang*, and as such, they can be used as methods of divination. Whereupon, Bing Zai is feted and called "Honorable Bing Zai," "Venerable Bing Zai," and even "Immortal Bing Zai."[37] But when the arbitrariness of his pronouncements proves too difficult to interpret, he is once more relegated to the position of village idiot. And if there is no underlying basis for Bing Zai's malaise or the ways his society treats him, there can, of course, be no solution.

Second, and more important, Bing Zai is immortal (if not eternal). At one point, the villagers want to use Bing Zai as human sacrifice to solicit the gods for a good harvest. But a clap of thunder just before the sacrifice convinces the villagers that the gods do not approve of such a cheap sacrifice. Even more striking, Bing Zai is one of the first to be poisoned at the end of the narrative. The people of Chicken Head Village, after losing several battles with Chicken Tail Village, decide to move elsewhere in imitation of the myth describing how their ancestors migrated from the coast. As a result the very old and the very young are poisoned so they do not drain the village's resources on the journey. Even poisoning, though, cannot kill Bing Zai.

> Bing Zai suddenly appeared from who knows where—amazingly he hadn't died, and the lesion on his forehead was even less red and had scabbed up. He sat on a wall with bare feet and stirred up the murky water in a broken jar with a stick so that sunlight flashed in its motion. He heard singing [his villagers sing as they leave] from afar, clumsily clapped his hands, and ever so softly, ever so softly mumbled the name of the person he never knew:
> "Dad."[38]

If Ah Q's death does not mark the cure for the social and cultural malaise which he represents, at least he is still human enough to die at his own execution. Bing Zai is not and has never been. Indeed, he is likened to a corpse in the narrative's very first sentence. And it is as animated corpse, as revenant of past (and current) sins haunting the community that we can understand the community's inability to kill Bing Zai. He is already the figure of a dead person (this is a more literal translation of *siren xiang*, which above I translated as corpse), so how can mere poisoning harm him?

The return of a spectral and vanishing past is, of course, a primary concern of this study. The recognition of Bing Zai as a reanimated corpse is related to this but also reveals a significant difference. While phantasmal pasts inform the present moment with their transformative, if insubstantial, presence, the fully corporeal return of the past in the form of Bing Zai is struck dumb and incapable of meaningfully interacting with the present. Arbitrary, as opposed to Niranjana's "strategically interventionist," repetition is all Bing Zai, or indeed the entire Chicken Head Village, can offer.

It is no surprise, then, when we realize that Chicken Head Village, located on the farthest margins of society, represents a space of the eternal present.

> What happened below the clouds seemed not to have much connection to the people in the village. The Qin Dynasty established the "Qianzhong Commandery," the Han Dynasty established the "Wuling Commandery," and afterwards "land reform" . . . This was all heard from some cow hide merchants and opium dealers who had come into the mountains. Talk is just talk, but you still need to rely on yourself to eat.[39]

History is impossible in such a space. Contingency and blind repetition cannot be made to signify a modernist historical notion of cause and effect much less the Benjaminian mutual illumination of past and present.

About the only thing the narrative can offer is a detached, ethnographic study of this society. As in "The Homecoming," the anonymous narrator of "Dad Dad Dad" takes pains to point out the archaisms of Chicken Head Village. For example, there is the term *huafen*:

> *Huafen* is another nebulous concept. It takes a long time for someone on his first visit to this region to grasp what it means. It seems that if one has money, skill, a beard, or a son or son-in-law with potential, then one has *huafen*. The young men all exert their utmost competing over *huafen*.[40]

Archaisms such as *huafen*, the inability for the villagers to understand modern terms such as *conservative*, the various superstitions, such as the one of the spider spirit related above, that the villagers indulge are all displayed as markers of their backwards and provincial world views. Indeed, although Ah Q's biographer seems surprised at himself (and a bit apologetic), he is nevertheless compelled to relate Ah Q's story. The narrator of "Dad Dad Dad," in contrast, is positively gleeful to display the villagers' eccentricities and shortcomings. As a result, the primitive in "Dad Dad Dad," marks the dystopian origins that are the roots of modern Chinese society. But this ethnographic jaunt, too, proves of no use in the attempt to orient the relationship of the primitive origin to the modern present. In part, this is surely due to the objectifying processes of modern ethnographic discourses.[41] But more important, for the purposes of this study, is the recognition that the past is thoroughly cut off from the present. If in Chicken Head Village, as origin, there is no development, only the replication of an eternal present, then there can be no relationship between it and modern society. Or, what is even worse, "Dad Dad Dad," as the modern parody reiterating and expanding the corruption described in "The True Story of Ah Q," indicates that modern society is only another arbitrary repetition of Chicken Head Village.

In "The Homecoming" and "Dad Dad Dad," Han Shaogong returns us to both the collective origins of Chinese culture and to foundational and constitutive texts of that culture. What is especially noteworthy about this is that while the *Zhuangzi* and "The True Story of Ah Q" are clearly both canonical texts in the Chinese tradition, they are in nearly all contexts located on opposite sides of the divide between the traditional and the modern. However, in this case, "The True Story of Ah Q" is, we could say, traditionalized in that it serves as source and primitive origin, an understanding of which, through the processes of modern, anthropological scrutiny, will serve to "explain" the present. This may be surprising until we remember the ways Maoist reading practices[42] codified Lu Xun's texts as primary—in both senses of the word—works of the revolution. In the post Cultural Revolution moment, "Dad Dad Dad," as parody of "The True Story of Ah Q," reveals the latter text's presence, as a reanimated corpse, at the foundations of modern Chinese society. Modernity, then, remains ever "an unfinished project"[43] which leads not forwards but to increasing stagnation.

As a final comment, then, it may be argued that because both "The Homecoming" and "Dad Dad Dad" fully incorporate their respective parodied texts in the modern parodies, the difference in terms of historical effect—of engagement with the past on the one hand and the cultivation of an eternal present cut off from the lessons of the past—lies in the differences between Zhuangzi's butterfly dream and "The True Story of Ah Q." That is to say, the full engagement of "The True Story of Ah Q" in "Dad Dad Dad" includes, ironically, the May Fourth totalistic rejection of the past. On the other hand, Zhuangzi's emphasis on the transformation of things places an explicit weight on precisely the connections and continuities between past and present.

Chapter 4
Interlude: The Maoist (Anti)Tradition and the Nationalist (Neo)Tradition

A noteworthy phenomenon of Communist China is that of the writers active since the May Fourth period, a remarkable number ceased literary production after 1949.[1] This is true of two of the authors discussed in other chapters of this study, namely Shi Zhecun and Shen Congwen, not to mention others such as Qian Zhongshu, Mao Dun, and Guo Moruo. Shi, Shen and Qian all retreated into scholarship; whereas Mao and Guo each took up official positions in the new government. On the other hand, of those who continued to write, many if not all eventually came under attack for various political crimes as displayed in their texts; these include, most notably, Ding Ling, Xiao Jun, and Lao She, the last of whom was hounded to death by red guards during the cultural revolution. Among all the other changes the communist revolution brought to China, the tightening of political control over cultural production was one that altered dramatically the writing of Chinese fiction.

In contrast, very few of the canonical authors of the first half of the Twentieth Century left the mainland for Taiwan when the Nationalist government retreated to that island. Perhaps the major exception to this last statement is Zhang Ailing (Eileen Chang), who did leave the mainland in 1952, but she did not live in Taiwan; rather, she went first to Hong Kong, moved through Taiwan and finally settled in the United States. To be sure, there were writers in the Nationalist fold, such as Jiang Gui (penname for Wang Yijian), discussed below, but it was not until after the Nationalist retreat to Taiwan that they gained prominence.

Irrespective of specific ideologies, for both the Communist and Nationalist parties, cultural activities, including literature, were important aspects of their respective claims to political legitimacy. On the one hand, the Communists, as a revolutionary party, sought to establish an entirely new cultural practice in Chinese society. On the other hand, the Nationalists, as a party in retreat/exile, sought to maintain a certain continuity with traditional Chinese customs, practices, and above all values, as a contrast to the Communist ethos, certainly, but perhaps more importantly, as a psychological anchor in a period of historical chaos when the world seemed to have been turned upside down. In what follows, I will offer some brief thoughts on the processes involved in the diverging evolutions of Chinese literature in the mainland and on Taiwan in order to set the stage for the chapters that follow.

The Fate of National Forms

The process of establishing party control over cultural production first took on full steam in May of 1942, when Mao Zedong addressed opening and closing remarks to a meeting of "workers in literature and art" (*wenyi gongzuozhe*) which lasted for several weeks. By virtue of Mao's leadership of the Chinese Communist Party (hereafter CCP), his remarks had an immediate impact on literary and artistic production, and by the following year when his speeches were published as *Zai Yanan wenyi zuotanhuishang de jianghua* (Talks at the Yan'an Forum on Literature and Art, hereafter *Talks*),[2] they represented official cultural policy for all communist controlled areas. In the *Talks*, Mao asserts that literature and art should be directed by political concerns: "Whether at a high level or a low one, our literature and art serve the popular masses, primarily workers, peasants, and soldiers; they are created for workers, peasants, and soldiers and are used by them."[3] Accordingly, the broad masses were to be the beneficiaries of literature and art, and the party, both in its role representing the masses as well as in its role leading the masses, thus claimed exclusive control over cultural production. David Holm makes two relevant points in this regard. First, in the *Talks* although Mao does not specifically call for the implementation of "national forms"—traditional folk forms or styles—that was clearly the effect the new direction laid out by his policy had. Second, the resistance of intellectuals to "national forms," as backwards or feudal, was very strong, not least because of support for this position from within Marxist-Leninist aesthetic theory.[4] Therefore, to effect a change, it required the implementation of new policy as embodied in the *Talks*, and in fact in the short term, Mao's remarks led to reprimands of, most prominently, Ding Ling and Hu Feng who had criticized the party and party control over intellectual and artistic work.

Despite the rectification campaign based on Mao's new policy,[5] this strain of literary theory had roots stretching back a decade and more. Debates on the popularization of literature (or literature for the broad masses) as well as on literary freedom (or the so-called "third-category writer") had risen and fallen with mixed results for the actual production of literature.[6] In the early 1930s, Qu Qiubai, formerly a CCP Politburo member and briefly chairman of the CCP, became a prominent spokesperson for the League of Left-Wing Writers and argued forcefully from a Marxist perspective both against the political independence of writers and for the popularization of literature.[7] The debate on popularization tended to revolve around two poles: the implementation in the new literature of traditional forms with which the (largely illiterate and semi-literate) masses were familiar and the raising of literary standards (or in other words, increasing the ability of readers to accept and understand what were felt to be more sophisticated—namely Europeanized—forms and styles) in this same audience. General consensus seems to have concluded that the former goal must be implemented first, and only then could standards be raised. Of course, the danger that traditional forms would bring with them feudal ideologies always loomed, and so, despite his sharp criticism of the May Fourth legacy, as Theodore Huters has said, "What Ch'ü [Qu] shared with the reformist tradition was, rather, the need to gain a conscious grasp of culture and society by creating a new category of writing that was precisely empty of vestiges of the past and into which new things could be poured without becoming contaminated."[8] Mao Zedong picked up on this strain of thought as early as October 1938, when in an address to the party's Central Committee he spoke to the need to link national forms to revolutionary goals to increase the acceptance of those goals by the broad masses.[9] Two years later, in "Xin minzhu zhuyi lun" (On New Democracy), Mao developed this concept of national form, urging comrades to "to reject [the old culture's] dross and assimilate its democratic essence."[10] This construction holds out the possibility that not all from the old society is necessarily feudal; hence, some is salvageable. And indeed it would seem needful to salvage what is useful rather than, as Huters says of Qu, to create completely new forms. Nevertheless, we should note that this construction, or indeed that of Mao's more pithy summation, "National form and new democratic content—this is our new culture of today,"[11] leaves unspecified what exactly is "dross" and what is not, therefore allowing a wide discretion (or narrow construction, as the case may be) in judgments on the success or failure of merging national forms with communist and revolutionary content. Over the course of the next three decades, this leeway consistently kept authors off balance, further reinforcing party-led political control of literary production.

Thus, it is no surprise that critics have consistently noted the similarities between traditional narrative forms and fiction produced in the communist base areas of the forties and in China as a whole in the fifties and sixties.[12] It was in this context that Zhao Shuli first came to prominence. Zhao was born into a poor farming family in Shanxi. As a child, Zhao had shown aptitude for music, had learned to play several instruments, and through this route became quite familiar with village art forms. In the 1920s, though, while studying at the Changzhi No. 4 Provincial Normal Academy, Zhao came into contact with May Fourth culture, and even wrote and published a few stories in the style of May Fourth literature. However, Zhao never seems to have been fully comfortable with this writing style. Before the war, Zhao was more or less destitute, performing all sorts of manual labor, and, although he had never met a communist, he was even arrested by the Nationalists as a communist sympathizer! With the outbreak of war, though, Zhao found a place working in a Communist propaganda department. And in 1943, he published the first of his acclaimed stories "Xiao Erhei jiehun" (Little Blacky Gets Married) and "Li Youcai banhua" (Rhymes of Li Youcai).[13]

"Little Blacky Gets Married" tells the story of how Xiao Erhei and Xiao Qin (Little Celery) come to be married. Xiao Erhei and Xiao Qin are both children of feudal remnants: Xiao Erhei's father is the local prognosticator[14] while

Xiao Qin's mother is the local shamaness. Both characters are ridiculed merci-
lessly and their practices exposed as superstitions. For example Xiao Erhei's
father determined that it was not auspicious to plant on a certain day, and so
while everyone else was out planting, he waited. Unfortunately, he was not to
get another chance to plant for several weeks; so, while all his neighbors were
nurturing their sprouts, only then were he and his sons finally getting their seeds
planted. As a result, neighbors made fun of Xiao Erhei's father by asking
whether it was a good day to plant or not and he is nicknamed, ironically, the
Second Zhuge (Zhuge Liang, the famous Chinese strategist). Xiao Qin's mother
on the other hand, nicknamed Aunty Fairy because of her occupation, supposed-
ly in the middle of a trance, matter-of-factly told Xiao Qin to mind the rice lest it
be ruined—thus exposing the fraud of her trade.

Xiao Erhei and Xiao Qin are both wholesome and hard-working youths who
despise their parents' eccentricities. They fall in love naturally enough as both
are the most attractive specimens of their respective sexes in the village. Their
parents, of course, oppose the match, Second Zhuge because the pair's horoscopes are ill-fated, and Aunty Fairy because she wants to sell Xiao Qin to an old
soldier living in the mountains. But the biggest obstacles in the way of their
marriage are the two brothers Jinwang and Xingwang, the local bullies, the first
of whom wants Xiao Qin for himself. These two conspire to kidnap Xiao Erhei
and Xiao Qin and take them to the district office for conducting an illicit extra-
marital affair. Of course, this is the communist controlled liberated area where
people have the freedom to choose whom they want to marry for themselves. So,
once they arrive at the district office, the bullies are themselves arrested, Xiao
Erhei and Xiao Qin are married and their parents are chastised.

There are several aspects of Zhao Shuli's narrative that I would like to point
out here. First is that the language, plot events, and character types are uncom-
plicated and ones with which local villagers would be familiar. Furthermore,
they illustrate the didactic message of communist support for the oppressed in
general and for freedom of marriage in particular. For example there is this passage at the beginning of the section, called "Get Them," in which Xiao Erhei
and Xiao Qin are kidnapped.

> Xiao Qin told Xiao Erhei all about her mother's plans for her marriage [i.e. to
> the old soldier]. Xiao Erhei said, "Don't pay any attention to her! I've asked a
> district comrade who said all it takes is for the man and woman themselves to
> be willing; if they go to the district [office] to register, no one can do anything
> about it . . ." When he had gotten this far, they heard some footsteps outside.
> Xiao Erhei stuck his head out to see, and in the darkness stood four or five
> people. One of them said, "Get them! Get them!" They both recognized Jin-
> wang's voice.[15]

As we can see, his description of events and dialogue is straightforward. Zhao
Shuli himself had this to say about his use of language.

> Since I am someone who grew up as a peasant and also have been to school,
> naturally I cannot avoid talking to farmers, nor can I avoid talking to intellec-
> tuals. Sometimes when I returned to the countryside from school, if I wasn't

careful, I would always bring a little school-boy accent [home with me] when talking with my parents and siblings. But as soon as that accent came out, it immediately became a topic of conversation. After this happened a few times, I learned my lesson. Later, even if I wanted to introduce intellectual language to them, I had to find a way to translate the intellectual language into their language. And after a while, it became a habit [for me]. If speaking is like this, then in writing I must also pay attention to this aspect—"however" is unusual so I change it to "but;" "hence" is a little bit new, so I change it to "because of this." If I don't change [this language] into appropriate words for them, then they will not want to read it. If this is true for words, then it is the same for sentences—since people cannot squeeze longer sentences into one clump [in their minds], why not shorten them and use a few more sentences? "The chicken clucks" and "the dog bites" are habitual, why must I write "the chicken is clucking" or "the dog is biting?" As for the structure of the plot, I also put the utmost effort into attending to the habits of the masses: the masses love to hear a story, so I emphasize plot; [the masses] love to hear chronological stories, so I seldom cut short a storyline for the sake of editing. I figure as long as the majority reads it I will not lose money selling [my stories]. As for whether this lowers the artistic quality of my work or not, well that is another question . . .[16]

There is much to comment on in this passage, but foremost is Zhao Shuli's concern for the way people *hear* language. As Huang Ke'an has said, "This is a type of oral transmission that emphasizes 'speaking and listening,' and not the May Fourth new fiction book-centered transmission of 'writing and reading.'"[17] Zhao is always concerned that the uneducated masses be able to understand his stories when they are read aloud, and so he bases his writing on colloquial speech. This, of course, meshes perfectly well with Mao Zedong's new policies for literature. Nevertheless, we must add that it is hard to say that Zhao Shuli's narrative style accurately recapitulates any particular national form. He drops most of the trappings of traditional vernacular fiction such as the story-teller stance while keeping traditional vernacular fiction's emphasis on plot. Indeed, rather than a combination of national form and revolutionary content, it may be better, as Huang Ke'an has suggested, to think of Zhao's fiction as combining May Fourth *xiangtu* fiction with "folk interest" to create a popular or mass style.[18] To this mass style is added revolutionary content, in the form of, as above, information on communist support for free marriage, and an illustration of how one goes about exercising this new right.[19]

Another aspect of Zhao Shuli's narrative that deserves note is his sense of humor. Of course, in addition to an emphasis on simple language and plot structure, humor is an important aspect of what Huang Ke'an identifies as "folk interest." One of the best examples is this scene in which Xiao Qin's mother goes to the district office dressed as a young woman despite her age.

An assistant led her into the district director's room, whereupon she prostrated herself and kowtowed, repeatedly saying, "Master District Director, you must resolve my difficulties!" The district director was just then bent over his table writing. When he saw her kneeling on the floor with bent head, the top of which was stuck with so many silver pins and decorations, he thought it was a young bride who two days before had quarreled with her mother-in-law. So he

said, "Doesn't your mother-in-law have a guarantor? Why don't you go bother
him?" Aunty Fairy was astounded and raised her head to glance at the district
director. Only when the director saw that she was an old lady wearing makeup
did he realize his mistake. The assistant said, "Excuse me, this is Yu Xiao
Qin's mother!" The director looked her up and down again and said, "So you're
Xiao Qin's mother, eh? Get up! There'll be no pretend ghosts or spirits here!
I'm clear on everything! Get up!" Aunty Fairy stood up. The director asked,
"How old are you?" Aunty Fairy said, "Forty-five." The director said, "Look at
yourself, is this Halloween?"[20] A teenaged girl standing by the door snig-
gered. . . ."[21]

Humor not only is one of the most enlivening of narrative techniques, but, as
here in the ridicule of Aunty Fairy, also diminishes class enemies and feudal
holdovers. We should note that Second Zhuge gets a similar comeuppance at the
district director's hands.

Moreover, while fellow villagers had laughed at these two old frauds, it is
only when the communist knocks them off their high horses that they reform:
Aunty Fairy dresses her age and Second Zhuge stops casting horoscopes. Likewise, though they are never mocked in the same way as Second Zhuge and Aunty Fairy, it is Jinwang and Xingwang who pose the biggest threat both to the two
lovers and to the community as a whole. However, once confronted by communist authority in the person of the district director, they too crumple like the paper
tigers they have always been.

Humor is put to a similar use in "Rhymes of Li Youcai," though here rather
than poking fun at feudal society, humor is used to expose the hypocrisies of
local leaders who usurp communist authority, through lax oversight, to maintain
their own private status and lifestyle. Li Youcai is a poor man who watches other people's cows for a living. However, he has a sharp wit which he uses to
compose verses (*kuaiban*) about various aspects of life in the village.

Before taking up the verses themselves, I would like to briefly discuss the
story's form. Like "Little Blacky Gets Married" before it, Zhao while never
completely conforming to the specifics of traditional narrative form, does give
voice to its spirit. For example, the story's opening line reads: "In Yanjiashan
there is a [person called] Li Youcai, whose nickname is 'Never Die.'"[22] This
construction imitates the opening of countless stories—based on the beginnings
of traditional biographies—while modernizing the language. That is, if Zhao
were to follow the national form as closely as possible, one might expect something like "Li Youcai, a man of Yanjiashan, nicknamed 'Never Die.'" Furthermore, as Cyril Birch has noted, the narrator in this story, as traditional narrators
are wont to do, on several occasions directly addresses his audience.[23] As with
"Little Blacky Gets Married," it is the recomposition of these traditional styles
and techniques with an infusion of pro-communist themes that signifies the
Maoist union of national form and "democratic" content. This also can be understood as the Benjaminian rearticulation of a fragmented and transformed past
with the present. Because of the modernist and revolutionary purposes of the
text, as we saw with "Mending Heaven" and "Shi Xiu" in Chapter Two, the past,
in the form of national form, and the present, in the form of democratic content

are not necessarily oriented towards the same ends. The ways the tension inherent in this sort of arrangement is dicussed in what follows.

Li Youcai's verses, likewise, add to the folk flavor of Zhao's narration. They also serve other functions such as summary and characterization.[24] But it is on the humor of the verses, directed at the story's antagonists, that I would like to focus here. For example

> Hooray for Yan, our village chief, who towers all above us;
> By all the years you've been our boss, it's plain to see you love us.
> Ten autumns now, the polling place has seen the folk in action:
> And each election proves once more that Yan's the big attraction.
> Yet times are getting harder now and labor we'd be saving,
> So I suggest we have your name cut on a wood engraving.
> Each voter then, instead of writing out the famous name,
> Can simply use the chop and the results will be the same.
> Then Yan, who's always first, can take the damn thing home and save it.
> For it will be a hundred years before we re-engrave it.[25]

This poem was written about the local boss, Yan Hengyuan who despite not actually being the village chief anymore, still controls the village through cronies. The following verse describes Yan's son, Yan Jiaxiang who has a nervous tic of excessive blinking.

> Freaky blinking eyes, Yan Jiaxiang
> His eyelashes are two inches long.
> Cheeks like eggs, and a nose just gone,
> When he speaks, his eyes go on and on
>
> His two eyes blink in a flash,
> But still he's got him some brains.
> Even when he's wrong, he'll get what he wants,
> And manage to increase his fame.
>
> He likes to get things real cheap,
> Or else he turns red like a beet.
> His eyes blink and blink,
> And he whines like a sow in heat.[26]

It is interesting to note that the way the story is constructed, these poems represent an expression of the masses' own discontent with corrupt leadership, which is to say, leadership not conforming to communist discipline. There are two points which need to be made in this regard. First, this construction harkens back to and re-embodies the mythical origins of Chinese poetry in the Guofeng (Airs of the States) section of the *Shijing* (Book of Odes) as the people's spontaneous expressions of content or discontent. Here, we should be reminded of Bonnie McDougall's suggestion that Mao's *Talks* best be understood as having its literary theoretical source in Mao's own practice of writing traditional poetry;[27] Mao's purity of vision precludes the possibility of the traditional form ever corrupting his content. The verses in "Li Youcai banhua," similarly because of their source in the propertyless class at the lowest stratum of Chinese society seem to perfectly embody Mao's prescription of national form (emptied, of course, of all traditional/feudal corrupting influence) fused with revolutionary content. Second, despite everything mentioned in the first point, this is only a construction. Zhao Shuli, the ultimate composer of Li Youcai's poetry, while never rich, did receive an education, which has always already removed him from the masses,[28] as he admits himself in the passage quoted above. Truly spontaneous expressions of the masses, as far as the Communists were concerned, always needed revisions, rectifications and purges.[29] It is precisely for this reason that Mao could not dispense with intellectuals altogether but had to settle for keeping them on a tight leash. Likewise, the revisions, rectifications and purges reveal the anxiety and slippage at the heart of the Maoist construction of National forms plus democratic (revolutionary) content: the modernist, teleological intentions of Maoist literature fear the eruptions of memory embodied in national forms and so submit them to discipline.

But to return to the story, these verses and others are composed fairly quickly (through long practice) and circulate through the community almost immediately. They allow the local poor peasant farmers an opportunity to laugh at those enforcing social control over them, and thereby vent some of their frustrations. But they do not in themselves alter the poor peasant farmers' material circumstances, to use the language of Marxism. For that, they must await the arrival of Old Comrade Yang. As with the district director in "Little Blacky," Yang (as the personification of communist authority) is the catalyst enabling the masses to shrug off their oppression, but it is the ostensible spontaneous expression of the people in the form of Li Youcai's verses which, as they were supposed to do in Confucian ideology, first alert him to the masses' complaints.

I will not go into the details of how the masses (under Yang's tutelage) assert their influence in society (fanshen, literally a reversal of situation). Suffice it to say that Yang's organizational experience and aid plus his access to district level authority ensure the poor farmers of success. What I would like to highlight here is that when Li Youcai's verses come to have active political intentions and meanings (as opposed to the earlier, reactive, commentary verses) they lose that playful humorous aspect so noticeable in the earlier samples of his poetry. I will cite two examples; the first is an attempt to organize the poor farmers into an agricultural association (nongjiuhui).

If you join the Farmers' Association, your power will increase several-fold;
Whoever dares to oppress us will be opposed by our unified [strength].
We will settle our debts with Old Hengyuan, settle them thoroughly;
He will repay ill-gotten money and return ill-gotten land,
He will enact real rent reduction: we will not allow him to hide anything.
All the inhumane cadres will be recalled,
We will never again suffer their abuses or be implicated by them.
When these tasks are completed, we will be several hundred times happier,
So to speed things up, hurry up and join the Association.[30]

The next example is a celebratory poem which comes at the very end of the story. Liu Guangju, who is mentioned in the poem, is one of Yan Hengyuan's cronies.

Yanjiashan is upside down,
For the masses have gained the crown.
Old Hengyuan has been deflated,
His money and lands all confiscated.
Liu Guangju, a great disgrace,
For his crimes, no one else will take the fall.
And the village all extols,
No more to be their fools.
From the village to the fields,
"A play! A play!" everyone yells.[31]

As these examples illustrate, while these later verses maintain the earlier meters and rhymes (though my translations seldom do these aspects justice), what humor remains continues to be directed at the now disgraced Yan Hengyuan clique, and in at least my own opinion is a pale shadow of the earlier ridicule, mockery, and sarcasm that were so effective in expressing the poor peasants' frustrations with their so-called social betters. Thus, while the national form (embodied by Li Youcai's verses) requires the communist party (embodied in Old Comrade Yang) to achieve political potency, it is precisely through the action of this increasing political relevance that the interest and indeed pleasure provided by the national form is emptied out along with any dangerous feudal elements. As we shift our attention to the literature of the Cultural Revolution, we will find, in fact, that without commenting on its loss, national form is all but dropped completely, resulting in increased emphasis on ideologically correct content.

The Primacy of Revolutionary Content

Despite being not only one of the first but also one of the best practitioners of Mao's theory urging the merger of national form with revolutionary content, Zhao Shuli came under fierce attack during the Cultural Revolution. Because of his tribulations, he became ill and eventually died in 1970.[32] In fact, from one point of view, the Cultural Revolution brought many things in China to an end, while from another it established a fresh beginning. This has been discussed in many forums and need not take up any more of our space here. Indeed, while Mao's *Talks* and its concomitant theory of national forms was heavily cited at the beginning of the Cultural Revolution ostensibly as an ideal which literature since Liberation had failed to meet,[33] I would suggest that the spirit of the *Talks* more or less faded away to be replaced by literary theory developed during the Cultural Revolution for the purposes of the Cultural Revolution. This is, perhaps, surprising since, in the period between 1943 and 1966, throughout the various loosenings and tightenings of literary control, Mao's *Talks* continually served as a baseline and, in fact, its increased citation tended to indicate coming rectifications of literary practice—as indeed was the case at the beginning of the Cultural

Revolution. By the Cultural Revolution, though, citation of the *Talks* seems to have had more to do with claims to authority rather than any elaboration of the theories laid out therein.

This is not to say that literary theory remained static through the roughly quarter century between the *Talks* and the Cultural Revolution. The Soviet import of socialist realism was important for a while (the 1953 revision of the *Talks* substitutes socialist realism for proletarian realism)[34] but it soon came to be superseded by the two-pronged approach of revolutionary realism and revolutionary romanticism, the first of which was said to provide a concrete manifestation of material life while the second was said to convey the revolutionary idealism of the proletariat.[35] Nevertheless, debates which tended to argue for or against the relative independence of writers and literature from ideological constraints, such as the one in the early 1960s on the utility of the so-called "middle character," one neither completely heroic nor completely villainous (eerily reminiscent of the 1930s debates on third-category writers, that is, those neither leftist nor rightist), invariably concluded with the reassertion of party control and purges, the first precedent for which was, of course, the *Talks*.

The effect of these repeated assertions of party control over literary output came to take the form of taboos to be avoided in literary production, thereby minimizing the potential for writers to be attacked on the basis of already-identified heresies. These included factuality, psychological analysis, humanism, love between the sexes, and the afore mentioned middle character.[36] We may note parenthetically that these taboos, like the draining of humor from Li Youcai's verses, reflect anxiety on the part of revolutionary (modernist) historical trends to contain and discipline the eruptions of non-progressive historical constellations of memory. The monologic[37] drive, the compulsion to weed out alternative voices, is prevalent throughout Maoist literary policies and practices. I will return to this subject again below.

But to return to the topic at hand, by the Cultural Revolution, strictures were expanded even more, limiting a writer to furthering the goals of the Great Proletarian Cultural Revolution with the unspoken caveat that the social disruptions of the early Cultural Revolution were off limits.[38] It was those very disruptions, however, which had an even larger impact on literary production. First of all, the presses were all but completely closed, and second, all literary production from the May Fourth on was denounced and even high ranking cultural officials such as Zhou Yang were criticized and dismissed, to say nothing of rank-and-file writers such as Zhao Shuli.[39] Therefore, when journals and presses resumed publication in 1972-1973, it was with a largely new set of authors. As the anonymous editor says on the "To the Reader" page at the end of one of the first new publications,

> The first issue of this *Series* [short for *Shanghai Art and Literature Series*] published here concentrates on fiction. The vast majority of the works were written by workers, peasants, and soldiers in their spare time, and of these, close to half have only just begun to try their hand at writing. It was the fierce struggle for survival that spurred them to take up their literary weapons. Molded in the form

of revolutionary heroes, [they] vigorously reflect the spirit of this great age of ours and laud passionately the victory of Chairman Mao's revolutionary line.[40]

Clearly, in the six intervening years, the slate had been wiped clean and prepared for a group of writers who could (finally) depict the new socialist utopia without any vestiges of the tainted past to obscure the brilliance of "Chairman Mao's revolutionary line." There was no more need for national forms since clearly the (formerly illiterate) workers, peasants, and soldiers were now not only reading but producing their own literature (Qu Qiubai's ultimate goal for literature).

As Richard King notes, the inexperience of these fresh voices often required "nurturing (*peiyang*)" by literary advisors and so forth. Indeed, Duan Ruixia called his story "Tebie guanzhong" (Not Just One of the Audience, 1973), which will be discussed below, a "thousand person cake" (*qianrengao*) because of all the "nurturing" he received during its composition.[41] I will argue that what we see in "Tebie guanzhong" and other stories from this period is a continuation of a trend in communist writing which Robert Hegel has identified (noticeable in our discussion of Zhao Shuli above) to confirm and proselytize views already current in political thought or enacted through social change.[42] In addition to this trend, I suggest that these stories mark a retreat from national forms as unnecessary distractions from the communication of correct communist thought and behavior.[43]

Foremost among the reasons for this change are the closely related concepts of the theory of the three prominences (*san tuchu*) and the model operas (*yangban xi*), both of which have their ultimate source in Mao Zedong's wife, Jiang Qing. The model operas (originally eight performance pieces—five operas, two ballets, and one instrumental suite—but whose number expanded over the course of the Cultural Revolution) represented the purest of political content, and as the term model opera suggests, were upheld as modern classics on which to base new cultural work, including film and literature.[44] One of the main aspects of these works which made them suitable to serve as models was their embodiment of the theory of the three prominences. The theory of the three prominences stipulated that "of all the characters, positive characters should be prominent; of positive characters, heroes should be prominent; of heroes, the central character should be prominent."[45]

The emphasis on heroism was not necessarily new (the debate over the "middle character" was precisely a debate over how large a role heroes should play); what was new was a matter of degree. The three prominences insisted that characters be delineated in stark black and white tones.[46] Furthermore, since stories set in the contemporary period depict the flowering of the socialist age, class struggle as such was not only anachronistic but actually inconceivable. Class struggle is replaced instead with line struggle, that is, contradictions between conflicting policy lines. Lest we be deceived, though, line struggle or the correct resolution to contradictions within the people, was every bit as crucial to the survival of communist society as class struggle was during the war and the immediate post-war period. In fact, the correct line is always that of Mao Zedong himself. "Comrade Jiang Qing's spirit in pointing out [the three prominences]," in the words of Yu Huiyong (who actually coined the term), "blazes the trail for socialist literature and art and takes up Mao Zedong thought as a weapon to establish a general scientific principal for literature and art."[47] Mao Zedong is the ultimate figure for the heroes encountered in these stories (and indeed in heroes from all of Chinese communist literature, including the district director and Old Comrade Yang discussed above). It is no surprise, then, that Gu Yuanqing notes that failure to reproduce the spirit of the model operas in literature was taken as betrayal.[48]

"Not Just One of the Audience" illustrates these points quite well. Indeed, its exemplary embodiment of the principals I have enumerated above probably accounts for its position heading the anthology *Zhaoxia* (Morning Clouds, 1973). *Morning Clouds* was the first in a series of anthologies put out by the Shanghai literary journal of the same name which began publication in 1973 but ceased with the fall of the Gang of Four. Duan Ruixia, the author of "Not Just One of the Audience," was a young electronics factory worker (one of the "workers, peasants, and soldiers" writing in their spare time mentioned above) who came to literary prominence in the pages of *Morning Clouds*. The journal as well as Duan himself increasingly came to engage in the internal party line struggle between the Gang of Four and the Deng Xiaoping faction, but in these earlier stories (with a few exceptions) such clear political allegories are not particularly evident.[49] Instead, I have chosen to discuss "Not Just One of the Audience" precisely because it seems more intended to urge readers to a general activity on behalf of the party and state rather than engage in a partisan battle. As the caption accompanying a portrait of Lu Xun at the beginning of the anthology says,

> This oil painting illustrates Lu Xun attentively studying Marxist philosophy in his "Secret Reading Room" [the title of the portrait]. An atmosphere of solitude, a darkened room, and moveable bookshelves in the style of wooden chests, call forth [a sense of] the disastrous political environment of those times. The hands of the clock have swept past 1 AM, and the ashtray is full of butts, but Lu Xun still has not gone to rest. Under the light of a lamp with an old paper shade, bent over a wicker chair he concentrates on his reading and his thoughts. His cigarette is about to burn his fingers, but he does not notice. The light of truth shines upon his heart.[50]

This portrait and the stories which follow it are intended as models, no less than the model operas were, to guide their readers' political actions and beliefs.

"Not Just One of the Audience"[51] tells the story of Li Changchun (Eternal Spring Li), a party branch committee member and quality control director for the Feiyue (advancing by leaps and bounds) Wireless Electric Factory, who attends a dress rehearsal of a performance of the model opera *Zhiqu weihushan* (Taking Tiger Mountain by Strategy). The opera is to be performed for the benefit of workers, peasants, and soldiers in celebration of the thirtieth anniversary of the publication of Mao's *Talks*. During the performance, Li notices that the sound system is not quite up to snuff, and when he discovers that an expert from the university had said only foreign models could fix the design, Li takes up the challenge. As he says to one of the actors, "Comrade, we should stage a revolution on your sound system, or else it will affect your performances."[52]

So Li and his friend, Su Qi (his surname Su is the same character used for the USSR), with the help of the entire factory (in their spare time since the normal workload cannot be postponed), get to work researching all the most modern electrical circuitry and speaker systems, designing and producing a prototype. In the story there is no Yan Hengyuan, nefariously subverting all the communist good will (although there is a doubter in the form of Su Qi, but more on this below); there is only the inanimate sound system and study which allows the workers led by Li Changchun to mold it into the advanced technology they require.

Still, there is a deadline because the first performances are coming up. In response to Su's suggestion that they may have bitten off more than they can chew, that science requires time for deliberate reflection, Li explains why it is so important to revolutionize the sound system.

> "Old Su, I started out as a soldier and when I have something to say it's like a bullet in the chamber, I don't fret but just come out and say [my thoughts] directly, so please forgive me. I think that we need a cool and deliberate scientific attitude, to start with reality and work conscientiously. But even more, we need to be full of passionate politics. People will always have spirit, and this spirit is nothing but the spirit of advancing revolution, of 'encouraging the strenuous struggle onward, the faster to erect socialism.' What we face is not the average research and design task but one of struggle to protect Chairman Mao's revolutionary arts and literature line. [Here Li goes into a long story about how theater in the old society demanded labor from poor people but did not allow them access to see performances]. After liberation, Liu Shaoqi, Zhou Yang and their crowd monopolized the arts and literature, putting on performances of feudal, capitalist, and revisionist black works, sounding a clarion and clearing a path for capitalism. Not until today's grand victory of the Great Proletarian Cultural Revolution have the workers, peasants, and soldiers—the subjects of literature and art—truly gained the stage. Warriors of art and literature, in order to better express the heroism of the workers, peasants, and soldiers, enter real life and laboriously study and train. We of the working class can only [try] to add brilliance to the model operas; there's absolutely no reason to diminish them by even the smallest amount. Think about it, could it be that this is a simple technical task?"[53]

I must note first that this passage recapitulates the marriage of the two revolutionaries with "a cool and deliberate scientific attitude" representing revolutionary realism, while "passionate politics" and all that follows represents revolutionary romanticism. This analogy also fits the dyad of national form and revolutionary content. That the marriage is heavily weighted towards the latter should be obvious.

Su Qi, faced with such an argument can only accede, although his doubts are not fully laid to rest until he hears the story of how Li Changchun's true life heroism—saving the radar apparatus on a navy vessel during exercises enabling the crew to complete their mission—inspired Lin Ying, the actor who plays Yang Zirong, the hero of the model opera, to a deeper understanding of heroism and hence the ability to perform Yang Zirong with such passion, energy, and (most importantly) verisimilitude (which here is conflated with truth). Indeed, it is the model opera, especially the line which says "the more difficult it is, the more [I/we] press ahead," which governs the development of the story (as model operas were intended to do).

The three prominences similarly work themselves out fairly straightforwardly in the story. Positive characters include the factory workers. Heroes include the actors, especially Lin Ying. And the central character certainly is Li Changchun. Su Qi's character falls both within and without the three prominences paradigm. He is clearly a hero for his help is indispensable to completing the new sound system. At the same time he plays the role of the turnaround character (*zhuanbian renwu*) who realizes his error through the recounting of Lin Ying's story and is thereby spurred to renewed exertion and devotion to the Chairman Mao line.[54] The discourse of heroism circulates on multiple levels through the story: between the model opera and the factory workers, especially Li Changchun (as displayed in the passage quoted above), between real life (although extradiegetically it is fiction) and the actor Lin Ying, between Lin Ying's recounting of Li Changchun's personal heroics and Su Qi, and of course between the text and the readers. At each point of circulation, the recipient is inspired to become a hero himself by the example given him, to take the instance of heroism as a model to guide his own future actions. But most importantly, each iteration of heroism can trace its source back to Mao Zedong (usually through quotations of Mao's works).[55] Perhaps most importantly, as this discourse circulates through the various narratives encapsulated in the story, it is constantly prevented from expanding beyond its surface level of meaning; that is to say, it signifies (repetitively) heroism and heroism alone. All other interpretations are denied by the discourse itself.

This discourse of heroism, in combination with the purging of established writers and cultural czars, the extended halt in literary publication, and the resulting reliance on amateur writers heavily "nurtured" by ideology, serves to flush all vestiges of the past (except as a negative example, as in Li Changchun's story cited above) from Cultural Revolution literature. The unanimous focus on a contemporary setting in these stories can only augment the separation of present from past. It is perhaps ironic, though not surprising, that *Morning Clouds*, both the journal and future anthologies, came more and more to be associated with the partisan politics of the Gang of Four. This can be understood as further elaboration of line struggle, but after the fact came to be seen as "conspiratorial literature" (*yinmou wenyi*) of the ultra-leftists. That is, it overstepped the bounds of selfless national hero and became self-serving propaganda wallowing in an excess of ideology. At the same time, though, in a way unexpected by its promulgators, the Cultural Revolution control of art and literature did, in fact, raise standards by first enforcing one common (political) standard which overrode all other considerations. In the post-Mao era, then, this standard could be raised quite easily, and indeed we find in the 1980s new and exciting literary voices of various styles, some quite experimental, that were fabulously popular, in part, because there was a reading public ready to branch out from the previous steady diet of communist ideology. Mo Yan and Han Shaogong, whose work has been discussed in earlier chapters, are two of these new voices.

From Literary Counterattacks to the "China Trope"

Although the government formed by the Nationalist party was forced to retreat to Taiwan in 1949, all of its attention remained fixed on the goal of retaking the mainland. In addition, millions of soldiers and party members as well as members of the business and intellectual classes accompanied the Nationalist government as it relocated from Nanjing to Taipei. The strains created by such a large and rapid increase in the population of China's second smallest province led the Nationalist regime to tighten its already authoritarian control over the island. To this end, policies—such as the promotion of Mandarin language education and media—begun since Taiwan was ceded back to China at the end of the Anti-Japanese war to foster connections to the Chinese nation and culture, were supplemented with official slogans and mobilization drives to rally the populace to support the objective of counterattack and defeat of the communist upstarts.[56]

Thus, in the field of literature, no less than their Communist counterparts, the Nationalist regime sought to develop and deploy a literature that served politics. From a certain perspective, the challenge facing the Nationalist cultural policymakers was not unlike that of their Communist enemies across the Taiwan Strait. There was an opportunity given Taiwan's small size to finally capitalize on the potential for literature and other cultural activities to bolster the acceptance of Nationalist rule and Nationalist goals for the future. In previous decades while on the mainland, the Nationalists had never been able to gain support from the majority of the intellectual class. Now on Taiwan, with a smaller geography and smaller population to police and with expanded governmental powers because of the declaration of martial law, a chance to start over and create a literature that could effectively support the Nationalists presented itself.

There were several obstacles in the way of achieving this goal, however. As I mentioned at the beginning of this chapter, very few established writers moved to Taiwan with the Nationalist regime. And in any case, writers steeped in May Fourth commitment to socially responsible literature had already proven difficult if not impossible to control. On the other hand, writers already present on Taiwan, or indeed anyone from the indigenous educated elite, had been educated in the Japanese language and culture and were not considered trustworthy by the Nationalists.[57] Instead, as the Communists did during the Cultural Revolution, the Nationalists found themselves nurturing an (almost) entirely new class of writers sympathetic to their cause.

As a first step, policies promoting Mandarin language and suppressing Japanese or the local Taiwanese dialect were implemented and enforced. Second, literature seen as subversive, especially literature in the May Fourth vein such as Lu Xun's writings or writings by authors who remained on the mainland, including even largely nonpolitical writers such as Shen Congwen, was banned. Finally and most important, the experience during the Anti-Japanese War of organiz-

ing writers' associations and enlisting them to aid in the national effort led naturally to continuing efforts along these lines.[58] Only now the aim was no longer to
defeat Japan; rather, it was to retake the mainland. The creation of parallel civi-
lian and military writers' groups to foster fledgling writers and administer government sponsored awards played an integral part in the mobilization of literature in support of counterattack.[59]

Again remarkably similar to what we have seen above in terms of communist literature, the literature produced in Taiwan under such conditions, not surprisingly, has largely propagandistic value. Still, the approach to the past revealed in these texts reflects a conservative bent in striking contrast to the
Communist valorization of revolution. As David Wang says,

> For . . . anti-Communist writers, given all the external contingencies, something
> quintessentially (Nationalist) Chinese remains intact. Whether it is called "tra-
> dition," "orthodoxy," or "humanity," this treasured essence of Chinese culture
> has been temporarily demolished by the Communists, its rehabilitation hinging
> on the recovery of the mainland by the Nationalist Party.[60]

The cultivation of uniquely Chinese characteristics in order to buttress conservative values certainly was not a new maneuver for the Nationalist state. The New
Life Movement of the 1930s had already attempted to counter Communist principles with a renewed emphasis on Chinese community based in (authoritarian)
Confucian norms. By the 1950s, counterattack texts from Taiwan cultivated this
"treasured essence" to the point of becoming a fetish. That is to say, the Chi-
neseness displayed as such a valued, and yet fragile, commodity in these texts
simultaneously marks and compensates for loss.

Let us turn to *Xuanfeng* (The Whirlwind, 1957) by Jiang Gui as an example
of counterattack writing. Beginning in the late 1920s, the novel tells the story of
Fang Xiangqian, an intellectual who has turned to communism and the Communist Party as the last, best path to save China. In cooperation with his nephew,
Fang Peilan, a former highwayman and current militia leader, Fang Xiangqian
brings revolution to his small town. But inexperience and naïve idealism prove
no match for the dictates of cold reality. The two Fangs lose control of their revolution, quickly becoming some of the first victims of their own success as they
are purged in internal party power struggles. Now under the leadership of more
self-serving masters, the revolution spirals into increasingly violent and destructive acts until the climax of a riot which costs the lives of hundreds in this one
local area.

From the description above, we can see that *The Whirlwind* depicts communism as a cure worse than the disease. The narrative exempts no one from
culpability; the novel is populated by scoundrels, prostitutes, sexual deviants,
brigands, opium addicts, and murderers, and these vices reflect the deeper moral
malaise infecting this society. But perhaps most important of all is the fact that
communism enables these disparate sectors of society to come together as a terrifying force that tears apart the foundations of a functional society. Individually,
the harm these socially malformed characters can inflict, while not negligible, is
still fairly limited. In *The Whirlwind*, however, the Communist Party gathers

these miscreants together under one banner, releasing them from all inhibitions and compounding the physical, emotional, and social damage they can inflict. For example, there is Shi Shenzhi, a Communist Party member who has been sent from Shanghai to lead Fang Xiangqian's local branch. When Fang balks at some of Shi's plans, the latter reveals the Communist Party's fundamental corruption hiding behind high flying rhetoric.

> "Xiangqian, this attitude of yours reflects the habits of the high and mighty; it's a classic petty bourgeois outlook and is absolutely unacceptable. You need to know that we concern ourselves only with the ends, never the means.[61]

Shi's plans include asking Dong Yinming, one of the Party members, to steal jewelry from his mother. When he has successfully stolen the jewelry, however, an innocent servant is accused of the crime. Rather than come to her defense, though, Dong lets her take the blame, and as a result she then hangs herself. Clearly, although the Communist Party claims to stand for the lowly and oppressed, it is these very downtrodden who pay the price for Communist hubris. Shi Shenzhi himself comes to a sticky end when he lavishes the money raised by this theft and other illicit means on a prostitute. When the money is gone, he is kicked out of her home. To raise more money he attempts to extort money from a banker, but instead is arrested and executed.

Jiang Gui himself certainly intended his novel to expose the evils of communism. In his "Author's Preface," he says,

> Here there are almost no orthodox characters. With some trouble, I made Fang Bagu this diehard (Nationalist Party Member) represent the true spirit of the nation to give people a thread of hope. It's a pity she battled alone, had too little strength, and instead was swallowed in this countercurrent. Yet, as far as the situation stands today, her stance still remains the correct one. Now when we speak of counterattack, it is impossible to deny the leadership of the Nationalist Party. This is a practical issue, not an ideological issue.[62]

We glimpse here one of the most intriguing aspects of this novel. Despite its clear anti-Communist stance, the novel remains ambivalent about the Nationalist Party.[63] Similarly, and yet contrary to what we would expect, Fang Xiangqian, the arch Communist, is not evil. In fact, he is full of good intentions to save the nation from catastrophe. But it is precisely his mediocrity which sets the impersonal and evil machine of Communism in motion. As David Wang says, "Fang Xiangqian is not a competent revolutionary, but he may cause society more harm precisely because of his imperfect villainy (or heroism)."[64] The novel's resistance to such stark black and white terms is most likely what kept it from garnering support from the establishment (Jiang Gui published *The Whirlwind* at his own expense after several years of trying to find a publisher for it) but is also what makes the novel appealing to scholars and critics.

Allow me to return for a moment to the notion of a "treasured essence" of Chinese tradition that is cultivated in counterattack novels such as *The Whirlwind*. Jiang Gui himself stresses the importance of the traditional chapter novel form (*zhanghuiti xiaoshuo*) and certainly engages that form from composing summarizing couplets at the head of chapters to deploying the traditional vernacular language of the classic Chinese novel. Moreover, David Wang has already traced connections between *The Whirlwind* and two other novels, one from the late Ming period and one from the late Qing period, much in line with the ways I have been delineating intertextual connections in my discussions of parody.[65] I will not repeat his effort here. Suffice it to say that Wang persuasively demonstrates the kinds of intertextual links and resonances that are a major concern of this study. Furthermore, Jiang Gui, in his "Author's Preface," finds the motivation for the writing of *The Whirlwind* in the classic Chinese historiographical notion of "recording evil to admonish [the world]."[66] In addition, it is not hard to place *The Whirlwind* in the tradition of classic Chinese novels of sexual manners such as *Jinpingmei* (The Plum in the Golden Vase, Ming dynasty) based on its depictions of sexual indulgence. Thus, *The Whirlwind*, in its structure reflects a certain continuity with traditional Chinese forms, styles, and themes, but in its content describes precisely the absence of a cohesive social system, of that "treasured essence." And it is that lack in society which allows for the debauchery (sexual and political) and violence described in the novel. That hole must be filled to restore society to its natural state.

Despite the similarities with their Communist counterparts already noted above, and despite their equally authoritarian proclivities, the Nationalists were never able to strike and maintain the same level of near total control over literary production as the Communists on the mainland achieved. For this reason Sung-sheng Yvonne Chang calls the Nationalist position "soft authoritarian rule."[67] There are several factors which contributed to the Nationalists' soft authoritarianism. First, in contrast to the Communists and despite the nationalization of certain key industries, the Nationalists never intended to create a state-directed economy in the socialist mold. Indeed the business class was one of the Nationalist Party's key constituents. As a result, market forces have always had a greater or lesser role to play in Taiwanese literary production and publication. An important example of this mix of political and market forces is the rise of newspaper literary supplements (*fukan*) as a crucial player in literary publication. While the supplements were supported by the government, they were also subject to market trends as represented in circulation numbers. Second, another key constituent of the Nationalist Party was the educated class (naturally excluding left-leaning intellectuals). Traditional literati and even May Fourth notions of the functions and value of literature remained powerful for this group and served to mitigate the overall ideological purposes for which the Party sought to employ literature and culture. Finally, as the drive to actually counterattack and retake the mainland drew on and on while the goal seemed further and further away, it increasingly felt less urgent to produce literature in the counterattack mode. By the 1960s, then, notions of pure literature, the importation of western modernist literary modes, and above all the conversion of the image of China from the locale of a successful counterattack to an ideal concept of cultural and

aesthetic value, which Chang calls the "China trope," had more or less sup-
planted counterattack literature in Taiwan.[68]

The "China Trope," in Chang's words, came into being when, "the signifier
['China'] was gradually dissociated from its physical referent, namely the Chinese mainland, emptied of its overt political contents, and reinvented as a potent
aesthetic trope."[69] In effect, the "treasured essence" discussed above in terms of
counterattack literature is preserved in this new, modernist trend but no longer
serves the political and military goal of retaking the mainland. Bai Xianyong's
collection *Taibei ren* (Taipei People, 1971) provides us an excellent example of
how the "China trope" is deployed in Taiwanese literature. In Chapter Six I discuss "Liang fu yin" (The Song of Liang Fu, 1967) and "Youyuan jingmeng"
(Wandering the Garden, Waking from Dream, 1966), both included in *Taipei
People*. Here, however, I would like to focus on "Yongyuan de Yin Xueyan"
(The Eternal Yin Xueyan, 1965) which is the first story in *Taipei People*. The
eponymous Yin Xueyan is a high class courtesan who has moved her location
and reputation from Shanghai to Taipei, but her life and her livelihood is firmly
based on her ability to maintain a Shanghai atmosphere even on what is considered the fringes of civilization.

> Yin Xueyan never aged. Of that class of affluent youth who had supported her
> ten years earlier in Shanghai's Paramount Dance Hall, some were balding;
> some had added frost at the temples; some had been reduced to serving as con-
> sultants to iron factories, or concrete factories, or synthetic fiber factories; and
> yet, a few had risen in the world to become bank executives or consortia lead-
> ers. Regardless of what changed, Yin Xueyan was eternally Yin Xueyan. In
> Taipei she still donned that pure white, fine muslin *qipao*, she still wore that
> faint, faint smile, and even her eyes refused to gain one wrinkle.[70]

This is how the narrative begins and indeed defines the (non)development of the
story which follows. It is precisely Yin Xueyan's changelessness, her ability to
preserve a "treasured essence," which captivates her patrons. Although her new
home, on Renai Rd, is located in one of Taipei's fashionable districts, once one
enters inside, one is transported to semicolonial Shanghai. From Yin's dress, to
her manners, to the objects—peach flower themed lacquered furniture, mandarin
duck embroidered cushions, antique flower vases with perfectly arranged flowers, and of course mahjong tables—decorating her home, everything is arranged
to suggest the continuity of Chinese leisure culture.

Yin does not sell sex, though the narrative does center around an affair she
conducts with a married man; rather, she sells memories of life before retreat to
Taiwan. That is, she sells the idea of China. And as we see, men are not her only
customers.

> Yin Xueyan received a twenty-five percent discount at Taipei's Hongxiang Silk
> Boutique; she could select the best quality embroidered slippers in The Flower
> Garden; she was expert in the Shaoxing Opera shown at The Red Mansion, so
> when Wu Yanli performed *Meng Lijun*, she was able to procure free front row
> seats; to speak of the Beijing or Shanghai snacks in Ximending [a fashionable
> shopping district in Taipei], there wasn't one with which she wasn't familiar.

Accordingly, whenever this group of ladies, with Yin Xueyan in the lead,
shopped in Ximending, watched Shaoxing Opera, or ate osmanthus flavored
tangyuan, they always forgot the troubles of the last ten or so years. It was as if
Yin Xueyan's body exuded the scent of Shanghai's multifarious splendor,
creating a half drunken state in these melancholy middle-aged women, so they
could not help happily discussing the wonderful taste of Shanghai crab roe
noodles.[71]

If these Taipei people can no longer live the life they once had on the mainland,
then they will relive it in brief moments of half drunken memories provided for
them expertly by Yin Xueyan.

Yin Xueyan's deployment and arrangement of things—antiques, flowers,
opera performances, snacks, clothes, even her own face—seems to almost create
a Benjaminian historical constellation, but the difference is significant. The
memories provoked in this manner by Yin do not produce history shot through
with "the presence of the now [*Jetztzeit*];"[72] instead it induces forgetfulness of
the present. This is precisely why Yin Xueyan is eternal; it is also why I said
above that the "treasured essence" of "China" cultivated in the Taiwanese literature of this period is a fetish. This body of literature raises an image of China: in
counterattack writing, China is a body suffering violence and waiting to be
healed, in later writings, although China has become an imaginary concept, it
still offers the tantalizing hope of plenitude. In neither case does this writing
actually put the past in contact with the present and set them in a dynamic relationship with each other. In this, again, the Maoist writing on the mainland
creates a strikingly similar effect to the writing from Taiwan even though one
fundamentally rejects the past while the other fully embraces it. Neither the single-minded focus on the present nor the single-minded focus on the past is adequate to establish a resonance between different eras and instigate messianic
time.

In the Time of the Post

After Mao and after Chiang Kai-shek, things began to change slowly in both the
mainland and on Taiwan. In the latter case, the rise of nativist and then localist
literature and politics challenged the hegemony of Mandarin language and Chi-
na-centered discourses that had predominated for the previous two decades. In
addition to a resurgence of interest in local Taiwanese history and culture, the
legacy of Japanese colonialism resurfaced after a long repression.[73] On the
mainland, a slow opening—economic, intellectual, and cultural—to the rest of
the world was accompanied by reexaminations of pasts and traditions that had
been denied in the Maoist era.[74] Above all, in both cases, market forces have
come to dominate in cultural fields, including, of course, literature.

The specific histories opened, explored, and informing different texts, naturally lead them in different directions, something which I will examine in the
chapters that follow. But before we delve into those differences, it is worth noting the convergences that exist. The turn to tradition that we find in the 1980s
and 1990s occurs on both sides of the Taiwan Strait. It is worth reiterating, how-

ever, what I hope this study has helped to make clear, namely, that while we often speak of "Chinese tradition" it is far from monolithic. A variety of wide-ranging influences have affected different strains of this continuing tradition: from the different regional and ethnic traditions explored by Roots writers to Japanese colonial (or postmodern) influences in Taiwanese literature. These differences, while important and necessary to take into account, to my mind cannot obscure other equally important similarities—parodic rewriting of earlier texts, for example—which we can then link in ways not unlike a Benjaminian constellation. Furthermore, the commercialization and commodification of culture affects both Taiwan and the mainland. And, as we will see in Chapters Seven and Eight, for two important texts both published in the mid 1990s, the depiction of these processes is crucial to the revelation of history in ruins, to borrow Benjamin's phrase.

Part II
Citation: Strategies of Intertextual Connection

Chapter 5
The Lyrical and the Local: Shen Congwen, Roots, and Temporality in the Lyrical Tradition

—These things seem to have no connection to history; it is as if the past hundred years or the next hundred years are the same as now.
Shen Congwen, *Random Sketches on a Trip to Hunan*

Since at least the work of Jaroslav Průšek, the category of the lyrical has played an important role in the analysis of modern Chinese literature. Indeed for Průšek, the pinnacle of Chinese letters (at least for the late imperial and modern period) culminates in texts which fuse the lyrical aspects of traditional poetry with the epic aspects of traditional prose and especially fiction.[1] A real benefit of Průšek's approach is that it allows the Chinese tradition an important role to play in the development of the new literature of the twentieth century in contrast to the ingrained, catalytic role usually assigned to European literature in literary histories. That being said, in today's world of free-floating signifiers unleashed from their signifieds, it is all but impossible to maintain the distinction between Průšek's lyrical (of the high poetic and/or subjective register) and his epic (lively but concrete description). That is to say, the epic turns out to be nothing if not lyrical.

More recently, therefore, lyricism has come to be contrasted not with the epic but with realism. Realism, which in Marston Anderson's words, posits "an optimal equivalency of the text and the real world" is ultimately undermined by the figurative (and thus lyrical) nature of language which, of course, is the stuff novels are made of.[2] David Wang, whose studies of Shen Congwen are important and influential predecessors for my analysis, suggests that Shen's fiction engages both the realism current in contemporary May Fourth writings and lyricism. Employing both realism and lyricism simultaneously allows him a critical purchase, in Wang's argument, from which Shen can hold in check both realism from too firm a belief in its own veracity and lyricism from a self-indulgent subjectivism.[3]

For the purposes of this study, lyricism or the lyrical will indicate a narrative style which tends to reveal and accentuate the figurative and representational nature of language. This definition does not intend to preclude that sense of the word *lyrical* (taken from its root in lyric poetry) to mean like poetry. Indeed, I use this understanding of the lyrical to explore intertextual resonances between and among traditional poems and modern narratives not unlike the parodic relationships discussed in previous chapters. At the same time, I feel that a broader definition allows the flexibility to grapple with the lyrical voice in modern narrative and the relationship it establishes with the past.

Here, as elsewhere in this study, I am interested in exploring the interactions between time and narrative, or in other words the different understandings of temporality (time and its passage) that narrative allows. As a result, I will argue that the literary technique of narrative lyricism can be variously deployed to create different sensibilities concerning time and connections possible between past, present, and future. One possibility is a pastoral atemporality which we might instinctively associate with lyricism; indeed, Shen Congwen's lyrical novel *The Border Town* is a prime example of this, as I will show below. Yet, there are other possibilities which I will also examine in the space below.

However, this question of lyricism and the temporal sense(s) it enables is simultaneously entangled with the issue of *xiangtu* (native soil) and the narratives written about it. Lu Xun's well known story, "Guxiang" (My Old Home, 1921),[4] is probably the first instance of native soil fiction in modern China. In this story the narrator, after a long absence in the city (Beijing) returns home one last time to bring his mother and nephew back to live with him in the city. The entire story is a continuous negotiation and contestation between the home of the narrator's memory and the home he finds on his return. Without exception, the home as it is fails to live up to his memory; yet, rather than being disabused of a nostalgic, idealized vision of home, we come away feeling the reality is an irrevocably diminished version of his home. The crux of the story, however, is embodied in the character of Runtu, a childhood friend of the narrator's. At the mere mention of Runtu's name a "wonderful picture flashed across my mind: a round and golden moon hanging in a sky of the deepest blue, below which was a seaside field planted as far as the eye could see with jade-green watermelon."[5] Bright, flashing memories such as this, though, sooner or later come face to face with the real thing: "This was Runtu. Although I knew he was Runtu as soon as I saw him, he wasn't anything like the Runtu of my memory. . . ."[6] The narrator goes on to describe how Runtu has been worn and wearied by a life of hard work growing melons in the salt air. Both men have changed, and the changes divide them from each other just as the present reality is divided from the past of the narrator's memory. As the narrator leaves with his mother and nephew he thinks to himself, "the countryside of my old home gradually receded; however, I did not feel any reluctance to leave. Only, I felt I was surrounded on all sides by an invisible wall, separating me from others and stifling me."[7] Nevertheless, the friendship which has sprung up between the narrator's nephew and Runtu's child is cause for some (possibly illusory) hope that these walls can eventually be torn down.

One of the major questions "My Old Home" asks is can we breach that wall? can we recover our past? but it comes away with a mixed answer. Following the model set up by "My Old Home," the native soil narratives examined in more detail below reattempt this question as well as others: can we recover our past or are we and it irretrievably alienated from each other? what is the relationship of the past to the present and future? what is memory and how does it mediate the past? how does literature from previous eras speak to us and to our contemporary literature?

Fundamentally, these questions with which native soil narratives concern themselves can be summarized with the question can we go home, that is can we recover our past? Often the attempted return to the past in the narrative, as in "My Old Home," is accompanied and mirrored by a physical journey from the urban center to the (childhood) home in the countryside. In this way tensions in the countryside/city opposition resonate with and compound tensions in the past/present opposition. David Wang, in his readings of Shen Congwen, has tended to discuss lyricism separately from the question of how one may return home, but for my readings, both of Shen and of Roots writers in the second half of the chapter, these two are inextricably intertwined.

Shen Congwen

Biancheng (*Border Town*, 1934), one of Shen Congwen's best known works, was written just before and finished during Shen's first trip back to his childhood home in West Hunan after almost seventeen years away,[8] first as a soldier and then as a writer in Beijing and Shanghai. *Biancheng* tells the story of Cuicui's coming of age in the hills of West Hunan. It is in many ways an idyllic story centered on the natural cycles of birth, life and death and the seasons on which they are modeled as well as the human cycles of annual festivals, and the birth, life and death of love. The following passage is taken from the beginning of the second chapter and is a description of the area around Chadong, the town in which the action of *Biancheng* is set.

> That river is none other than the You River of historical significance, which has been renamed the Bai River. The Bai river, after it flows to Zhenzhou and joins with the Yuan River, becomes slightly turbid like a mountain spring. If we move upstream, pools of three or five *zhang* are so clear you can see their floor. In these deep pools you can see the white sun shining on all the small, white stones on the bottom like agate. Fish swim here and there in the water as if floating through the air. On the two banks are such tall mountains, on the mountains are so many bamboo sprouts which can be woven to make paper and when they grow old create a deep blue-green (*cui* the same character as that which makes up Cuicui's name), coercing peoples' eyes [to look at them]. Homes for the people who use the river are found amid the peach and apricot flowers. In the spring-time, all it takes is to look carefully, anywhere you see peach blossoms you will find peoples' homes, and anywhere people live you can buy liquor. In the summer, the dazzling, purple patterned clothes drying in the sun can serve as a banner for habitation. And in the autumn and winter, the

homes, whether on the cliffs or on the water's edge, without exception all flash bright. Walls of yellow mud, roofs of raven-black tile, set in eternally firm locations, and in perfect harmony with their environs, leave you with a welcoming and happy impression. A traveler who has even a slight interest in poetry, music or painting, curled up in a small boat on this river for a thirty-day journey would not feel any boredom, because there are wonders everywhere, places of majestic and fabulous nature, each scene will cause him to be absorbed in admiration.[9]

Like a Chinese landscape painting, the scene is laid out according to the topography, starting with the river and the mountains and only then coming to human settlements. The description employs a certain reliance on metaphor (bright colors and the people's happiness), simile (stones like agate), metonymy (the flowers with people's homes), and vivid images ("as if floating through the air," "coercing peoples' eyes," "purple patterned clothes drying in the sun"). Shen also employs a certain rhythm and in some instances repetition which unfortunately is necessarily altered in the translation. These, nevertheless, contribute to the overall lyrical effect of his prose. Furthermore, images of fish swimming, peach blossoms, bamboo groves and so on are omnipresent in Chinese poetry starting from its very beginnings in the *Shijing* (Book of Odes) and memorably captured in such Tang Dynasty favorites as "Yugezi" (Fishing Song) by Zhang Zhihe: "Before Mt. Xisai the white egrets fly / Peach blossoms, flowing stream, and thriving mandarin fish"; "Zhuli guan" (In the Bamboo) by Wang Wei: "No one knows I am here in the deep [bamboo] grove / Only the bright moon comes to shine"; or "Guan youyu" (Gazing on Swimming Fish) by Bo Juyi: "Rounding the pond in a leisurely stroll, watching the fish play / When a child's fishing boat arrives" to name just three. Another common poetic theme is touched upon in this passage in the reference to a traveler passing through on boat which recalls Su Shi's "Zhouzhong yeqi" (Waking in the Night on the Boat): "Boatmen and waterfowl all dreaming / suddenly a large fish, fast as a running fox, splashes"; and especially Zhang Ji's "Fengqiao yebo" (Mooring for the Night by Maple Bridge): "The Hanshan Temple outside old Suzhou / The midnight chime reaches this guest boat" both of which were written during boat journeys. Moreover, the traveler mentioned at the end of the passage is, perhaps, autobiographical since *Border Town* was completed during Shen Congwen's first trip back to Hunan after leaving for Beijing in 1922.[10] More than ten years away from his birthplace has left Shen feeling like an outsider, as if every scene is new and fresh, as if he had never laid eyes on it before.

Furthermore, I would like to draw attention to the quick catalogue of the seasons which the narrative recites. Natural cycles and rhythms play a crucial role in this novel to such an extent that they are almost an unnamed character. The seasons themselves, it must be added, are not the focus of attention; rather, the ways in which people interrelate with the seasons, the ways in which their lives also circulate is of much more importance. In the spring, they make liquor, in the summer wear bright clothing, and in the autumn and winter abide in their homes. For the rest of the novel, whether it be the annual dragon boat races to celebrate the Dragon Boat Festival or the simple event of growing up and finding a mate, natural rhythms govern the lives of Shen's characters just as they govern the novel's form. That is, the lyricism of Shen's prose, the rhythms it performs on a formal level reinforce and resonate with the natural cycles which play such an important role in the novel.

It almost goes without saying, moreover, that the clearest allusion to a traditional text in this passage is certainly to *Taohuayuan ji* (*Peach Blossom Spring*). Above and beyond the list I have given above, *Border Town*, on a more systematic basis, cultivates intertextual resonances with Qu Yuan's masterpiece *Chuci* (*Songs of Chu*),[11] but even more importantly with Tao Qian's classic *Peach Blossom Spring*. Both of these texts, of course, were written in and about the area of Western Hunan that Shen called home, but it is the latter text which provides a model and an interpretive framework for *Border Town*. In the passage above, the association between human habitation and peach blossoms makes the connection between the people of this place and the people of Peach Blossom Spring. *Peach Blossom Spring* is, of course, the classic Chinese utopian text which tells the story of a fisherman who stumbles upon a peaceful hamlet with no connection to the outside world. The people here are descendants of people who fled the chaos of the Qin Dynasty (221-207 BCE): "When they asked him what age it was now, they did not [even] know of the Han [Dynasty, 206 BCE-220] much less the Wei or Jin [Dynasties, 220-316]."[12] Shen, by associating Peach Blossom Spring with Chadong (or we might even say, relocating Peach Blossom Spring to Chadong) not only claims their utopian lives for his characters (modified, though, as we will see), but also, and perhaps more importantly for the purposes of this study, he reasserts this utopian disconnection from the passage of linear time.

Therefore, we will notice that there is nothing in the passage quoted above which would give us any indication when the action of the novel takes place. Indeed, there is one brief mention of revolution just a page or so after the passage quoted above, but unless one is looking for it, it is easily glossed over. Besides this one place, there is hardly anything which would indicate that the novel is set in early Republican China as opposed to the Ming or Qing Dynasty: vehicles are all powered by men or animals, there is no mention of electricity or steam power, clothing is plain and ordinary. There is a timeless quality to the narration which is almost in inverse proportion to the specificity of place; it could be almost anytime in Western Hunan. In fact, at the beginning of the third chapter, the narrative claims that events in the rest of China have next to no effect on the lives of the people who live in this little town:

For these people, excepting the death of the family cow, an overturned boat, or some other fatal accident or bad fortune which might distress them, whatever strife or misfortune might be affecting the rest of China seemed never to penetrate the lives of the people who lived in this border town.

In any year, the days full of the most excitement for the border town were the Dragon Boat festival, the Mid-Autumn festival and the New Year's festival. The pleasure and excitement these people felt during these three holidays thirty or fifty years ago has not seen the slightest change even up to the present.[13]

In this way, timelessness is intertwined with the rhythms and cycles discussed above. The lyrical rhythms and the connections drawn to classic texts (particularly *Peach Blossom Spring*) redouble the sense of a frozen past or more appropriately an eternal present, a temporal disjuncture with what the (urban) reader is familiar in the present.

It is no mistake, moreover, that *Border Town* is set in a rural community, indeed on the borders of Chinese civilization (if not the actual borders of the modern Chinese state). The utopia that is Peach Blossom Spring and the border town of Cuicui and her grandfather is unthinkable in an urban center, for that claim to a cyclical present is in fact predicated on isolation. Ethnic tensions[14]—which could destroy the utopian eternal present of Chadong—are completely elided in the narrative in favor of maintaining utopian isolation, cyclical renewal, and timelessness. All of this is largely propelled through the narrative's lyrical voice, both as it recalls earlier literature—and thus a sense of the persistence of earlier styles and stories—and in its close identification with the eternal cycle of the seasons, as well as in its interactions with the locality of Western Hunan. The links that the narrative thus forges with the past, in turn, are implicitly contrastive with the modern, the realist, and the urban. The past, therefore, becomes an effective tool for keeping the contemporary at bay and/or a vantage from which to scrutinize the present as well as modern urban life.

The creation of an eternal present that we can see here in *Border Town*'s narrative does allow a platform from which we may contrast the contemporary present (of the novel's composition/publication or indeed of the early twenty-first century). However, as we saw in Han Shaogong's "Dad Dad Dad," it cannot lead to historical understanding. If we recall that, for Benjamin, history works as a connection between the present and certain moments from the past, we will see that Shen's narrative cannot serve as a historical constellation in Benjamin's sense precisely because the past is absent from *Border Town*. Rather the temporality—and thus, historicity—of *Border Town* is spatialized into the utopian space of Chadong which remains eternally pristine.

In this detached setting where the contemporary is thoroughly flushed from the story, Shen tells a story of a love triangle, which may owe a certain amount to the seventeenth century classic *Hongloumeng* (Dream of the Red Chamber), and a heroine whose inaction, reminiscent of Zhang Dihua in Wu Jianren's *Henhai* (*The Sea of Regret*, 1906), dooms the three to an unhappy end. Despite this, the love between Cuicui and Nuosong is a natural love, one unencumbered by social distinctions, etiquette or decorum. Her grandfather, who insists on allowing Cuicui to choose her mate for herself, is fond of saying "Carts go on the road, horses take the horse path."[15] To take the road, one should employ a match-maker and arrange the marriage in a Confucian style, assuming Cuicui is amenable. Horses, on the other hand, are their own masters; they sing for their brides and win their hearts through their songs and devotion.[16] Nuosong takes the horse path, and though their relationship is not consummated (at least in the text of the novel), he does win Cuicui's heart. The subtle, though clear, anti-Confucian tendency in this novel seems to link Shen to his contemporaries in the May Fourth Movement. Yet the lyricism of his prose, the idyllic landscape he paints oppose the realism and naturalism insisted upon by those very same authors and critics. Indeed, what I just termed an anti-Confucian tendency, perhaps, would be more aptly called an anti-authoritarian tendency, which might have further angered the often dogmatic and intolerant advocates of the new literature.[17]

The novel's ending, Cuicui alone and waiting for Nuosong perhaps to return after the death of his brother, Tianbao, who was the third corner of this love triangle, is noteworthy for its desultory tone. It seems almost to suggest change and forward progress. Nevertheless, I would argue the opposite, namely that the novel, ending as it does on the down swing of the cycle implies a resurgence and the continuation of the eternal present into the next cycle.[18]

If in *Border Town* Shen (potentially as that traveler mentioned above) claims an ability to return at will to an everlasting present of cyclic changes that have always already come full circle for his homeland, in *Xiangxing sanji* (*Random Sketches on a Trip to Hunan*, 1934) he comes to the opposite conclusion. *Random Sketches* is a collection of essays based on the same trip home of 1934 that saw the completion of *Border Town*. The essays were written after his return to Beijing with reference to letters written to his wife during this trip.[19] Here again, *Peach Blossom Spring* is reinvoked as a model for how *Random Sketches* is structured and against which it should be read. In *Random Sketches*, however, the utopia that was Peach Blossom Spring has been invaded by external forces and compelled into a linear time frame.

Perhaps the starkest example is Shen's meeting with the model for Cuicui in the chapter called "Laoban" (Old Friend). As a young soldier, he and a friend, Nuoyou (note the similarity to Nuosong), had been stationed for a while in Luxi, and his friend had fallen in love with a shop girl named Xiaocui. When Shen comes back through Luxi, he seeks out this shop where, lo and behold, there she is unchanged from all those years ago. He soon discovers, though, that his friend has actually come back and married Xiaocui, and thus the young girl keeping shop is their daughter. Nuoyou, meanwhile, has been devastated by the years and opium; so much so, in fact, that Shen can't bear to even identify himself to his old friend.

> My heart seemed to be in a tumult, but I felt that my disquiet was unreasonable. With a heart leaping such that even had I forcefully suppressed it I could not restrain [my heart from racing], I had truly stood upon the mud bank where seventeen years ago I had lain. But, as for the past, who can fence it in and keep it from passing? who can deny it permission to return? Time had oppressed my heart with all kinds of mutations in human events; I must bear it and be silent. In another seventeen years, who can say that I will not come back to this little town?
>
> Because of this springtime [i.e. to celebrate the Chinese New Year] return, I was a bit despondent, a bit lonely. . . .[20]

Time has irrevocably changed both Shen himself and his friend, Nuoyou. It truly is, as they say, that you can't go home again.

Nevertheless, Shen often invokes the sense that history has not touched these towns or these people. The epigraph at the beginning of this chapter is one example; another is in the chapter titled "Xiangziyan" (Box Cliff) in which he says,

> But if you carefully think about it, again, these people fundamentally *seem* to have no connection with history. If we look from the perspective of how they approach life and the entertainment through which they release their emotions, then it is *as if* the ancient and the modern are the same with no distinction. What my eyes see now *perhaps* is exactly the same as what Qu Yuan saw two thousand years ago.[21]

This chapter follows a more or less standard procedure for *Random Sketches* in that Shen arrives in a place, remembers what it was like when he had been there many years before, and then depicts the place now. The contrast is usually telling. In the case of "Box Cliff," Shen had witnessed the annual dragon boat races here fourteen years earlier (ca. 1920) and remembers the fantastically beautiful boats, the racers who refused to leave their boat after the race so that liquor had to be brought to them for their celebration on the river. So he goes ashore to "refresh" his memories.[22] However, instead of reliving his happy memories, Shen is confronted with a twenty-one year old man who has been crippled in anti-Communist fighting.

However, I would like to stress all those *seems* (*sihu*), *as ifs* (*haoxiang*), and *perhapses* (*huoxu*). These words are at the heart of the figurality that is the crux of what I have been calling lyricism. Shen establishes these comparisons and invokes his memories almost as straw men which are then refuted and reversed by the conclusion of the chapter. That is to say, the description of these people living an unchanging life for hundreds and even thousands of years is a metaphor. But the reality of these people's lived lives cannot be completely covered by metaphors passing for descriptions, and in the end must be revealed.[23] The revelation of the inadequacy of Shen's metaphors and memories to current reality simultaneously marks his difference, especially his urban and even cosmopolitan culture, as well as the local populace's difference from what they were in the past. If in *Border Town* Shen conjures a sense of timelessness by avoiding the explicit contrast of urban to rural (though we must admit that this contrast remains implicit at least on the extradiegetic level of narrator and readers), in *Random Sketches*, Shen makes this contrast explicit and as a result moves his characters into a modern, linear time frame.

This argument finds an important parallel in David Wang's notion of imaginary nostalgia which, in part, invokes an "aesthetic of the residue or the fragment . . . The fragmentary image serves as a synecdoche, suggesting what the missing whole might have been as well as the impossibility of restoring it."[24] Such a description, of course, recalls Benjamin's conception of a past in ruins as we have been using it here.[25] The fragment truly is an "index of absences,"[26] but it simultaneously is itself a presence carried over from the past. Thus, even as it marks loss and change, the fragment also preserves and connects to this (ruined) past. From this perspective, the fragments of memory juxtaposed in *Random*

Sketches with present conditions more or less explicitly mark Benjaminian constellations which draw our attention to the vanishing of the past. The utopian *Border Town* cannot engage such a temporal vantage precisely because utopia is beyond history. It is only in the memoir *Random Sketches* that highlights the loss of the past that those past moments, as phantasmal memories, are activated and put into contact with the present.

Roots

With the consolidation of political power, and therefore the power to direct cultural expression, in Communist hands, Shen Congwen's fiction was denounced as reactionary and pornographic and was put aside for the better part of thirty years.[27] Beginning in the 1980s, however, Shen's writings slowly began to be rehabilitated and reconsidered. In the mid 1980s, the Roots movement (*xungen*) entered the literary scene. Root Seeking was exactly what its name implies, an attempt to unearth and recover a sense of China's past which, it was felt, had been lost through all the tumult of the twentieth century. At the same time, Root Seeking was also a form of literary dialogue with a more recent past and with immediate forebears such as Lu Xun and Shen Congwen. Or in other words, Root Seeking as a movement was trying to recover much of what had been discarded by the reformers earlier in the century (many of whom entered the Communist Party), but at the same time, they owe much of their own literary viewpoint to their more recent precursors. Thus the authors writing during this period, and especially those considered part of the Roots movement, were seeking both literal and literary predecessors. As I discussed in Chapter Three, the parody of Lu Xun's "The True Story of Ah Q" in Han Shaogong's "Dad Dad Dad" is one example of the reuse and reconnection to May Fourth literary forefathers. When we remember that most of the people of this generation had put their educations on hold (often without any choice in the matter) to spend years in the countryside "learning from the peasants," it is no surprise to find that they wanted to reconnect to something both of value and arguably more permanent than the Cultural Revolution, in whose name they had gone to the countryside in the first place.

In 1985 Han Shaogong wrote an essay called "Wenxue de 'gen'" (The "Roots" of Literature) in which rather than proposing a new direction for literature, Han identifies a trend already in progress and describes (and praises) its salient characteristics. Though Han did not coin the phrase *xungen* in the article, it is this essay which is the *locus classicus* for the name of the literary movement. Han begins with the now famous question "Where has the splendorous culture of Chu gone?" and answers that question with Western Hunan![28] Han employs the botanical metaphor of roots to argue that "if the roots [of literature] are not deep, the leaves are unlikely to flourish."[29] Thus, to produce a flourishing literature, one must cultivate strong and deep roots. What is interesting is that "the countryside [*xiangtu*] is the past of the city, is a museum of folk history."[30] Or in other words, time is displaced into space so that the modern city, which "regardless of north or south, to a greater or lesser extent lacks personality, and where transient history all too easily switches [direction],"[31] is cut off from the past, tradition, and cultural roots whereas the countryside preserves and nurtures them. Before moving on, I would like to note that by schematizing time along a spatial axis, Han implicitly endorses a modern teleology of rupture with the past not unlike the Communist teleology he hopes to overleap. Han seems to suggest that by leaving the city behind, one can reconnect to tradition and cultural roots, but as we saw in the discussion of *Random Sketches* above, linear time, once it enters the picture, cannot be halted.

In the introduction to a collection of Roots stories, Wang Zengqi, who had been one of Shen Congwen's students in the 1940s, says "'searching' for what 'roots'? Searching for cultural roots. Simply put, it is an attempt to bring contemporary literature into contact with the veins of traditional culture, or so I think."[32] He goes on to say,

> Some people say that "May Fourth" is the dividing line in Chinese culture. This is not necessarily so. The "May Fourth" era experienced a certain amount of radicalism, but, in truth, the focus of the "May Fourth" movement lay not in an absolute denial of traditional culture. The true dividing line, perhaps, began in the 1940s. For quite a while now, we have emphasized only that a culture is the reflection of politics and economics, and we have relatively ignored culture's independence and continuity. When discussing traditional culture, we have mostly spoken of criticism, but seldom of continuity.[33]

Thus the cultural roots with which Roots authors are trying to connect includes traditional culture up to and including May Fourth. Indeed, it is not, as we have been taught, May Fourth which enacted an irrevocable break with tradition (though the seeds of that break certainly were planted during the May Fourth period);[34] rather, it was the rise of communism which finally succeeded in separating the modern from the traditional. Elsewhere, Li Tuo, the well known critic, has said that in linguistic terms *menglong* (misty or obscure) poetry, Roots Seeking fiction and experimental fiction "all challenge 'mainstream language' with 'marginal language.'"[35] He goes on to say that even the most conservative of Roots writers "emphasize the seductiveness of the Chinese language, and bind up [today's] spoken language with the aesthetic mindset of late Ming Dynasty *sanwen* prose writers."[36] Finally, Li expands on Wang Zengqi's intuition that the rise of communism is the true gulf that Roots writers are trying to bridge when he notes that it is precisely this focus on language, and the concurrent deemphasization of realism, which infuriates the official critics.[37]

To be sure, what is perhaps most striking when reading these Roots stories, is the degree to which they seem to have eschewed realism and embraced lyricism, as Shen Congwen had done before. For example, there is "Shangzhou chutan" (First Visit to Shangzhou, 1987) by Jia Pingwa, which owes much to Shen Congwen.

> This canyon has no road signs, has never been measured. Some people say it is sixty *li*, some say eighty. But the population is absolutely certain: sixteen households. Sixteen households make up the population of two counties. However, some of the people from Danfeng live in Luonan, and some people from

Luonan plow fields in Danfeng. Ever since ancient times, Luonan people have had black faces, whereas those from Danfeng are red. They are black, red, black, red, extremely fierce visages. From the southern end to the northern, they spit the same language from start to finish; in everyplace and in every lane it is the same jumble of accents. Perhaps the mountains surround them too thickly, the forests smother them too severely. They were almost completely cut off from the outside world. It was only with the Cultural Revolution, when line after line of people fled to Luonan from the struggles in Danfeng, that the people in the canyon first saw groups of people filing through. And it was not until two years after the collapse of the Gang of Four that they first had a telephone. The poles slant and wind from the peak down to the river bank, while the lines always limply, limply droop with the weight of countless birds. And it was only then that their first paper was established. [Now you can] read the news for half a month fifteen days later. The canyon is too big, too big, but the road is frightfully narrow, frightfully narrow and frequently forces you to wade the river. The water isn't all that deep, but it is furious and agitated, as if it is no longer water but a lane of flowing iron. When outsiders cross, even if they are not knocked down, very few escape without injury to their legs or the loss of toenails from the sand and rocks sweeping along the river. Sixteen households, you almost can't tell where they live. Occasionally rounding over the lip of the mountain [you will find] an old pine tree as thick as an embrace growing from the crevice in a split boulder which will cause you to stare wide-eyed and tongue-tied. Behind the old pine tree, below a boulder hanging in the air, suddenly there is someone's home. The roof, however, has a front half but no rear half; that half is the boulder. Half of the floor is dirt, half is a cave bored into the rock. If you push on the door and enter, the inside is as dark as night. Perhaps there is an oil lantern, perhaps not. There is a large *kang*, split wood piled in a rack, red red firelight casting a man's shadow on the wall, suddenly large, suddenly small, like the dance of a jumping ghost. The owner stands there like the character *da*, broad body, eyes flashing, teeth white as snow. Smoked meat hangs one by one from the rafters; if you're not careful you will bump your head against one. This is their sign of wealth: every year they slaughter a few pigs, smoke them pale yellow with fragrant wood. To eat a piece simply cut it off. Spring, summer, autumn and winter, swooning or sober without end. If you enter, sit on the edge of the *kang*, if they offer food, eat, if they offer water, drink. This is what they consider showing respect to friends, give a foot and get a yard. With two hands they will offer you the liquor they brewed themselves. Mostly they don't think much of talking, a face full of honest smiles. If you ask them anything, they'll answer you in a voice loud from shouting across the mountains. What they are most interested in is news from the county, province and even national and international happenings. One thing is for certain, if a huckster from the city came here he would be very popular. When they hear something they like, they laugh loudly, "Ha Ha." When they hear something that makes them angry, they cuss and swear. Without knowing it, they'll stuff a bowl of beans roasted in the fire and shucked into your hands. If you eat them, your mouth will be as dry as a chestnut. Drink three gulps of water and you're full.[38]

We can see in this passage an almost line-by-line transposition (and expansion) of the passage I quoted earlier from *Border Town*. That passage begins with a historical and geographical reference to the river, this one with a political and geographical description of the canyon. That passage then traces the flow of the river; this one traces the length of the canyon and the flow of people through it (as well as the river). That passage then discusses the people and their homes, as this one does, and like Shen's description goes on to speak of the annual cycle of their lives. Jia carefully avoids the obvious poetic allusions, but his language is just as vivid and energetic as Shen's is, not to mention his use of poetic techniques, notably repetition, parallelism and metaphor. Furthermore, despite the references to the Cultural Revolution, the Gang of Four, telephones and so on, this region is almost as untouched by linear time as Western Hunan in *Border Town* is. Indeed, it is precisely the references to those modern/contemporary things and events that demonstrate how untouched by the outside world the sixteen households in these two counties are. It took slightly more than one hundred years for the telephone (Bell's patent was issued in 1876) to make it from the United States to Shangzhou.

But here we see the crucial difference between these two stories, in *Border Town* linear time never makes and never can make that advance into the secluded area. For Jia Pingwa and his Shangzhou, time is slowed down so that we can still see what life was like a hundred or two hundred years ago. Nevertheless, time does eventually catch up, alter (spoil is too harsh a word for Jia Pingwa, though Li Hangyu, see below, might be comfortable with it) and eventually begin to homogenize the area. One suspects that the visitor mentioned at the end of the passage quoted above (reminiscent of the traveler to western Hunan in *Border Town*) is another agent of change and homogenization, namely the author (or reader) himself who is connected to the outside world and has brought tendrils of that creeping vine, globalization, into this area. Thus "First Visit to Shangzhou" though it resembles *Border Town* in its narrative structure is actually more like *Random Sketches* since it brings past and present together and allows a comparison of the two. Indeed, the divide which separates the Roots writers from traditional culture, namely the Communist revolution, necessitates the injection of linear time into the attempt to reconnect to traditional culture.[39] We saw this in Han Shaogong's discussion of cultural roots, and we see it again here in "First Visit to Shangzhou." We may explain this in the following way: since the Roots movement is working from the assumption that traditional culture has not been passed down to their generation, an assumption not shared by Shen Congwen, the attempt to reestablish contact with traditional culture must necessarily contain the consciousness of its distance, of the changes which have occurred in the meantime.

Jia Pingwa's story does not have a singular plot line; instead, it is split into several sections each telling its own story. Several of these sections can be linked parodically to *Border Town*, not only in stylistic and thematic ways as in the passage above, but also in terms of character and plot. At the same time, the story continues to juxtapose and compare past and present. First there is, for example the section entitled "Taochong" (a place name which means Peach Wash or Peach Flood)[40] which tells the story of a ferryman and his family. The ferryman is clearly based on Cuicui's grandfather, with some important differences. Foremost among these is that this ferryman has most certainly chosen this line of work for the money he can make. And he makes quite a bit, enough to elicit the jealousy of his neighbors and eventually to get him labeled a Capitalist Roader and banished from the region. I quote a section below which clearly shows that, afterwards, his formerly jealous neighbors now miss him for the simple reason that crossing the river was easier when there was a ferry. Here, although the narrative tone is neutral, there is an implicit criticism of the present (not to mention the Communist Party if not communism itself) as well as nostalgia and a sense that the past is irretrievably lost.

Second, there is the section called "Xiao Baicai" (Little Cabbage) which tells the story of the region's most talented opera performer, Xiao Baicai. She, meanwhile, is clearly modeled on Cuicui, as the ferryman above is modeled on her grandfather. She is a young girl alone in the world who has too many suitors and as a result ends up alone and loveless. However, again like the ferryman above, her story has significant differences from Cuicui's. First, in both sequence and perhaps in importance, it is not men who sing to her but she who sings (men hear themselves as her target, though whether they truly are remains debatable). At first she is beset by fans, love letters and eventually more brazen suitors. Then, when she does not settle down with any of them (in fact she is told that she is too young by her director) she is assumed to be wanton. And thus, in the Cultural Revolution, she is denounced despite the fact that she is a simple performer and more or less apolitical. Again, especially from a feminist perspective, we can find implicit criticism of the present, of what has come to pass in the area, in this storyline. In fact, I do not think it is going too far to say that Xiao Baicai is a parody of Cuicui, one who is swept up in the flow of time, very similar to the ways that "Mending Heaven" and "Shi Xiu" are parodies of traditional texts.[41]

It is also worth mentioning that the process of bringing past and present, model and copy, together that Jia engages works in line with the Benjaminian historical constellation we have been occupied with delineating in this book. The past cannot be captured, for it is in the process of vanishing. But it can be revitalized so that it informs the present and reveals the ruins of the past, specifically in this case, the violence perpetrated as a matter of course during recent historical events.

The majority of Roots stories are explicitly set in the present or recent past. Instead of employing a sense of timelessness, like *Random Sketches* they tend to contrast, sometimes implicitly sometimes explicitly, the present with the past— the branches with the roots, if you will. "First Visit to Shangzhou," as mentioned earlier, seems almost in its entirety to enact just such a juxtaposition of the old and the new.

> Ten years had passed, eighteen years had passed, the Shimen River and the Luo River still were flowing, still flowed together, Taochong [a small peninsula between the two rivers] still had not been washed away. Only, a lot of electricity plants and reservoirs had been built upriver on the Luo, and the water had gradually declined. That small ferry boat was gone. People once again had to walk up seven *li* and return to those long stepping stones or that long bridge made of bound planks. The brave still used this path, but the timid had to wind

> ten *li* to arrive at a concrete bridge. . . . The peach blossoms on Taochong
> bloomed and wilted. The people in the village couldn't help but think of the old
> man and his family [who had lived on Taochong]. They felt that family had
> been wronged and regretted the jealousy they had felt at the time. . . .[42]

There are some clear differences from the way things used to be, and the local
people even consciously regret at least some of what has been lost. Yet, rather
than seeing some real change, these people simply revert to an even earlier mode
of life. The tone here, as it is throughout the story, is neutral, and, on the next
page, the past is somewhat restored by the return of the old man's son to resume
running a ferry across the rivers (a second reversion). Elsewhere we see city folk
traveling into the region (in the same way that we the readers do as well) and
comparing their life in the city to the lives they find here in Shangzhou. In fact
that comparison is implicit throughout the story, surfacing at various moments,
like the one quoted above or in statements such as "Although communism was
never fully realized, people's goodness was preserved here and developed into
an exquisite virtue which can cause outsiders to marvel, sigh, and catch the bug,
learn [from them] and act accordingly [in their own lives]."[43]

If there is one character, however, who is unable or unwilling to make peace
with new events, it can be none other than Chai Fukui in Li Hangyu's "Zuihou
yige yulaor" (The Last Fisherman, 1982). Chai is the last fisherman left on the
Gechuan River, which has seen its fish population decline drastically because of
pollution from upstream. All the other fishermen have found other jobs and deserted the river, but Chai stays on. It is how his forebears had lived before him,
and it is all he understands. When he needs new hooks for his lines, the shop
clerk, who doesn't carry hooks anymore since all the fishermen have gone,
sends him to Dagui who has a set of hooks. But Dagui is holding on to them
because they are hand-made folk craft of museum quality. "Museum, antique,
foreigners whatever, these things were one hundred eight thousand *li* removed
from him. What he could grasp was eating, sleeping, tending his lines . . . ."[44]
Chai has out-lived his times, and new vocabulary such as *museum* or *antique*
marks this change. His former mistress, Ahqi, still hopes to marry Chai but insists that he find a more stable and reliable line of work. She even finds a job for
him in a local MSG factory, but his response is firm and final, "I certainly don't
want to be miserable in a factory. . . . At a certain time go to work and at a certain time get off, work in a conch shell, how is that better than the freedom of
fishing? [Do you think] I could live such a repressed life?"[45]

Chai's fierce resistance to change, to linear time, is, of course, futile. But in
an important sense, his struggle preserves the tradition of fishing with which he
is so familiar in a more human way than a set of hooks on display in a museum
could ever do.[46] We see here even more explicitly than in "First Visit to
Shangzhou" another incarnation of the aesthetic of the fragment, which simultaneously fetishizes the loss of plenitude and conserves a splinter of the original.
The struggle to preserve an embodied connection to the past through Chai's
memories and daily practices is ultimately imperfect, but without it, no translation of or historical connection to the past (in a Benjaminian sense) is possible.

Chai and his dedication to a dying way of life force us to witness the vanishing of the past.

In this chapter, I have focused on lyricism and its connection to local places. In the process we have seen that the interaction between the lyrical and the local is also often enmeshed in themes of utopia and dystopia. Indeed, we might schematize the texts we have examined in this chapter and say that *Border Town* reflects a fully utopian view, "First Visit to Shangzhou" depicts a declining utopia, *Random Sketches* and "The Last Fisherman" illustrate fallen utopias (perhaps something close to reality?). To push this schematization one step further, the extradiegetic contrast between *Border Town*'s readers' (most likely urban) lives and the story recapitulates the inability to find Peach Blossom Spring again. Thus we can imagine the spectrum of possibility I have laid out turning back on itself, becoming a circle oscillating between utopia and dystopia.

An important aspect of these explorations of utopia and dystopia is that, as we have seen, they are intricately concerned with the displacement of the temporal into spatial terms. Specifically, this displacement opposes urban to rural, relegating the rural to the past. This is true regardless of whether the past/rural is valorized or denigrated. Of course, the modernist discourse appropriated by Communist teleology makes more or less the same displacement (though the argument could be made that it is made the other way around—displacing space into time).[47] What is striking in this comparison, however, is that for modernizers and Communists alike, utopia is to be found in the perfected future. For these texts, as we have seen though, utopia, or the lost utopia is sought for in the rural/past. There is, certainly, a long and venerable history in China of looking to the past for perfect models for society, one not fully displaced until the twentieth century, largely through the efforts of May Fourth modernizers and their successors. What I am hoping to highlight here is the resistance to that modern orientation towards the future, but at the same time, the ways in which it becomes inescapable for these Twentieth Century texts. One of my main arguments in this study, of course, is that it is with the Communists that this modernist discourse is most fully implemented. As a result, the Roots writings are perhaps mired even more deeply in this discourse, even as they struggle to extricate themselves from it. Yet, Shen Congwen, while he may exhibit more latitude in this regard, certainly is not exempt. This may help explain why *Border Town* is the only text I have examined here which comes close to embodying again the utopia of *Peach Blossom Spring*. In so doing, though, it removes itself from the kind of Benjaminian historical discourse which puts past and present into communication with each other that we have been tracing in this space.

However, the aesthetics of the fragment, embodied in Chai Fukui's fierce but futile resistance to change as well as in Shen Congwen's memories recounted in *Random Sketches*, attests to the perseverance of at least a portion of the past or of tradition. This fragment is translated into a modern idiom marking loss simultaneously as it incorporates and sustains within itself what it once was. Thus, the fragment allows a partial continuity, one that I would argue makes possible discerning the contours of the absent whole. The fragment, of course, is also the basic unit which is used to construct a Benjaminian historical constellation. For Shen on his trip back home or for Chai as he traverses the river, the past is clearly in ruins. But linking to that ruined past, in memory or vocation, helps to infuse it with liberatory power for the individuals involved and blast it out of the homogenous continuum of modernist history so that the past can be preserved, even if only as a fragment, and inform the present with its vitality.

Chapter 6
Tradition in Exile: Allusion and Quotation in Bai Xianyong's *Taipei People*

—One evening when I was on night patrol, I discovered an old soldier sitting alone on a boulder on the beach outside the base playing an erhu. *That night the moon was clear and bright, there was no breeze off the ocean. I couldn't tell if it was his slumped, brooding posture or that terribly sad sound of the* erhu, *but suddenly I realized the misery and worry he felt over his lost home must be as deep and as far away as that felt by frontier guards in ancient times.*

Bai Xianyong, "A Sea of Blood Red Azaleas," from *Taipei People*

In Chapter Four, I discussed "The Eternal Yin Xueyan," one of the stories collected in Bai Xianyong's short story collection *Taibei ren* (Taipei People, 1971). There I focused on the "China trope" and the ways the characters populating the narrative close off communication between past and present, choosing to live, for all intents and purposes, in the past. In this chapter, I look specifically at two other stories from *Taipei People*, "Liang fu yin" (The Song of Liang Fu, 1967) and "Youyuan jingmeng" (Wandering the Garden, Waking from Dream, 1966), but in my analysis, I show that they produce slightly different effects. While from a certain point of view the characters in these two stories are equally blinkered to the present, instead focusing all their attention on the past, the narratives also allow for certain lines of communication to open between past and present, allowing the past to powerfully, and in the case of "Wandering the Garden, Waking from Dream" viscerally, affect the present.

The stories in *Taipei People* depict a wide range of characters from all social classes and from various different Chinese provinces, and each story needs to be considered individually as well as part of a collection. Still, in aggregate the stories of *Taipei People* describe the lives of mainlanders who have retreated to Taiwan with the Nationalist regime. Already a decade or more has passed since they arrived in Taiwan, as they originally thought only temporarily, and they have settled into routines, accumulated petty grievances, made new acquaintances and so on. But though their lives may be located in Taipei, they are not and can never be Taipei people—their hearts and minds reside elsewhere: in Sichuan, in Guilin, in Jiangnan.

These other locales and the histories attached to them make their ghostly return in the memories of these exiles. Already, though they would not dare to consciously acknowledge the fact, they realize there will be no triumphant military conquest or spectacular resumption of their former lives. Still, the phantasmal and fantastic image of China—which stands for so many different things for different people, but mostly indicates home—flashes brilliantly in their imaginations. And they cling to any fragment—a snippet of song or poetry, scars, food, mahjong—that can help them stoke those memories, no matter how much pain those same memories may bring them.

Individually, the stories which comprise *Taipei People* describe different types of mainlander exiles. But it seems to me, and the analysis below reflects this, that each story also experiments with different notions of the past or tradition and different ways, successful or unsuccessful, of keeping the past fresh and active in the present. Yin Xueyan, as discussed in Chapter Four, cultivates a singleminded focus on the past which leaves no room for the present; the young narrator in "A Sea of Blood Red Azaleas," as we see in the epigraph above, experiences a moment of recognition and sympathy for the loss the older generation has suffered; Pu Gong in "The Song of Liang Fu" nurtures the past, like his orchids, in the hopes of passing it on to future generations; and Madame Qian in "Wandering the Garden, Waking from Dream" is physically and emotionally seized by an uncontrollable eruption of memory into her present moment.

"The Song of Liang Fu"

At the end of "The Song of Liang Fu," a story which mostly consists of two people sharing memories of a mutual friend who has just passed away, we find the following description.

> A breeze picked up as Pu Gong[1] returned to the courtyard at the end of this winter's day, and the purple bamboo that filled the yard began to shiver and rustle. Blood red was smeared across the western sky, cold and congealed up there. Pu Gong stepped across the courtyard, but then stopped. There was a three-tiered, black iron rack with nine pots of orchids neatly arranged on it. They were all the best quality of Pure Heart orchid; the nine porcelain pots were square, filled with cold fir wood mulch, and were decorated with a blue and white pattern of dragons. The orchids had already passed their period of lush blooms; three or five wretched petals hung from dry, brown stalks and exuded a slight strand of cold fragrance. But each of the leaves radiated a lush green. Pu Gong stopped in front of those several dejected, potted orchids, hands clasped behind his back, lost in reverie for quite a while; the full, silver beard that lay upon his chest was blown about by the wind. He thought again of many things from half a century before, during the 1911 Revolution, that he had long ago forgotten. Not until his grandson, Xiaoxian, came and pulled on his sleeve did he lean on his grandson's shoulder, and the two of them, grandfather and grandson, went in together to share dinner.[2]

The parallels—and parallel contrasts—are neatly orchestrated in this passage. The season, winter, and time of day, sunset, both nicely mirror not only the state of the orchids, entering dormancy, but also Pu Gong's stage in life, nearing death.[3] Likewise, the few petals—hanging listlessly—mimic Pu Gong's beard, which in turn flutters in the wind like the bamboos around him. In contrast to this, there are the green leaves and Pu Gong's grandson, Xiaoxian, counterbalancing the decay and decline of the flowers and Pu Gong himself.

The ghostly appearance of otherwise forgotten memories from so long ago clearly has a strong impact on Pu Gong as he stands oblivious to the wind or the passing moments. If we take Pu Gong, then, perhaps especially because of his indulgence in memory (which has made up the bulk of the preceding story) as a representative of the past and his grandson as a representative of the future, it seems to me to be very indicative of Bai Xianyong's approach to this issue in this story that the two should go together to share a meal. The intimacy which this interaction reveals is telling, and indeed, may figure one of the major functions carried out by this collection of short stories: the transmission of a (nearly forgotten) tradition. Indeed, Xiaoxian's name might be roughly translated as "following in the steps of ancestors." And true to his name, earlier in the story Xiaoxian displays his ability to memorize the Tang poems his grandfather has taught him despite the fact that he was born in America and did not speak a word of Chinese when his grandmother first brought him back to Taiwan.

Indeed, although the narrative merely touches upon certain poems, classical poetry bears great signifying power in this story. And because the narrative does not linger over these references, it requires a certain amount of unraveling to reveal the layers of contexts which inform the poetry's meaning and therefore resonate with the larger narrative surrounding it. Take, for instance, the couplets which, in the finest calligraphy, adorn Pu Gong's study walls. It is worth mentioning that the configuration of Pu Gong's study is a visual and spatial model of the sorts of links and juxtapositions Benjamin envisions when he speaks of historical constellations which remove eras from linear notions of cause and effect. Instead, new associations are created and dialogues established in order to bring certain meanings and resonances to the fore. In this way, as we will see, the lines which hang on Pu Gong's walls intersect not only with each other but also with the people who enter the room to create new configurations of signification and reveal new vantages on history.

As a former general in the nationalist army, one who served during both the 1911 Revolution and the 1927 Northern Expedition, it is no surprise that Sun Yat-sen's famous last enjoinder to his party, "The Revolution is not yet complete / Comrades, we must still be diligent" is hung on one wall. Paired with this on another wall is a couplet from Du Fu's poem "Deng lou" (Climbing the Tower): "The Jin River spreads spring across the land / The clouds above Yulei Mountain substitute ancient times for the present." These lines are particularly difficult to translate;[4] Du Fu is cultivating a certain sensual isomorphism (the coming of spring which every year is the same and clouds eternally floating above Yulei peak) which seems to transport the poet back in time (or perhaps transport the past into the present). The sensation of being unable to distinguish the present from the past is oddly sympathetic to Sun Yat-sen's notion of revolution in the future perfect tense, for an eternally incomplete revolution makes no distinction between past or present. Thus what on first glance are merely the sort of commonplace quotations to hang on the study walls of an elite member of this society actually fit together and reinforce each other as we would expect from a Benjaminian constellation. Despite this, there is also an important contrast set up by the juxtaposition of these two couplets. While Du Fu yearns for ancient times, Sun Yat-sen urges his followers on to the (ever incomplete) bright future. This sort of temporal disjuncture—indulging in memories of the past to the extent of nearly forgetting (or ignoring) the present even as the goal of retaking the mainland is constantly invoked—infects most of the characters in *Taipei People*, perhaps especially Pu Gong and Madame Qian (who will be discussed below), and leaves them in a certain state of limbo in which they indulge in nostalgia of the future tense: looking forward to the restoration of a remembered past. The fragmentary nature of that re-membered past is reflected in the fragmentary nature of this couplet from Du Fu which is taken out of the poem in which it was composed to be displayed on Pu Gong's wall. Of course, for those well versed in Classical Chinese poetry, like most of Pu Gong's peers, the invocation of a couplet is enough to recall a mental (phantasmal) image of the entire poem, a fact which Bai Xianyong counts on in this case. Still, as we saw in our discussion of Roots literature in Chapter Five, the fragment may resonate with the present in powerful ways, but as fragment it precludes the possibility of truly recapitulating the past in the present. Instead it relies on the Benjaminian transformation to give it a second life in the present.

Du Fu, of course, is the great poet of exile in the Chinese tradition. In "Climbing the Tower," written in 764 when he was living in Chengdu, the capital of the ancient state of Shu, Du Fu, as in many of his poems, bemoans the war-torn state of China in the mid eighth century. In this case, he compares the situation to that of the Three Kingdoms period and likens himself to the great (but unsuccessful) minister of Shu, Zhuge Liang. Moreover, a line from Du Fu's "Shu xiang" (Prime Minister of Shu) is used in a memorial scroll at the funeral of Pu Gong's friend, Wang Mengyang. Such assiduous cultivation of associations and allusions both to Du Fu and to Zhuge Liang contributes to what Joseph Lau calls a "foreboding vision of catastrophe,"[5] but which I might rather say is a pervading sense—not only in this story but also throughout the collection—of elegy and indeed in many cases even anticlimax after the catastrophe has already occurred. Neither Du Fu nor Zhuge Liang were successful in their political endeavors. Du Fu's one goal was to serve in government, but he was only ever able to attain minor positions at infrequent intervals. Zhuge Liang, although rising to the position of Prime Minister in the state of Shu, never was able to restore the Han Dynasty (the rulers of Shu were of the same lineage as the Han emperors). Given the abiding and indeed all-consuming ambition to retake the mainland, it may seem inauspicious to link oneself to Du Fu or Zhuge Liang given their failures.[6]

And yet, given the cultural stature of both Du Fu and Zhuge Liang, we can hardly say that the use of their figures is in any way unusual.[7] In fact, Cao Cao, the ruler of Wei, another of the Three Kingdoms—ultimately, it was his son who was able to unify the country—might be a better figure to emulate if we are concerned with military and political triumph. However, the fact that he is always seen as the villain of this period makes Cao Cao an almost impossible choice. So we return to Du Fu and Zhuge Liang to assert cultural and civilizational superiority even in the face of hopeless struggle. It is worth remembering that, at the time of the composition of "The Song of Liang Fu," the Communists were sweeping all this feudal dross away in the Cultural Revolution,[8] and as mark of their difference from the Communists, it is no surprise that the mainlander exiles on Taiwan would emphasize connections to traditional culture.

To further complicate the poetic references cultivated here, this poem, "Climbing the Tower," ends with the poet reciting "The Song of Liang Fu," which was said to be one of Zhuge's favorites.[9] "The Song of Liang Fu," which gives this story its name, is a Han Dynasty Yuefu poem that concerns events from the Warring States period. The poem laments the plot hatched by the Prime Minister of Qi, Yanzi, to kill three unsurpassed warriors by causing them to vie among themselves for two peaches. Since the three are so formidable, they actually pose a threat to the Duke of Qi. To negate the threat, Yanzi persuades the duke to offer two peaches to anyone who can claim merit. Naturally, since all three have shown valor and skill, but since there are only two peaches, one is shamed. The other two, likewise, are shamed that they stepped forward to claim the peaches themselves. All three commit suicide to maintain their honor.[10]

As in its namesake, Bai Xianyong's story tells the tale of three valorous soldiers: Pu Gong, Zhong Gong, and Wang Mengyang. While all three had been cadets in the Sichuan Military Academy, they did not become friends until they all served together during the 1911 Revolution. Now, as an old retired general, after the loss of the mainland and the last of the three still alive, Pu Gong recalls their glory days on the afternoon after Wang Mengyang's funeral. He reminisces how they smuggled munitions into Wuchang (now, part of Wuhan) in a bridal procession in which Zhong Gong played the part of the groom, Zhong Gong's wife played the bride, and Pu Gong and Wang Mengyang were sedan bearers. Afterwards, the three swore brotherhood to each other. Pu Gong relates his memories in the following manner.

[Wang Mengyang] was the most heated, I still remember, he had drunk so much his face was completely red. He slapped his sword on the table and pulled me and Zhongmo [Zhong Gong] outside into the courtyard where we swore a blood oath after the fashion of Liu [Bei], Guan [Yu], and Zhang [Fei] in the Peach Garden. We raised our heads to heaven and swore "If we don't kill the Manchu swine, may we not return alive." And we agreed, come what may in the years to come, to enjoy fortune and face troubles together.[11]

The reference here, of course, is again to the Three Kingdoms period when Liu Bei, Guan Yu, and Zhang Fei swore brotherhood to each other. Again we see parallels and contrasts between the two stories to which Bai alludes. Both "The

Song of Liang Fu" and the friendship between Liu Bei, Guan Yu and Zhang Fei concern three outstanding military men. But the story of the oath in Peach Garden concerns the beginnings of their careers while "The Song of Liang Fu" concerns the end. Likewise, Pu Gong relates the story of the beginning of his and his two best friends' careers long after those careers are over. And, as we saw in the story's ending passage, it is precisely this tension—between flourishing and decline—that Bai's story taps.

It is clear from the narrative that present decline clearly has the upper hand over Pu Gong's memories of his youth: he falls asleep in the middle of a game of go. Still, he is remarkably vigorous for a man of his age: the narrative makes a special point of noting his purposive stride and erect bearing on several occasions. Those moments of reverie, however, stand out not only for the youth and dynamism they demonstrate in contrast to Pu Gong's current life but especially because they mark moments when he was at the center of China's momentous history of the twentieth century; whereas now, Pu Gong is at both a spatial and temporal remove from that center. And what is worse, like his friends Zhongmo and Mengyang, there is little likelihood of Pu Gong's ever returning to the mainland alive.

Nevertheless, because these memories stand out starkly against Pu Gong's current situation, they can be grouped into something like a Benjaminian historical constellation. As such they are reinfused with life and, what's more, meaning for Pu Gong. Most important of all, Pu Gong does not recount his memories in solitude; he is accompanied by a younger (though now in his fifties) former assistant and student of Wang Mengyang's, Commissioner Lei. Invoking the mode of historical biography, in the vein of Sima Qian, Commissioner Lei seeks this information to be included in a (semi-official) biography of Wang Mengyang, a former Chief of Staff in the military. Indeed Pu Gong says, "'You may include it,' Pu Gong nodded in approving permission, 'I'm the only one left who knows all the valiant deeds of your teacher's youth. At the time we swore brotherhood, although things were slapdash and we were just a bunch of hot-blooded fellows rushing about for revolution, still, it was precisely that rushing about that established the Republic.'"[12] We see here a moment of the personal historical constellation resonating on the level of greater society. And this is why I focus our attention on the presence of Commissioner Lei, because, while his character remains fairly undeveloped in the story, he is the conduit through which this particular tradition can be preserved and passed on—analogously to the way that on an extradiegetic level, the collection *Taipei People* is a conduit for passing on tradition as well.

It is a tradition with few heirs, however. Wang Mengyang's son, recently returned from America, created trouble with the funeral: "Probably he has lived abroad for too long and so he doesn't really understand our Chinese customs and rituals [that maintain] human relationships."[13] He shows no consideration for his father's second wife who cared for him as his health failed, and he spurns Buddhist rituals that disperse bad karma because the family has converted to Christianity. That indifference to and (perhaps) incomprehension of Chinese modes of human interaction is attributed to American (non)culture and its ability to appropriate traditions and drain them of their specificity. Indeed, Americanization—universal shorthand for the creeping homogenization of global capital—and communism are the two peaches offered to the Chinese people that bring death with them. Caught between the millennial fervor of communist anti-tradition and the whitewashing of American style non-tradition, the only safe path is to choose not to eat a peach, as it seems Pu Gong has done. But of course this choice leads to passivity and eventually to irrelevance; tradition no longer has any bearing on modern life.

In contrast, the other example of an Americanized member of the younger generation is so fascinating. Xiaoxian, it seems, has been rescued from the fate of Americanization. He has been brought back to a place where he can be steeped in Chinese tradition: both the sorts of oral histories Pu Gong can relate to him as well as the Tang dynasty poetry Pu Gong teaches him. And so we come again to the ending of this story and the scene in which Pu Gong leans on his young grandson as they enter the house together to eat dinner. Against the backdrop of a winter evening that had seen the funeral of one of the last of the generation of the 1911 Revolution, all things for Pu Gong seem to be at an end. But then there is his grandson come to help him inside and perhaps to continue his grandfather's legacy, as his name would indicate.

"Wandering the Garden, Waking from Dream"

If in "The Song of Liang Fu" we see the possibility of continuity for a tradition uprooted and transplanted into new and hostile ground, in "Wandering the Garden, Waking from Dream" we see that tradition brought to crisis. As with "The Song of Liang Fu," the title of this story, "Wandering the Garden, Waking from Dream," is an allusion to a classical text, in this case scene 10 of the famous Ming dynasty drama *Mudan ting* (Peony Pavilion). In this scene the heroine of *Peony Pavilion*, Du Liniang, visits for the first time a garden housed in her father's official residence (he is a government official) which she had not known of before her maid told her. Moved by the abundance, beauty, and above all the flowers in the garden, Liniang falls asleep and dreams of a romantic encounter with a young examination candidate, Liu Mengmei, before she is startled awake by the entrance of her mother. *Peony Pavilion* goes on to describe how Liniang dies of longing for her dream lover, but is reincarnated when Liu Mengmei happens upon the garden (now her grave). After some trials—and Mengmei's successful examination—the two lovers marry and live happily ever after.

"Wandering the Garden, Waking from Dream" relates the events of an evening soiree at the home of Madame Dou, wife of the important General Dou, told from the perspective of Madame Qian, widow of General Qian. Although Madame Dou's fortunes have risen dramatically in recent years, things were not always so.

> You could count only one or two of the ladies and wives in Nanjing whose status was higher than [Madame Qian's]. Don't even mention the concubines of officials. She was openly married as Qian Pengzhi's official wife. Pitiful "Cas-

sia Fragrance [Madame Dou's stage name]," she didn't even have the standing
to invite her own guests to a party, so she had to serve as hostess at "Cassia
Fragrance's" birthday party. Not until coming to Taiwan has "Cassia Fragrance"
had the nerve to throw a party like this. And she was only in her early twenties
then; a sing-song girl became the wife of a general overnight. How many singing girls can marry into an average household? How much rarer, then, to marry
nobility? Even her own sister, Number Seventeen, "Red Moon," had said to her,
unkindly: "Sister, you should put up your hair. Tomorrow when you walk together with General Qian, people will think you are his granddaughter!" Qian
Pengzhi was approaching sixty the year he married her, but no matter what you
said about it, she was still his officially recognized wife.[14]

Madame Dou had been one of those "concubines of officials" while they still
lived in Nanjing, only recently being raised to the position of first wife of General Dou. Despite her former prominence, since moving to Taiwan, Madame
Qian has been living in the south, away from Taipei's high society. For this reason Joseph Lau calls her a "double exile."[15] The narrative reflects her unease
with this kind of social situation from the very beginning when she arrives at the
Dou's mansion in a taxi only to find a double row of parked, government owned,
black sedans of the kind given to high ranking officials for their use.

Her disquiet continues as she enters the mansion and is introduced to new
acquaintances and reunited with old friends; among the latter are most prominently Madame Dou and her younger sister Jiang Biyue, both of whom had also
been performers in Nanjing with Madame Qian. In fact, the fun prepared at this
party is precisely the performance and enjoyment of Chinese opera, for all the
guests are themselves connoisseurs and performers. Madame Qian, though away
from society for years now, is still renowned for her singing.

> Qian Pengzhi had said that, after returning to Shanghai, he had thought night
> and day about hearing her sing "Wandering the Garden, Waking from Dream"
> when he had visited the Captured Moon Theater in Nanjing. No matter what he
> did, she stuck in his heart, so he turned around, went back, and married her.
> Qian Pengzhi always said to her, he could ask for nothing more in his later
> years than to have her by his side singing a few lines of Kunqu [opera]. She had
> only just become a favorite at the Captured Moon Theater. From her first line
> of Kunqu, the entire hall was filled with cheers. One of the teachers said: "Of
> everyone in the [district of the] Confucian temple, only "Blue Field Jade [Ma-
> dame Qian's stage name]" is the true inheritor of the Kunqu tradition.[16]

So we see that it is precisely Madame Qian's singing of "Wandering the Garden,
Waking from Dream" that propels her to stardom and from there to officially
recognized status as General Qian's wife. And we learn early on in the story that
Jiang Biyue has set up a sort of competition between Madame Qian and another
guest, Mrs. Xu, in which the latter would sing "Wandering the Garden" while
Madame Qian sings "Waking from Dream."

Still the connection between Madame Qian and this scene from *Peony Pavilion* is stronger, and indeed, more visceral—at least on the night of Madame
Dou's party—than merely the fact that she is known for performing it. And as
we saw in "The Song of Liang Fu," the impact of "Wandering the Garden, Wak-

ing from Dream" on Madame Qian is augmented and refracted through layers of other dramatic works which touch upon the narrative. The first of these is *Luo shen* (Goddess of the Luo River) which tells the romantic story of Cao Zhi's (one of Cao Cao's sons) encounter with a goddess. The story is based on a poem Cao Zhi wrote. Traditionally there has been much speculation that the goddess in the poem is a covert reference to the empress, that is to say Cao Zhi's brother's wife.

Goddess of the Luo River is brought up in conversation before dinner by Colonel Cheng, the young, handsome officer who is quite knowledgeable about opera and whom Madame Dou had asked to make sure Madame Qian enjoys herself. As the narrative reveals a bit later, Colonel Cheng shares many of the same traits as one of the officers formerly serving under General Qian, Colonel Zheng Yanqing.[17] More importantly, the reference to *Goddess of the Luo River* resonates on several levels with Madame Qian's own life. First, there is the affair she had with Colonel Zheng, a younger man's illicit courtship of an elder's wife. This has been the one moment in Madame Qian's life for romance. In comparison to General Qian, who dotes on her, but as we have seen is long past his prime, the affair with Colonel Zheng is described in a moment of stream-of-consciousness ecstasy which conflates two events: a toast at a party and a horse ride.

> Then he raised his wine glass saying: Madame. That pair of oiled, black riding boots snapped together with a *pa da*, a pair of nickel spurs flashed in the eyes. He was so drunk his eyelids blinked peach blossoms, yet still he called: Madame. I'll help you onto your horse, Madame, he said, his tight riding pants revealed the rippling muscles of his legs, like tongs clamped on the horse's belly. His horse was white, the road was also white, the tree trunks were also white, that white horse of his flashed under the fierce sun. They said: both sides of the road to the Sun Yat-sen Memorial are lined with white birch trees. That white horse of his began to run between the rows of birch, just like a white rabbit dashing back and forth through a patch of wheat. The sun shone on the horses' backs steaming out tendrils of white mist. One white horse. One black horse—both horses foamed with sweat. His body was covered in the pungent scent of horse sweat. His eyebrows became jade green, his eyes were like two balls of black flame, pearls of sweat streamed from his forehead to his flushed cheeks. The sun, I called. The sun glares so brightly I can't open my eyes. The tree trunks, pure white and slender, bark peeling away, revealed naked and tender flesh within . . .[18]

While the narrative does not give an explicit account of the actual consummation of their affair, the eroticism of this passage hardly needs further elaboration. Second, and here we see again the sort of twist that Bai imposes on the classical allusions he employs, instead of brothers competing for the same woman, the affair with Colonel Zheng ends tragically when Madame Qian's own sister, Red Moon, steals him away from her.

Of course, when *Goddess of the Luo River* is brought up by Colonel Cheng, there is no indication of the echoes it will recall later in the narrative. It remains a bit of polite conversation at a party of opera cognoscenti which primes the pump, so to speak, for the emotional disarray which Madame Qian, lost in her reveries, experiences as the party progresses. After a splendid dinner, the performances, the highlight of the party, begin. And it is at this point that Bai's story begins to actually quote sections of the several operas. It is also at this point that the dramatic texts evoke responses in Madame Qian's mind and memories. First, Jiang Biyue performs the part of Yang Yuhuan from *Guifei zuijiu* (The Drunken Beauty).[19] In this scene Yang Yuhuan, the emperor's favorite consort, becomes drunk when the emperor visits another of his wives instead of Yang.

> Jiang Biyue naturally played drunk, wobbling all about at precarious angles, like a fish flopping on dry land. She picked the wine cup up with her lips, and then with a *dang lang* tossed it to the floor, singing:
> Life is but a spring dream
> Thus, to open my heart, I'll drink a few cups
> The guests immediately fell about laughing. Madame Dou, out of breath from laughing, shouted to Madame Lai in a hoarse voice: "It looks like Biyue is really dunk!"[20]

While the rest of the party enjoys this revelry, we know that Madame Qian, long absent from this sort of social gathering, has just been toasted many times by friends old and new and is herself uncomfortably drunk. At the same time, all these toasts have reminded Madame Qian of a farewell party on the mainland when her sister and Colonel Zheng both toasted her, announcing obliquely the end of her affair with the young officer and simultaneously injuring her voice even though she needed to perform later that evening.

We begin to see a pattern in the ways the traditional texts interact with the modern narrative. As before with *Goddess of the Luo River*, the inclusion of *The Drunken Beauty* simultaneously reflects Madame Qian's state of mind as well as an important difference. In this case, Madame Qian, like Yang Yuhuan, is drunk. And like the emperor's favorite, she is drunk in connection to a disappointment in love. However, unlike Yang, Madame Qian has no desire to be drunk, and indeed finds her drunkenness able only to hamper her singing. This is true both in her memory of the farewell party and in the present party at Madame Dou's home. That is to say, life may be a spring dream, but Madame Qian is not living for the moment with open heart; rather, she is locked away in her memories even if those memories are to some extent spurred by the activities going on around her.

With Madame Qian's emotional stage set, the narrative turns to "Wandering the Garden, Waking from Dream." As Joseph Lau remarks, the next section of this story is a tour de force for Bai Xianyong and his use of the western, modernist literary technique, stream-of-consciousness (part of which I have quoted above), without, at the same time, also disrupting the thoroughly Chinese voice of his writing.[21] What transpires here is that as Mrs. Xu takes the stage, the narrative dives into Madame Qian's consciousness, juxtaposing and conflating, in a truly Benjaminian manner, the present with several crucial moments in the history of her marriage and the affair with Colonel Zheng: General Qian's love and care for her (though not passion), Madame Dou's party in which Jiang Biyue and Colonel Cheng (among others) both toast her, the party in Nanjing in which both her sister and Colonel Zheng toast her, the horse riding episode, the performance after the Nanjing party when she begged the music instructor to play the music in a lower key because she had drunk too much earlier, and the fortune telling of a blind, female musician suggesting that a misplaced bone will lead to tragedy for Madame Qian.

Punctuating these chaotic and repeated images are lines from (Mrs. Xu's performance of) "Wandering the Garden." These lines both reflect Madame Qian's state of mind and spur her frantic emotions into further confusion. So while Mrs. Xu plays Du Liniang, in a very real sense Madame Qian has become Du Lininag, suffering the same emotional tumult and misgivings as the fictional heroine. The effect created here is not unlike that created in Han Shaogong' parodies discussed in Chapter Three. There is an important difference, however, in that while from one point of view Madame Qian recapitulates Du Liniang's emotional state, from another point of view, Madame Qian's state of mind is at odds with Du Liniang's. For example, Mrs. Xu sings,

> From turbulent heart these springtime thoughts of love
> will not be banished
> —O with what suddenness
> comes this discontent!
> I was a pretty child and so
> of equal eminence must the family be
> truly immortals, no less
> to receive me in marriage.
> But for what grand alliance
> is this springtime of my youth
> so cast away?
> What eyes may light upon my sleeping form?[22]

If for Du Liniang these lines refer to the possibility of spinsterhood, for Madame Qian they reflect the difference in age between General Qian and herself and from there lead to the memory of the day she and Colonel Zheng rode to the Sun Yat-sen Memorial and finally to the following declaration:

> Glory and wealth—it's just too bad you have a misplaced bone. Fated tragic love, sister, he is elder sister's fated tragic love. Listen to me, sister, fated tragic love. Glory and wealth—but I lived only that once. Do you understand? Sister, he's my fated tragic love. Glory and wealth—only that once. Glory and wealth—I lived only once.[23]

So like Du Lininag, Madame Qian is suited to marry into a family of eminence, but in contrast to her fictional counterpart, it is precisely because of that marriage that "the springtime of [her] youth [is] so cast away." Only once in her life has Madame Qian truly experienced a love as passionate as Du Lininag's, and even if it is better to have loved and lost, for Madame Qian, it still does not seem to have made up for a passionless marriage. Finally, Madame Qian reacts to the lines, "Lingering / where to reveal my true desires! / Suffering / this wasting, / where but to Heaven shall my lament be made!"[24]

> It was in that moment, a discarded, wasted life—in that moment, she sat down next to him, dressed in gold and red, in that moment, those two flushed, drunken faces drew together, in that moment, I saw their eyes: her eyes, his eyes. Finished, I knew, in that moment, where but to Heaven—[25]

Again, though the words to express her emotions, "discarded, wasted life" and "where but to Heaven" are drawn from Du Liniang's aria, the sentiments are diametrically opposite of those for Du Lininag. While the young Liniang is excited for the first time by the riot of a spring garden in full bloom and aroused in response to that excitement—an arousal which is confirmed and consummated in the dream—the middle aged Madame Qian, in a kind of perverse *memoire involuntaire*, relives, perhaps for the last time, that moment of arousal as a loss.

As with Liniang, the narrative recounting of Madame Qian's encounter with Colonel Zheng occurs in a dream. And as with Liniang, Madame Qian is startled back to the present by the completion of Mrs. Xu's performance and Jiang Biyue's insistence that she then sing "Waking from Dream." Abruptly, with the claim that she has become hoarse, Madame Qian absolutely refuses to sing. Thus while the narrative describes Madame Qian waking to the present, there is no performance of "Waking from Dream." In a sense, then, especially as we have seen that Madame Qian's dream is of a much more desolate variety than Du Liniang's, there is no waking; the dream continues. That is to say, even startled from her dream-like state, Madame Qian remains mired in those memories and defined by them in her everyday life.

The term, *cansheng*, which Birch translates as "this wasting" and I translate as "wasted life," as Lau notes, could also very well be translated as "residual life."[26] From this vantage it is appropriate to view Madame Qian as a displaced revenant, haunting a new locale with memories of another time and place. And the compulsive return of phantasmal memories of another place is a major reason these Taipei people cannot put down roots in their new home. In this Madame Qian is unquestionably representative of all the various Taipei people considered in Bai's collection. Madame Qian may be situated on the island of Taiwan, but her life, and more importantly, the meaning she can attribute to that life, remains located on the mainland.

What may be worse—and this is certainly a possibility that Pu Gong would refuse to contemplate—the meaning of their lives remains to be found only in *memories* of the mainland; for even if they were to return, China is an irretrievably altered place. It is for this reason, more than the assertion of some putative civilizational superiority over the Communists, that these Taipei people rely so heavily on traditional texts in order to buttress their self-identity. Figures like Du Fu, Zhuge Liang, and Du Liniang, seem eternal and timeless in the ways we commonly speak of them. So, to establish a Benjaminian historical constellation with the likes of these (or the cultural works associated with them) is precisely an assertion of continuity in an era of turbulent change.

However, as we have seen here, this sort of linking, making the traditional text speak to a modern age also changes it, whether it be the altered context in which Madame Qian understands Du Liniang's complaints or the three valorous soldiers who, unlike the three in the poem "Song of Liang Fu," live long past the time of their glory, indeed, live long enough to see all that they fought for lost. These sorts of changes are inevitable; in fact, it is precisely these changes which Benjamin found so powerful in his notion of history, for they allow communication, a link to be established, between past and present, even as the ruins of the past are brought to light through the action of that very communication.

As I have suggested above, if this is true of the individual stories in *Taipei People*, it is also true of the collection as a whole. That is to say, the arrangement of these stories which open themselves to transformed pasts in a variety of ways becomes a (second-order) Benjaminian constellation. The juxtaposition and recombination of Pu Gong's memories with Madame Qian's memories, with Yin Xueyan's, and with those of the other stories in the collection augment the effects of each individual story. And this new historical constellation establishes its own resonance and rapport with *Taipei People*'s readership enabling a collective experience of a transformed and fragmentary Chinese tradition. In this way the past in ruins can be transmitted.

Chapter 7
Back to the Future: Temporality and Cliché in Wang Anyi's *Song of Everlasting Sorrow*

—Who can appreciate time like Wang Qiyao? Don't be fooled into thinking she passes her days in a haze, uncomprehendingly, that is just subterfuge. When the curtains jostle, what you see is the wind, what Wang Qiyao sees is time. Or in the holes in the floor or the stairs, what you see are ants, what Wang Qiyao sees is time. When Wang Qiyao lingers before going to bed on Sunday night, who says she is passing the night alone? She is carting the flow of time!
Wang Anyi, *Song of Everlasting Sorrow*

This chapter aims to provide a reading of the temporal role cliché plays in one contemporary Chinese novel, *Changhenge* (Song of Everlasting Sorrow, 1995) by Wang Anyi. Specifically, I attend to the two clichéd death scenes—the second of which ends the novel—as the culmination of a historical sentiment which is also observable at other levels in the narrative. To set the stage for the examination of these death scenes, I first note other repetitions and link this to a nostalgic conception of time which, rather than looking to the future, emphasizes return. My use of the term *cliché*, then, in addition to its common meaning of a pat or overused idea or expression, is also meant to indicate a nostalgic process of reiteration and repetition which (re)circulates time and opens onto a non-progressive sense of history. I will have more to say on this below.

There are several reasons why *Song of Everlasting Sorrow* is especially fertile ground for an inquiry into repetition and the circulation of time. First, its title is the same as the Tang Dynasty poem "Song of Everlasting Sorrow" by Bo Juyi, and there is a clear but complex intertextual relationship between the novel, the poem, and a third text, the Qing Dynasty drama *Changshengdian* (Palace of Everlasting Life) by Hong Sheng. The citation and circulation of this story, in addition to being a venerable literary tradition, provides a template for other citations and circulations of other temporalities in the novel. However and second, rather than retell the Tang Dynasty story, the novel traces the personal history of its protagonist, Wang Qiyao, over four decades from the mid 1940s to the mid 1980s, and the effects this historical era has on Wang Qiyao's experience also help us organize reflections on the interactions between past and present or past and future. Finally, the language, style, and themes that Wang Anyi employs, as we can see in the epigraph above, continuously evoke issues of time and its passage.

I am certainly not the first critic to note the nostalgic tone that suffuses the novel, nor that this nostalgia links to a consumer culture which both is depicted in the novel and marks the book itself as a consumable vessel for such nostalgia. Coming in the aftermath of the post-Tiananmen, heady economic boom jumpstarted by Deng Xiaoping's trip to the Shenzhen stock market in 1992, the novel helped fill a need, in an apparently apolitical way, for an easy reconnection to a time which seemed lost.[1] Dai Jinhua's words on the "Mao Zedong fever" which was more or less contemporary to the novel's publication are, thus, also apropos of *Song of Everlasting Sorrow*: "It truly was a process of ideological production and reproduction and at the same time a very typical process of production/consumption."[2] For these reasons the novel appeals both to a popular audience because it taps into the contemporary fad for nostalgia and to critics who see in it a bellwether for cultural life in the mid 1990s.

While I have learned much from these other critics, and in places echo and build from some of their observations, my concerns largely lie elsewhere. I believe what sets this analysis apart is the close attention paid to cliché and the alternative historical form based in repetition and reiteration that it enables. This alternative historical form, in turn, allows an understanding of women in Chinese culture which reads somewhat like a twenty-first century "J'accuse!" revealing a crime of murder committed against women again and again over the years. Such a feminist theme fits in well with concerns expressed elsewhere in Wang Anyi's writing, both essays and fiction,[3] but in discussions of *Song of Everlasting Sorrow* seems to be lost amid analyses of nostalgia, desire, and consumerism and the resonances that can be drawn with 1980s and 1990s Chinese society and culture. Hence, I discuss nostalgia not so much as a reflection on the production or indeed the reception of the novel but rather as a means to illuminate the historical work cliché undertakes in the novel.

Cliché and Nonprogressive History

In earlier chapters we have already been concerned with how the passage of time or interactions between past, present, and future are intricately intertwined with notions of history. Expanding upon that, I will briefly discuss how the issue of cliché is also wrapped up with Benjaminian conceptions of history before moving on to a consideration of the novel. In a reading of Benjamin reading Baudelaire, Elissa Marder finds history in the medium of repetition and cliché. Benjamin has said that Baudelaire was the last lyric poet but also that his poetry "render[s] the possibility of lyric poetry questionable . . . He went so far as to proclaim his goal 'the creation of a cliché.'"[4] The contradiction of a lyric poet whose poetry highlights the impossibility of lyricism leads Marder to note that this construction makes Baudelaire not a lyric poet but a "simulacrum" and a "stuttering ghost"[5] who marks the passing of lyric poetry through the creation of cliché.

The sense of cliché which Benjamin attributes to Baudelaire and on which Marder builds is not merely an overused and hackneyed mode of expression; rather, it marks the shock of experience which comes to define modernity for Benjamin.

> Baudelaire battled the crowd—with the impotent rage of someone fighting the rain or the wind. This is the nature of something lived through (*Erlebnis*) to which Baudelaire has given the weight of experience (*Erfahrung*). He indicated the price for which the sensation of the modern age may be had: the disintegration of the aura in the experience of shock. He paid dearly for consenting to this disintegration . . .[6]

Earlier, Benjamin relates this shock, which in Baudelaire's poetry is given form in cliché, to the fragmentation of experience created by industrialization: "The shock experience which the passer-by has in the crowd corresponds to what the worker 'experiences' at his machine."[7] That is to say, the shock destroys any inherent, cohesive sense of life on a human scale and, in its place, establishes life set to mechanical rhythms, to which people, like factory workers, must adjust. The arbitrary, from the individual perspective, flows of crowds along the boulevards, then, correspond to the equally arbitrary flows of industrial products towards and away from the worker's station as they make their way through the process of production. In this understanding, the cliché embodies the shock experience and makes it comprehensible at the price of knocking it out of the temporality of "something lived through" and freezing it as "experience," which can now only be understood as a disembodied fragment left over from a lost whole.

For both Benjamin and Marder, Baudelaire's poem "A une passante" is critical to this understanding of cliché and linking it with temporality. The poem of unrequited love (already a clichéd sentiment), in the form of a sonnet with two quatrains and two tercets, turns on the fabulous cliché in the middle of the poem (the first line of the first tercet) which reads, "Un éclair . . . puis la nuit! [A flash . . . then night!]" This instantaneous flash, as in a photographic flash, marks the unattainable moment between passing and past; as Marder says, "The poem attempts to arrest, photographically, the impossible temporal disjunction evoked by [the woman's] passage."[8] The ellipses, equally important to the cliché constructed here, like the flash, also mark the seemingly instantaneous yet actually lengthy passage of time. The sonnet becomes, then, a stuttering freeze-frame eternally marking the woman's passing, linking us to a fleeting presence, yet one, in truth, which is already gone. The flash and ellipses, we must also note, are the supreme cliché, seen in countless films, poems, or other narratives to signify what otherwise escapes the power of language to describe, that is, an incomprehensible yet powerful realization or recognition which stops the individual's sense of temporality even while time sweeps on in the real world. Or in other words, the shock of experience.

Clichés of this nature abound in *Song of Everlasting Sorrow*; indeed the novel revels in them in a way not unlike Baudelaire. The fifth chapter of the novel, "Wang Qiyao," which introduces the heroine of the novel, begins by noting Wang Qiyao's very clichédness: "Wang Qiyao is the typical daughter of Shanghai's alleys."[9] The word which I have translated as "typical," *dianxing*, can also mean stereotypical or cliché, and as a type or cliché, Wang Qiyao is spoken of in general terms as a representative for all the other girls like her. Furthermore, by my count, in the four pages which make up this chapter there are fifty-seven clichéd idioms, many of which are four-word *chengyu*, including, for example, *xinghuo liaoyuan* (setting the prairie ablaze), *posuo dengguang* (dancing lamplight), *chuochuo yueying* (overflowing moonlight), *chuchu dongren* (enticing), and *yaoxiang miman* (the fragrance of the herbal medicine fills the air). Even for those that may not be included in a *chengyu* dictionary per se, to the extent that they encourage and engage in the lilting four character rhythm of the Chinese language, in which *chengyu* plays such an important role, these turns of phrase significantly add to the narrative's deployment of cliché on the linguistic level. In addition, these clichés, as we can see in several of the examples I have listed above, evoke a certain romantic sentimentalism which itself has by this time become hackneyed and strained. For example,

> Wang Qiyao is the typical [*dianxing*] unbetrothed [*daizi guizhong*] daughter; the girls that the apprentices in the foreign firms follow with their eyes are all Wang Qiyao. On days when they air out clothes [*futian shaidu*], Wang Qiyao gazes into her mother's trunk and longs for [*chongjing*] her own trousseau. The girls wearing their wedding trains in the photos of photo studio display windows are the final Wang Qiyao on her way to be married. Wang Qiyao always outshines flowers and the moon [*bihua xiuyue*]: wearing a blue patterned *qipao*, she is voluptuous [*shenying yingying*], her ink black hair covering a pair of eyes that can speak.[10]

The overwrought and overused images of outshining the moon and flowers or eyes that can speak, and so on, hardly need to be pointed out. The narrative itself even notes that this sentimentalism is clichéd.

> There is not one Wang Qiyao who is not a sentimentalist, a fashionable kind of sentimentalism. Their affectations are all studied. Pressing fallen leaves in books, preserving butterflies in rouge jars, and the tears that they cause themselves to cry are all done in imitation of the crowd. That sentimentalism is predetermined, conviction following form, but we can't say that it is entirely false, only that the sequence is reversed; it is a true thing when it is done. Every sort of thing in this place is a facsimile and has a guide.[11]

But this admission on the part of the narrative, as we can see, is not apologetic or even condemning; it is, rather, indulgent and accepting.

The facsimile with which this last quotation ends is important to keep in mind as we come to a further understanding of cliché. If we follow Marder, the customary understanding of cliché as this sort of pat turn of phrase, image, or idea is augmented through a focus on its etymological root indicating "the mechanical reproduction of letters [or] photographs, coupled with an emphasis upon an image which is cast in relief."[12] Cliché, then, is the negative image which enables a positive production (as in the development of a photograph) by replacing darkness with light and absence with presence. Like a photographic negative, history as negative image is captured in an instant, in a flash, but remains to be endlessly reiterated in static and rigid form: "The true picture of the past flits by. The past can be seized only as an image which flashes up at the instant when it can be recognized and is never seen again."[13] Baudelaire's poetry as cliché, in this conception, is the negative image that (re)inscribes history on its audience, and this is possible precisely because Baudelaire is no longer a lyric poet but a modern one. The flash in "A une passante" is such a cliché, (re)counting the impossible or imaginary connection between the poet and his paramour (since she is veiled in the poem, and thus cannot return his gaze) and marking the poem not as lyrical, nor yet as parody of lyricism, but as modern. The cliché snaps the image of the past, transforming and freezing it as "experience," thereby preserving and enabling its connection to the present moment.

Cliché, then, conceived of as a rigid framework enabling history through multiple reconnections to a "flashing" image of the past, is marked by the same anti-progressive notion of history as is expressed in Benjamin's "Theses on the Philosophy of History." To reiterate, in the "Theses," Benjamin argues that the job of the historian is to "[grasp] the constellation which his own era has formed with a definite earlier one."[14] In this way history is removed from base chronology or a simplified notion of cause and effect. Instead, history is a process of linking eras on the basis of echoes, repercussions, and resonances and establishing thereby constellations through which the mutual implications not only of the past in the present but also the present in the past are illuminated.

For Benjamin, non-progressive history is radical, liberating, and messianic. In *Song of Everlasting Sorrow*, however, the radicalism of the nonprogressive historical urge is found in a focus on the everyday and the feminine. That is, it is clear that one of the main contrasts to Wang Qiyao's personal history is the official history of the Communist state which, in the 1960s and 1970s, was so exuberant in its millennial zeal. Given this contrast, and indeed the implicit valorization of the former and criticism of the latter, historical liberation in the novel appears in the form of a quiet and homey emphasis on the individual rather than the collective, and especially on the feminine rather than the masculine. Likewise, its radicalism is to be found in its emphasis on quotidian, domestic life and the exemplarity of the mundane. *Song of Everlasting Sorrow*, then, deploys this nonprogressive historical sense for specifically feminist ends which reflect personal, not political, desires. However, when we draw a contrast to the largely absent official history, in a sense orienting the historical constellation against the dark background of the rest of the night's sky, we can see how the personal and individual liberation of such a feminist nonprogressive history is able to expose the violence underpinning official history.

Since I am borrowing Marder's metaphor of the negative image and photography, we should note, briefly, the important role that cinema and especially photography play in *Song of Everlasting Sorrow*. "The story of forty years began on the day they went to the movie studio."[15] This is the opening line of Chapter Six of the novel which begins Wang Qiyao's individual story and which is titled "The Studio." While at the studio she witnesses the filming of a death scene which proves central to Wang Qiyao's story. More importantly for our immediate purposes, a director who meets Wang Qiyao on the day of her visit sends her to be photographed, an activity to which Wang Qiyao took "like a fish to water,"[16] yet another cliché. And Wang Qiyao's minor fame is launched when a magazine decides to include one of those photographs in its publication.

> The photo which later was selected for the inside cover of *Shanghai Life* was of her in an everyday *qipao* with a flower pattern. She was sitting on a stone bench next to a stone table, her face in a slight profile, as if she was listening to someone speaking outside the frame. In the background was a round window with the silhouette of flowers and leaves; it was clearly a screen. Although the scenery was of the outdoors, the light was indoors and manmade. And as for her posture, even if she was speaking with someone, it was a posed conversation. Actually, this photograph was of the most common sort, even a touch vulgar, every studio display window had one. It was pretty but not the epitome of pretty. But this photo had something which stuck to people's hearts. There is only one word which can describe the Wang Qiyao in the photo: compliant. That compliance can be tailored to different people's hearts, men's hearts and women's hearts. Her visage was compliant, her figure was compliant, the pattern of flowers on her *qipao* was the most compliant type, fine, a flower here a flower there, wanting to be friends with you. The scenery was fake, the light was fake, her posture was fake, the entire photo, to be honest, was fake, but precisely because it was fake, the woman in it became real.[17]

The false note struck by this photo is analogous to the false note struck by a tired cliché. It captures a moment, posed and common as it is, that resonates with her fellow citizens of Shanghai. And in its countless reiterations (in magazine copies and display windows), as negative image, it makes that moment palpable to its viewers, inscribing on them the salience of a common and compliant sort of prettiness. As we saw above, the fragment of time captured in this photograph and in this cliché opens onto a personal and familiar historical sense in which the salvational power is found precisely in the individual or minor effects and emotions it elicits in its audience.

Photography and especially film are, of course, the preeminent examples Benjamin uses to discuss his theory of the transformations art undergoes in the "age of mechanical reproduction." Film and photography, like cliché in Baudelaire's poetry, also mark the shock of experience and the destruction of the aura which before the modern period had inhered in art.[18] These are mass art forms which, Benjamin argues, find their value in exhibition which, in turn, is enabled by the reproductive technologies which lie at the heart of photography and film. Benjamin says,

> There is a tremendous difference between the pictures [a painter or a cameraman] obtain. That of the painter is a total one, that of the cameraman consists of multiple fragments which are assembled under a new law. Thus, for contemporary man the representation of reality by the film is incomparably more signifi-

cant than that of the painter, since it offers, precisely because of the thorough-going permeation of reality with mechanical equipment, an aspect of reality which is free of all equipment.[19]

Benjamin's emphasis on "multiple fragments which are assembled under a new law" naturally parallels the work of establishing historical constellations be-tween eras that has been a major focus of this book. A photograph, such as the one of Wang Qiyao described above, is constructed, through framing, screens, props, and so on, in such a way as to offer "an aspect of reality which is free of all equipment" so that, as the narrative says, "the woman in it became real." In a sense this is a reauthorization of the aura, but in such a way that it inheres not in the photo itself but in its effects on its audience. That is, through its exhibition, in shop display windows and magazine covers, as a rigid, materialized es-sence—in this case of compliance—it comes to make an impact on the masses, creating resonance with a memory of a (lost) past; that is to say, nostalgia. Like the imaginary connection between Baudelaire and the *passante*, the imaginary connection drawn between the photo (or the cliché) and its mass audience is the dynamic force which puts the experience in motion and infuses it with historical significance or aura.

There are two aspects of this approach to history and cliché that are espe-cially important for my treatment of *Song of Everlasting Sorrow*. First, the no-tion that cliché is a device which reveals the presence of an absent object is rele-vant in particular in regards to the several death scenes in the novel which the narrative explicitly marks as hackneyed and staged. Indeed it is this very clichéd presentation of death, which strikes Wang Qiyao as so uninspired but which, nevertheless, in the flash of the final moment, shows the murder of a woman to be the one eternal and unavoidable historical fact. Second, the multiple iterations of love, of women, of the city, and of fashion which circulate through the novel, like multiple prints of a photo, likewise render the past visible—instill it with exhibition value—and infuse the present with its liberating presence.

From Everlasting Sorrow to Everlasting Life and Back Again

The love story of Tang Xuanzong (Emperor Xuanzong of the Tang Dynasty, also known as Tang Minghuang or Emperor Ming of the Tang Dynasty, r. 712-756) and Yang Guifei (Imperial Consort Yang, also known as Yang Yuhuan) has its beginnings in history. As in other stories in Chinese history of the cata-strophic consequences for the State of love which exceeds Confucian bounds (stories such as those of Baosi or Xishi), love for a beautiful woman distracts the ruler from governing which in turn leads to revolt and the fall of proper rule.[20] The An Lushan rebellion (755-763) caused the court to flee the capital as well as the executions of Yang and her cousin, Yang Guozhong, who had been the prime minister. Xuanzong abdicated in favor of his son, and lived out the re-mainder of his life in retirement and grief for the loss of China as well as Yang.

The official historical take on the femme fatale would have ended here (as, indeed, the precedents mentioned above do) with clear censure of the emperor for neglecting his duties. However, in the Mid-Tang period, a discourse of *qing* (*eros*, love, passion) was on the rise, a discourse whose development owed much to Bo Juyi's participation.[21] "Song of Everlasting Sorrow," as a result, goes on to tell of a Daoist who travels to an island of the immortals on the emperor's behalf. There he meets with Yang (in the afterlife renamed Taizhen [Ultimate Truth]), and takes back to the emperor two tokens of her love, a gold hairpin and a shell box, each of which she has broken, keeping a piece herself. She also reminds the emperor of a vow they swore of unfailing love. The poem ends with these lines, "Ancient Heaven and old Earth in time will cease / Only this sorrow goes on without end."[22] The poem, thus, ends with the lovers parted and endless sorrow resulting from their separation.

Hong Sheng's *Palace of Everlasting Life* takes Bo Juyi's "Song of Everlasting Sorrow" one step further, for here the lovers are reunited after death in the celestial realm. In their own ways, both Wai-yee Li and Stephen Owen have argued that the drama stages an elaborate separation (through juxtaposition and contrast) of the mythic and the historic (for Li) or the poetic and the ironic (for Owen). For both scholars the circulation of the musical piece *Nichang yuyi* (Coats of feathers, rainbow skirts) through the different realms (mythic, poetic, historic, ironic) is crucial to their ultimate separation and therefore the reunification of the lovers as an apotheosis of the mythic or poetic.[23] Only through such a separation of two distinct realms (whatever their provenance) can Hong Sheng validate the *qing* of Xuanzong and Yang Guifei without opening that validation to Confucian censure and, in turn, enable their ultimate and eternal reunion.

Before moving on, I would like to draw our attention to the iteration and reiteration of the same material among and between different registers which is apparent in these two tellings of the Yang Guifei story. Such iteration simultaneously marks a separation and distancing. This is true in terms of the overall story which, in the transition from "Changhenge" to *Changshengdian*, is transposed from poetry to drama and from separation to reunion, as well as in the iteration of the music *Nichang yuyi*, which, as Li and Owen indicate, distinguishes the transcendent from the mundane. As with the parodies examined in Part One, this separation attendant upon iteration is analogous to the Derridean *supplement*: both necessary and excessive.[24] That is, there is no lack inherent in Bo Juyi's poem except precisely the lack that Hong Sheng reads into the narrative—namely a need for the lovers to be united eternally in the transcendent realm, if not in this one—and supplements through his reiteration of the story.

The *supplement* we see here, marking the poem "Changhenge" and the drama *Changshengdian* as both the same and yet different, relates to our earlier discussion of cliché as repetition linking the present to a particular past. The repetition of sameness in cliché certainly serves to expose the past within the present. But this mutual implication, as an attentive reading of Benjamin reveals, does not indicate the collapse of past and present; rather, the present is thereby valorized as a moment of liberation. With this understanding, we can say that *Palace of Everlasting Life* is liberated through the supplement of its reiteration of the Yang Guifei story to uphold *qing* and its power in human life as a virtue. This issue resurfaces in the novel *Song of Everlasting Sorrow* in the paradox of

Wang Qiyao being simultaneously both an individual and a (stereo)type. Related to this, as we will see in my discussion below, is the seeming contradiction of taking Wang Qiyao's life as both the epitome of a minor history and as representative of Shanghai as a whole (and therefore not minor). In the following, I will recall our attention to the Derridean *supplement* as it is appropriate to highlight the oscillation between various positions without the negation of one or the other.

We see a further iteration of the story in Wang Anyi's novel. Naturally, we also see a further separation, for here, while Wang Anyi adopts the theme of *qing* as exemplified in the story-cycle of "Song of Everlasting Sorrow" and *Palace of Everlasting Life*, she removes her story from that of Tang Xuanzong and Yang Guifei. Instead, she tells the story of Wang Qiyao, who, in 1946, at the age of seventeen placed third in the first Miss Shanghai beauty pageant after the end of the anti-Japanese war. The first and second place winners, one can infer, possess striking beauty, but Wang Qiyao places third specifically because of her "girl-next-door" loveliness:

> Wang Qiyao came in third place, [and so was] commonly called Third Miss. This name specifically referred to Wang Qiyao. Her beauty and refinement were subtle, not enough to place first, but were appreciated by regular people and encapsulated by the name Third Miss. . . . We could say that she was the true representative of the majority; this majority, though silent, is the most basic element of romance and beauty in this elegant city. Those walking on the boulevards are all Third Misses. The first and second place winners were for formal occasions, they took responsibility for the tasks of young ladies' diplomacy. We never saw them unless it was a special occasion. They were [an integral] part of special occasions. Third Misses, however, are familiar and everyday images; seeing them in *qipao* warms the heart. Third Miss, in truth, best embodies the people's view. The first and second place winners were idols, our ideals and beliefs. But Third Miss is related to our everyday activities, she makes us think of things like marriage, life, and family.[25]

Not only are Wang's charms down-home, familiar and above all comforting, but it is the (self)recognition of them by Shanghai's citizens[26] that links her to the city itself and that makes her the embodiment of all the other Third Misses in Shanghai.

Simultaneously, it is her election as Third Miss that brings Wang Qiyao to prominence and to the notice of Li zhuren who takes her as a mistress. Wan Yan notes that correspondences between the Yang Guifei story and *Song of Everlasting Sorrow* start and end with the universal recognition of Wang's beauty in the pageant and her subsequent sexual monopolization by state authority (in the person of Li zhuren, a military official—we may also note that Li was the imperial surname of the emperors during the Tang Dynasty[27]). However, while the relationship between Yang Guifei and Tang Xuanzong leads to national crisis and Yang's execution, the national crisis contemporary with Wang Qiyao, namely the civil war, takes no interest in her relationship with Li zhuren, and, in contrast to Bo Juyi's "Song of Everlasting Sorrow," it is Li who dies, in this case in a plane crash.[28] For Wang Qiyao there is no reunion in the afterlife; indeed, her relationship with Li zhuren could hardly be called passionate, it is more aptly described as a merger of two congruent forms of capital: Wang's cultural capital in the form of her beauty and the resulting title as Third Miss and Li's political capital in the form of his official position and the resulting economic capital that position enables him to control. Instead of reunion in the transcendent realm, Wang is forced to make her way through the vastly altered world of Communist China which officially sanctions the destruction of all the various forms of capital she had accumulated herself and as a result of her relationship with Li zhuren. The parallels between the plots of the two stories, thus, are confined to Book One of the novel while Books Two and Three go on to tell the story of the modern Yang Guifei unleashed not only from the imperatives of history but also from her emperor.[29] Nevertheless, Wang Qiyao is not therefore able to escape Yang Guifei's fate; it is only delayed. While Yang was hanged by the roadside at Mawei, Wang is strangled in her bed by an acquaintance who then goes on to steal the few remaining pieces of jewelry Li zhuren had given Wang Qiyao.

Despite this extended hiatus in the parallels between the two storylines, thematic similarities remain. Notable among these are the fairly evenly spaced references to *Nichang yuyi* (here reversed to *yuyi nichang*).[30] Instead of referring to a piece of music, however, Wang Anyi restores *yuyi nichang*—feathered skirts and rainbow jacket—to its literal sense of extravagant and decorative clothing so that she can then immediately raise this image as a figure for women, Shanghai, and Wang Qiyao herself. For example, there is this first mention of feathered skirts and rainbow jacket in the narrative's discussion of the beauty pageant.

> At least half of Shanghai's splendor is based on the desire for fame and wealth [on the part of women like those competing in the pageant]. If this desire did not exist, more than half of this city's shops would fail. Shanghai's splendor, in truth, is the elegance of women: what the breeze wafts is the scent of women's perfume, and women's outfits outnumber men's outfits in the display windows. The shade of a French parasol tree is feminine, and the fragrant peach blossoms framed by bamboo in the garden are symbols for women. The damp breeze in the season of spring drizzles is the petty tantrum of a woman, and the *jiji nong-nong* of the Shanghai dialect is specifically designed for a woman to express herself. This city itself is like a great woman, [clad in] feathered skirts and rainbow jacket; the gold and silver spread across the sky and the multi-colored clouds are the costume of a woman ascending to heaven.[31]

We see in this passage those venerable Chinese clichés of peach blossoms and bamboo, and indeed the final reference to a woman ascending to heaven is itself a reminder of Hong Sheng's modification of the Yang Guifei tale. At the same time, Wang Anyi has subjected this story to a further transformation by specifically linking women (primarily represented by Wang Qiyao) to the city, taking them as two sides of the same coin or, we might say, as each other's supplement. Furthermore, while in *Palace of Everlasting Life* the circulation of the music *Rainbow Jacket and Feathered Skirts* through the various registers separated high and low, mythic and historic, or poetic and ironic, in *Song of Everlasting*

Sorrow, Wang Anyi takes its inversion, feathered skirts and rainbow jacket, literally a kind of dress, as sign and symbol for one part of such a division: the low (as opposed to the high), minor or personal history (as opposed to major or national history), and women (as opposed to men). The narrative thereby emphasizes the minority of Wang Qiyao's personal history and links it specifically to the lives of women as well as to the city in implicit contrast to concerns of national history.

Both Shanghai and women faced ambivalent challenges and aid from the Communist state. Undoubtedly, women gained much from Communist rule: the right to divorce, to right to free marriage, the right to equal work and respect, and so on. Nevertheless, at the same time that the famous adage "women hold up half the sky" was used to support extending such rights to women, it also gave ideological sustenance to the reshaping of women in the form of men. These effects notwithstanding, women also continued to be held to different standards especially in terms of sexual mores.[32] On the other hand, for various reasons, not least of which was fear of contamination from its semi-colonial atmosphere, "Shanghai was transformed from a financial service center to the workshop of Red China."[33] While this quotation is almost certainly an oversimplification, Shanghai has always been a manufacturing center and has always been more than that too, it is true that the Communist authorities felt the need to deemphasize certain aspects of Shanghai life. In this way, not unlike the way women were made to be like men, the attempt was made to pave over differences between Shanghai and the rest of China. By insisting on the minority of Shanghai and Wang Qiyao's history, Wang Anyi is upholding difference to resist homogenizing national history and as a supplement to it.

An important link both in binding Wang Qiyao and Shanghai together and in highlighting the aspects of minor history in this story are the first five allegorical chapters of the novel. These five chapters, "Nongtang" [The alleys, pronounced *longtang* in the Shanghai dialect], "Liuyan" [Gossip], "Guige" [The inner chamber], "Gezi" [Pigeons], and "Wang Qiyao," constitute the whole of Book 1, Part 1 (*diyibu diyizhang*), and it is only in Book 1, Part 2 that Wang Qiyao's individual story is begun. We begin, then, with the *nongtang*, Shanghai's back alleyways, dark, dirty and yet homey. We move on to gossip, that form of communication which, according to the novel, is particularly suited to women. Next is a description of the girls and young women of the *nongtang*. Then the pigeons who are ubiquitous throughout the city, and finally Wang Qiyao who, as we saw in the discussion of cliché above, is here taken as a figure for all of the young women in Shanghai.

Throughout these opening chapters, any concern with major history or the national stage—including most of Shanghai's own robust economic activity, which the narrative, with the exception of consumerism, largely seems to associate with masculinity—is scrupulously expunged to make way for personal, local, private, and especially feminine concerns. These are then concentrated in the person of Wang Qiyao that "typical daughter of Shanghai's *nongtang*." While, Yang Guifei was sought and found precisely because of her exceptional beauty, Wang Qiyao is the archetype of the average Shanghai women. Despite this important difference, both women's stories crucially revolve around the intersection of public and private time, of major and minor history. That is to say, while life in the *nongtang*, full of gossip and pigeons, does shelter the Wang Qiyaos of petty urban Shanghai from major history and public time—as the imperial palace sheltered Yang Guifei—the effects of public time and major history do filter down—as, of course, they also did into Yang Guifei's personal life during the An Lushan rebellion. Thus, while private time and minor history may largely ignore the major history of public time in everyday life, the latter affects the broad contours of the former, sometimes dramatically as when Wang Qiyao's friend and sometimes lover, Mr. Cheng, commits suicide at the beginning of the Cultural Revolution.

A Conflict of Time

A careful reading of *Song of Everlasting Sorrow* reveals an intriguing phenomenon: Wang Anyi is surprisingly stingy with explicit time markers. In dramatic contrast to the specificity of the novel's spatial setting (Shanghai is the focus of the very first phrase of the novel: "Shanghai, when viewed from an extreme height. . . "),[34] time has to wait until page 31, in Book One, Part Two, Chapter Seven to make its first appearance. And even there, the time is far from explicit: "taking advantage of the current nostalgia for Ruan Lingyu. . . ." It is not until Chapter Nine that a specific date is mentioned: "Shanghai at the end of 1945. . . ."[35]

Of course, Shanghai is, relatively speaking, a young city, so it would be hard to guess wrong by more than a hundred years or so. Furthermore, the narrative, through mention of, say, trams but not rickshaws, and most prominently movies and movie studios, or indeed the end of the Anti-Japanese War, reveals nearly exactly when the story takes place. Thus, it is not a question of confusion for the reader, or poor narrative construction on the part of the author; rather, it is an issue of narrative emphasis and revelation: what does the narrative reveal to its audience, and when does it disclose this information? That is, the narrative chooses to emphasize minor history both by focusing on the small events in private lives and by neglecting the clear markers—that is, dates based in a concept of "homogenous, empty time,"[36] to use Benjamin's phrase—of official history.

The novel is divided into three overarching sections (what I have translated as Books 1-3) which correspond to pre-Communist Shanghai, Communist Shanghai, and post-Mao Shanghai, or roughly 1945-1949, 1949-1976, and 1977-1986 respectively. By my count, in all of Book One, there are six points at which the temporal setting is indicated (one of these being the vague indication of a period of nostalgia for Ruan Lingyu cited above). Book Two, on the other hand, has eleven, though five of these are merely specifications of the season with no date given. In contrast to Books One and Two, Book Three has nine references to specific dates, one to a nonspecific time, and two in close proximity to a specific reference thus implying their attachment to that specific date.[37]

Similarly, Wang Qiyao's age is kept in a certain ambiguity until the beginning of Book Three. That is to say, we know that Wang Qiyao has recently graduated from high school when she competes in the Miss Shanghai pageant, and so her affair with Li zhuren would take her into her early twenties. While the text does mention Wang Qiyao "at the age of 25,"[38] there is no year to compare with here. It is not until page 266, however, that we discover "In 1976, Wang Qiyao was 47 years old," which allows us to calculate in retrospect that she was born in 1929 and was seventeen when she became Third Miss in 1946. The allegorical tendencies of the novel, that is of treating people, activities, and locations as representative of higher-level narrative issues, is in large part driven by this de-emphasis of public time, for it is their very generalizability that enables them to resonate on higher planes of meaning.[39]

The first conclusion to be drawn from these observations is that the instances in which the narrative notes explicit dates mark those moments when public time intrudes on private time: 1945-1946, the end of the Anti-Japanese War and the Miss Shanghai pageant; 1948-1949, the establishment of the communist state and the death of Li zhuren; 1958, the Great Leap Forward and shortage of food everywhere; 1966, the start of the Cultural Revolution and Mr. Cheng's suicide; 1976-1978, the fall of the Gang of Four and Weiwei's (Wang Qiyao's daughter) early adulthood; the 1980s, the Deng Xiaoping era modernizations and the return of retro fashions from Wang Qiyao's youth.

The second conclusion to be drawn from these observations is that, at the risk of stating the obvious, this neglect of specific dates is most marked at the beginning of the novel, lessened slightly in the middle, and most remedied in Book Three. This is certainly not to say that in Book Three dates are suddenly crystal clear. Dates here are, however, noted more frequently and in greater specificity than earlier in the novel. In other words, we are never in doubt as to in which era of modern Chinese history the events of the narrative take place. Indeed, it is important that the narrative be roughly plottable according to the historical arc of the development of the PRC. Rather the central aspect to which I want to draw our attention is that the narrative consistently deflects concern away from major history, in part, by deemphasizing the importance of one of major history's essential tools, namely specific dates. As a result, events, people, and places further in the past are more generalizable and time is dissolved into the referentiality of allegory; whereas, as the text approaches the contemporary period, the uniqueness of moments, indicated by an increasing frequency of specific dates, precipitates out of the flow of time until the final singular moment of death. Again, this is not a full blown effect, but a noticeable trend resulting from increased specificity in the public temporal setting of the novel.

On the other hand, rather than think in terms of such an opposition as that between allegory and realism, we can also see that during the Maoist period (and to some extent the late Republican period as well), the opposition is between public time and private time in which the latter is marginalized, ignored, and finally erased in the discourses of the former. In the post-Mao period, however, because of the conscious reaction to the excesses of the Cultural Revolution and the discourses which lent it ideological support, there is a certain alignment between public and private interests.[40] Thus, the increased frequency of dates in Book 3 could be taken as an indication of this mutual referentiality and imbrication of private and public time. As a side note, the congruence of public and private interests as depicted here would likely also engender, extradiagetically, a sense of nostalgia in the novel's readers, even for a period so close to their own, for in the post June Fourth China of the novel's publication, while public and private were not necessarily in opposition, there surely were and are certain areas of public discourse which are off limits, and this fact has repercussions for private life and is qualitatively different from the ethos of the 1980s.

The allowances public time and major history make for private time and minor history in this new era of alignment and cooperation between these forces leads to a sense, especially to Weiwei's younger generation, that is, those without memories of a "time before," that everything seems different and new. Indeed, the newfound space for private time represented a dramatic break with public time discourses, such as the socialist hero—especially the Cultural Revolution version. Yet, things are not so much new as renewed: fashions from cosmopolitan (semi-colonial), Republican Shanghai return to shop display windows on the main boulevards and Wang Qiyao's minor celebrity as Third Miss is revived in newspaper articles on old Shanghai. At the same time, things are not so much renewed as renewed in diminished form: the new age in Wang Qiyao's opinion had

> become coarse. . . . Let's say that everything is restored, everything has come back, but even so, what has come back is not the original but an indistinctly different other thing. The neon lights were shining again, but the evenings were not those evenings; the old signs were hung up, but this shop was not that shop; the street names had been restored; but even more so, the people walking along the street were not those people.[41]

And, we might add, Wang Qiyao herself is no longer the young woman she once was. Likewise, Weiwei, her daughter, is a different and diminished iteration of herself. The new reincarnations of that past are (merely) facsimiles and clichés of former glory. But as I have already begun to argue, it is precisely in these clichés that we can find nonprogressive history and connection to the past.

In this way, the minor history of the alleys in earlier sections can be seen as a pattern of life which had been suppressed during the Maoist years and which comes to be incompletely revived in the post-Mao era. This incompleteness is, of course, a function of the inalienable pastness of the past. But it also reflects the influence of progressive public history on the memories of private history, which when they return, return as fashion. Fashion is one of the human endeavors which best reveal the tension between novelty and imitation, or, in terms I have discussed above, the supplementary connection and separation inherent in iteration. In contrast to the commodified return of the past as fashion in the 1980s, during the Maoist period, these minor histories are already the site of old Shanghai preserved amidst the new communist order and thus mark a historical constellation, in the Benjaminain sense, drawn with this past. Hence, we find that Kang Mingxun, Weiwei's biological father, falls in love with Wang Qiyao precisely for the memories that she, as Third Miss, recalls in him.

He felt a stimulation and pleasure in his breast that seemed to have been lost and regained. He thought: it's a new city, the streets all have new names. The buildings and lights are still here, but that's just a shell; there's a new heart inside. In the old days, when the wind blew it was romantic, and French parasol trees were emissaries [of romance]. But today, the wind is the wind, and trees are trees; everything has retaken its original shape. He felt that his person moved along with the times, but his heart remained in earlier times, and so his breast was hollow. Wang Qiyao was a remnant of the former era, and she brought his heart back to him.[42]

The new Communist regime and the importance it frequently placed on thoroughly literal discourses ("the wind is the wind, and trees are trees")[43] have destroyed the romance of old Shanghai; the romance lives on, now, only in remnants and traces such as Wang Qiyao. We see in both the leftover fragments of old Shanghai in the Maoist period, and in their new blossoming in the post-Mao period the cycling and recycling of the past in the creation and recreation of historical constellations full of personal significance to the denizens of Shanghai. As supplements to the current moment, these bits of the past lift the present out of the normal sequence of events to infuse it, as for Kang Mingxun above, with salvation. It is noteworthy that both of the passages I have quoted here cite the same aspects of the city, street names and lights, as empty signifiers waiting to be filled with meaning. We can see, then, in these empty signifiers the negative image of history which goes through multiple iterations: in the 50s, the heart and soul of Shanghai has been stripped away; in the 80s, a coarse facsimile of old Shanghai is erected. It is in the minor histories, another and different negative image, that an authentic Shanghai is preserved; but only imperfectly as its restoration in the 80s illustrates. Thus, Wang Anyi's manipulation of time in *Song of Everlasting Sorrow* leads directly to a sense of longing for a past fullness, as exemplified by Kang Mingxun's love for Wang Qiyao, and the inability to realize it, as exemplified in 80s Shanghai.

Nostalgia

Nostalgia, or the longing for past fullness mentioned above, is clearly the dominant framework with which critics approach *Song of Everlasting Sorrow*. In part, this stems from comparisons of Wang Anyi to Zhang Ailing. One of the first to make such a comparison was David Wang, who praises the former for reviving a Shanghai literary school which had been in decline during the Maoist years.[44] The comparison is perhaps natural since both are women writing in and about Shanghai, and so it is no surprise that Xudong Zhang followed Wang in a more detailed comparison of Zhang Ailing and Wang Anyi titled "Shanghai Nostalgia." There are several kinds of nostalgia involved here: the looking back at Zhang Ailing in comparison to Wang Anyi, the looking back, in Books Two and Three of the novel, at Wang Qiyao's life in the 1940s, and Zhang's own clear, if unacknowledged, looking back at a (lost) socialist mode of production.[45] Indeed, Zhang stresses the "ideological short circuit"[46] nostalgia performs by joining the proto-capitalist Shanghai of the 1940s with the market-oriented Shanghai of the

1980s (and on). At the same time, Zhang praises *Song of Everlasting Sorrow* for reflecting on the "archeological layers of the social history of the city."[47]

Since I have already begun to argue that the novel redeploys various pasts in multiple configurations to create historical constellations meaningful to, resonant with, and liberatory for present concerns, it will be no surprise that I should take issue with Zhang's notion of "ideological short circuit." Instead, I feel that Ban Wang's discussion of nostalgia in the novel is more fruitful for the approach I want to take here. Wang defines nostalgia as "alternative temporalities of remembrance" which resist the totalizing official discourse of national history.[48]

> The novel's historical acuity lies in its ability to open time to alternative versions of temporality. Wang Qiyao and her confidants live in the interstices of two kinds of temporality: one of constant revolutionary change and the other of the residual way of living previously based on the market economy. The fact that the glamorous commercial world is in the midst of ruins strips it of an imputed continuity in a submerged half-life, waiting in the wings for its future comeback, as many "market" nostalgics would have it. Yet the relics of the commodity are being recollected as memory, which opens onto a different stratum of time. It is this time, the lived temporality of the common people in their daily life, nourished on the memory of a previous, lost commodified world, that cuts through both the glorious time of revolution and the fanatic, teleological time of triumphant capitalism (which is believed to be the future now unfolding before us).[49]

It should be clear that my discussion of longing and the inability to realize that desire shares much with this conception of nostalgia. For both Wang and Zhang, the interest of the novel, and indeed their sense that it is successful literature, comes from the recognition of Wang Anyi's ability to walk the tightrope between official discourse and "alternative temporalities," not unlike what I have called public and private time, never fully embracing or denouncing either. David Wang's sense of Wang's "sarcasm" (*chaonong*) works along similar lines.[50] Thus, nostalgia in *Song of Everlasting Sorrow* is rooted in the "relics of commodity," the detritus of private time, and takes form in the accumulated details of quotidian life.

And yet, despite Ban Wang's careful analysis, it is precisely the sense of the return of a previous future (even if not that of capitalism) that enables nostalgic sentiment from within the novel. In this regard, Li Feng distinguishes nostalgia from a Proustian *mémoire involontaire* by highlighting the ability of the individual to consciously engage in nostalgia whenever desired. This, in turn, logically leads to a recognition of the duplicability and iterability of nostalgia.[51] In *Song of Everlasting Sorrow*, we see this played out at the level of the chapter headings, such as "Gossip," "Alice Apartments" (*Ailisi gongyu*), "Regular Guests" (*Shouke*), "Chatting around the Stove" (*Weilu zaihua*), "Dances" (*Wuhui*), or "Weddings" (*Hunli*) to name only six, which describe activities, places, and people with a sense of regularity and routine which is repeated at stable intervals. Wang Qiyao is herself, moreover, the primary example of iterability in the novel. The eponymous chapter 5 establishes her qualifications to represent any and every young girl from the alley, and she is frequently referred to in the plural as (all) the Wang Qiyaos (Wang Qiyaomen). More specifically, at the birth of her daughter, Weiwei, the text states, "It seemed as if the former time had returned, only with the addition of the little person on the bed"[52] and the birth marks the return into Wang Qiyao's life of Mr. Cheng, who muses "it felt like it was not the baby who was newly born, but himself."[53] At still another level, on several occasions Wang Qiyao's resemblance to the famous 1930s movie star Ruan Lingyu is remarked, and we have already plumbed her parallels to Yang Guifei. These multiple referentialities and iterations build up a sense of déjà-vu, of the circularity of private time, and the return of an all-too-familiar past. Yet this returned past is a supplement, always already different too: "It seemed as if the former time had returned, *only with the addition of the little person on the bed.*" That is, these iterations reveal the paradox inherent in renewal: the return to an original newness, like the dual nature of the supplement, can only be different in its similarity. This apparent contradiction can be resolved, though, when we think of it as the negative image of a cliché, revealing presence in absence. While these differences mark the imperfection of each iteration, they also estab-lish the historical connections between eras, inscribing each on the others and liberating them from the cause and effect sequence of official history so that they may resonate on a personal level for individuals in the flash of recognition.

Likewise, the correspondence between the two scenes of death, one at the beginning and one at the end of the novel, is a frequent focus of the critics' con-cern as a return-to-go moment. As a school girl, Wang Qiyao visits a movie stu-dio to observe filming.

Clearly the three-walled room was a set, but every item was thoroughly famili-ar. The quilt on the bed was almost new, the ashtray was half full with cigarette butts, and the handkerchief on the bedside table had been used and crumpled up, just like everyday life, except one wall was missing. It was pleasing to see, but also somewhat wearisome. Since they were standing off a ways, they could not hear what was being said; they could only see a woman in a nightgown lying on the bed. She tried different positions: profile, head raised, and with her low-er half sliding off the bed. Her nearly transparent nightgown clung to her body, and the bed was rumpled; this was also a bit wearisome. . . . The scene in the room seemed to retreat a little, but also became more lively and familiar. Wang Qiyao noticed the lamp on the set throwing realistic light; the lotus flower shade cast undulating shadows on the three walls. It was like an old scene rep-layed, but she couldn't remember where or when the old scene had happened. Wang Qiyao returned her gaze to the woman under the lights. She suddenly understood that this woman was performing the role of a dying person, but she couldn't tell if it was suicide or murder. The strange thing was, the scene was not terrifying at all; rather, it was so familiar that it became wearisome. . . . The studio was as noisy as the docks, shouts of "Camera!" over here and "OK" over there. Only the woman remained still, as if she wouldn't wake for thousands of years.[54]

The familiarity of this scene is at once comforting and boring. It is rehashed and trite; indeed, it is almost the very embodiment of cliché. Of course it is also an artistic representation, even if especially verisimilar, as the missing fourth wall makes explicit. This scene makes its return, however, at the very end of the novel as Wang Qiyao lies dying on her own bed.

> The last thing Wang Qiyao saw was the hanging lamp. Big Feet's [her murderer, and a slight acquaintance] broad shoulders brushed against it and it started to swing back and forth. This scene seemed very familiar, so she searched her memory. In the last moment, her thoughts traversed the tunnel of time and the movie studio of forty years before appeared before her eyes. Yes, it was the movie studio, a room with three walls, a bed with a woman displayed across it, a hanging lamp ceaselessly swinging over her head, casting undulating light down upon the three walls. She finally understood, the woman on the bed was herself dying of murder. Then nothing, fade to black.[55]

Shu-mei Shih has called this an instance of "negative nostalgia": "a sense of repetition that repeats what was already perceived as repetition in the past. It is a repetition that repeats the past that repeats the future."[56] It is precisely these circular movements back and forth through time that Xudong Zhang labeled "short circuits" but which I argue are creative reconnections, almost like neurons in the brain extending their links to other neurons. Like the return of older fashions in the 1980s, the return of a previous future delayed marks an instance of an "alternative temporality of remembrance," of conscious iteration and linking to a Benjaminian historical constellation. "Travers[ing] the tunnel of time" explicitly marks this reconnection as such a constellation and, in turn, infuses the memory with revelatory and revolutionary meaning, namely that this death is murder, a meaning, moreover, which remained elusive until this historical flash. Simultaneously, the creation of this historical constellation reinscribes this meaning—murder—on all the previous deaths going back to Yang Guifei.

The feminist accusation inherent in the historical meaning of murder stands out. That is to say, Wang Qiyao's death is murder, clearly, but the official historical discourse would, of course, pay no attention to it. Ruan Lingyu and Yang Guifei's deaths, however, though called suicide or execution by the official histories, as well as the countless other reiterations of this death in real life and in cultural products such as film reveal in this flash of historical meaning that they too are crimes committed against women. Further, this meaning includes a recognition (and implicit condemnation) that these crimes are accepted as cliché and mundane, that they occur with the acceptance if not approval of official historical discourses, and as a result go unremarked by society. While alternative narratives, such as Bo Juyi's "Song of Everlasting Sorrow," Hong Sheng's *Palace of Everlasting Life*, or indeed Stanley Kwan's film *Ruan Lingyu*[57] may also have exposed the events described within them as instances of state or patriarchal violence, it is only through the nonprogressive historical form created in *Song of Everlasting Sorrow*'s narrative that this crime can be revealed as multiply iterated across eras and perpetrated not only on famous movie stars or prized consorts, but also on those everyday women who thought they were ignored by official history.

At the same time, the final stage direction reminds us of the staging of the story and the wearisomeness that Wang Qiyao associated with the scene (replayed once again) in the movie studio. Wang Qiyao's death repeats the clichéd death scene witnessed in the movie studio, which repeats Ruan Lingyu's death, which, in turn, repeats the death of Ruan's character, Wei Ming, in the film *Xin nüxing* (New Woman), which was based on the real-life death of Ai Xia.[58] And all of these relate to/repeat the classic death of Yang Guifei. The iterations of this murder mark the cliché both in their maudlin ordinariness and in their staged nature. Nevertheless, with our Benjaminian understanding of cliché, we can see that it is precisely in such staged—that is, actively constructed— reiterations of the past that that past is authorized to become active in the present and a historical constellation is created infusing both present and past with mutual significance. Indeed, this meaning is impossible without the negative image of cliché and the positive history it engenders.

Despite the foregoing discussion, there is a sense in which nostalgia is misleading as a rubric with which to approach *Song of Everlasting Sorrow*.[59] Wang Qiyao herself is hardly ever reflective on her own life. Instead, as the epigraph heading this chapter indicates, she seems to merely mark the time of her life as it passes and, with the exception of a certain ennui during her time with Li zhuren, accepting what comes her way with remarkable unflappability. The nostalgia, in the sense of longing, of the novel, then, is not that of Wang Qiyao; it is, rather, expressed by several characters, such as Kang Mingxun, mentioned above, and most notably by Lao Kela (Old Color), who falls in love with Wang Qiyao because of all that she represents of old Shanghai, as well as Zhang Yonghong, Weiwei's friend, who plumbs Wang Qiyao for fashion information and taste rooted in a 1940s sensibility. Both of these eventually fade from Wang Qiyao's life; Lao Kela even develops a dread of his growing compulsion for what he calls Wang Qiyao's agelessness[60] before finally leaving for good.[61] Wang Qiyao herself, then, in all her iterations, is the cliché, the negative image which inscribes itself in these characters' hearts and minds, enabling personal historical constellations replete with private meanings for themselves.

There is a *double entendre* in the title of this chapter, "Back to the Future." On the one hand, Wang Qiyao, as the modern day Yang Guifei, inevitably returns in the end to the future prepared for her. Without this (final) iteration, the historical and fundamentally feminist accusation of abuse at the hands of public time and official history, now revealed as servants of a patriarchal society, would be impossible. On the other hand, as cliché and negative image, Wang Qiyao enables us to embody Benjamin's angel of history whose back is eternally turned to the future and thus sees only the ruins of the past. That is, she and the novel which constitutes her story establish the rigid framework of the negative image of cliché enabling us as readers to perceive this nonprogressive history. As a product of the mid 1990s, this surely is a protest and attempt at resistance to the official promotion of the headlong "progress" at all costs of Chinese economic resurgence. Yet, we would be wrong to limit our understanding to only this or only the historical moment of the novel's composition and first publication. As Benjamin's nonprogressive history shows us, the past moments which are contained within the constellation are likewise authorized and liberated through this historical work. For us as readers of the novel, then, this cliché (re)inscribes, reiterates, and reveals the pat and hackneyed historical truth of the murder of a woman (and of all the Wang Qiyaos), when she has outlived her time, for social and public expedience, whether it be Confucian notions of proper rule or bourgeois prudery or capitalist desire for excess value in the form of gold.

Chapter 8
Globalized Traditions: Zhu Tianxin's *The Ancient Capital*

— Could it be that none of your memories count . . .
Zhu Tianxin, *The Ancient Capital*

Zhu Tianxin's (Chu T'ien-hsin) 1997 novella *Gudu* (The Ancient Capital)[1] is an extended musing on the transformations Taipei has undergone from colonial Japanese rule to the mid 1990s. The novella's heroine, after returning from Kyoto, takes on the persona of a Japanese tourist and roams Taipei following the directions of a colonial-era Japanese guidebook and map. As she tours the city, she contrasts what she actually sees with her own adolescent memories of the Martial Law period cityscape as well as with the descriptions of the various locales in the guidebook. At the same time, the novel establishes multiple intertextual resonances with, most prominently but not exclusively, the Nobel prize winner Kawabata Yasunari's novel *The Ancient Capital* (Koto, the same Chinese characters as Zhu's novel) as well as Tao Qian's "Peach Blossom Spring" by quoting from those two texts (among others) on many occasions. These resonances construct an implicit comparison between *Koto*'s heroine (and her relationship with her sister) and *Gudu*'s heroine (and her relationship with her daughter and her friend A) and alternatively between Tao Qian's fisherman and the roaming heroine of the novella. I focus on the novella in this chapter, then, as a palimpsest of "the ancient capital" superimposing Taipei of the Japanese colonial era, Kyoto, Martial Law era Taipei, and contemporary Taipei on one another through memory, architecture, intertextual connections, and a guidebook.

As with previous chapters, I take the citation of previous literature in *The Ancient Capital* as the creation of a Benjaminian historical constellation, one which, in the end, reveals the destruction that the modern present has visited on the past. What distinguishes Zhu's novella is that the citation and circulation of these literary texts, while prominently including classic Chinese texts like "Peach Blossom Spring" and the first history of Taiwan, *General History of*

Taiwan, also includes non-Chinese texts such as Kawabata's *The Ancient Capital*, as well as Robert Frost's poetry or Frank Lloyd Wright's writings. The globalization of literary traditions to be tapped in this text, certainly, reflects the penetration of global capitalist flows of goods and information as well as Taipei's inclusion as one of the points of exchange along these flows. While the broadening of literary heritages could be seen as enriching, the imbrication of these heritages with capitalist modes of exchange ultimately shows the heroine to be a consumer which isolates her from her society and renders her defenses against the alienation of modernity impotent. As with several of the other texts discussed in Section Two, it is only at the extradiegetic level of text and readership that the Benjaminian constellation can create a certain kind of community that often remains elusive for the characters themselves.

Narration and the Politics of Identity

A striking fact about Zhu's novella is that it is written as a second-person narrative, an aspect of the text which, given the relative rarity of this narrative type, surprisingly goes largely unremarked by the vast majority of scholars.[2] While some mention this fact but place no critical emphasis on it, like Tang Xiaobing, others, like Lingchei Letty Chen, conflate the narrator with the narratee.[3]

In contrast to these scholars, I argue that it is important that we recognize this second-person narrative structure for what it is and for the effects it creates in the narrative. For example

> You simply don't understand why, from that moment, you started unceasingly dreaming of far-away places, always wanting to travel, travel far and fly high. In truth, you have never been away from this island for more than a month, like a savage islander or pirate. For several years now, from time to time, in order to pass through you have found it necessary to fantasize that a certain part of this city, a certain stretch of road, a certain street scene was a city you had been to or even one you have not visited yet, like a lot of men who, no matter how good their relationship is, need to think of some other woman before they can make love to their wife.
>
> You have never attempted to organize these kinds of feelings, and you do not dare to mention them to anyone, especially in a time when people are always verifying how much you love this place and even demanding that you leave if you don't like it.
>
> If you want to go just leave, or Scram back to such-and-such a place, as if you all had some great place to go, some great place to live, and it's only out of spite that you don't go.
>
> . . .
>
> Is there a place like that?[4]

The politics of identity that we see dramatized in this quotation is a central factor in the heroine's story. Her relationship with her homeland is conflicted in no small part because a certain, large portion of her community considers her alien and rejects her. She is forcefully unhomed, not by a recognition of the uncanny but by others around her. And the basis for this rejection is not any action she has taken or speech she has made, but her parentage. She is the daughter of mainlanders who came to Taiwan with the Nationalist retreat. The question ending this section nicely reveals the fallacy at the heart of this identity politics as well as the impossibility of the heroine's predicament.

More to our immediate purposes, though, when we read this passage, and I feel it is representative of the entire text, it is not difficult to understand why critics such as Chen merely speak of the heroine, drawing no distinction with the narrator. That is, the knowledge about the narratee's internal life and the compassion with which it is put on display here by the narrator strongly suggest an identification between the two, so that the text can be seen as a sort of internal monologue or a letter to oneself. The objectification of the self helps the self in accurate analysis of her emotions, her memories, and her situation. Indeed, especially given Zhu's personal status as the daughter of mainland immigrants to Taiwan, it is also a very small step from this conflation to the larger conflation of the author with the narrator leading to the implicit identity of all three. The emotions elicited by the rejection of second generation mainlanders, like Zhu and like the heroine of the novella, by self-identified local Taiwanese, as described above, must surely have been felt by Zhu herself on occasion.

The ease with which we seem to be able to identify the narrator with the heroine and both of them with the author, raises a whole host of issues of narratology and fictionality, most prominently including questions which Jaroslav Průšek was the first to raise, questions of the lyrical and the epic modes of Chinese writing and the ways they intersect in modern fiction.[5] These issues, however, are beyond the scope of this study. Rather, what I would like to stress is that when the fact of the second-person narrative is glossed over in our rush to find Zhu, the author, in her text, we disregard the ways that this structure includes and envelopes the narrative's audience into the story.[6] The constant reiteration of the word "you" in the text, as the grammatical subject of the action narrated in the story, increases the likelihood of the narrative's audience—who as recipient of the discourse, then, also should be addressed as "you"—to identify with the story's heroine. While this identification between naratee and audience may be especially true of other second generation mainlanders, it is no less true of other local subgroups in the narrative's audience. That is, the access to the heroine's interior life provided by the narrative dispels the effectiveness (or at least the continued effectiveness) of the pseudo-ethnic argument that (second generation) mainlanders are not full-fledged members of Taiwanese society. The knowledge the audience gains about the heroine's feelings, especially strong feelings of nostalgia and conservation of Taiwanese locales, is weighty evidence in favor of her deep connection to the island. For instance, the heroine repeatedly displays her concern for the preservation of local, Taiwanese space, as we can see in the following example taken from the section of the text in which the heroine tours Taipei with the aid of her Japanese guidebook and map.

> Nogi-machi. A four-wheel drive Jeep was parked in front of a large home shaded by banyan and sweet gum trees, the Jeep was covered in bumper stick-

ers expressing the ideology of a military state, unchanged for several decades like the Spanish-style home of Zhou Zhirou in the next block. One can tell that things have never changed by the trees growing unfettered in the courtyards (usually, yes, South Pacific trees planted by the original owners such as coconut, betel nut, mango, banyan . . .) shading the tiled roofs and courtyard walls to block out people's notice. There are many such families who wish to avoid attention mostly because, despite having retired from service to the ancien régime, they still were living in official residences. The more discrete and humble among them feared only that their children and grandchildren would cause a stir; there were not a few of this younger generation, however, who perversely drove their four-wheel drive Jeeps or sports cars home in the wee hours of the morning, honking the horn to rouse the retired aides-de-camp or old A-mas to open the gate for them. There were some of the second generation who had studied abroad and were willing to return, who began secret renovations, such as the brick facing added to the houses on Fuxing South Road, Section 1, Alley 295 that used to have fourteen large coconut trees and on Xinsheng South Road, Section 1, Alley 97 that used to be overgrown with magnolia, nightshade and camphor; then, in the last few years of the '80s, acquiescing to the demands of a third generation bored over the summer break, they cut the trees, threw down a slab of concrete, and erected a basketball net so their obese grandchildren could imagine themselves as NBA stars; don't believe it? take a trip on the mass transit, the official residences on both sides of Fuxing South Road and Da'an Road are proof.[7]

In passages like this we see how difficult it can be to distinguish clearly between the narrator and the heroine. But again, what seems more important to my way of thinking is the way the narrative draws its audience into, if not identification, then into its confidences, as we can see in the direct address, "don't believe it?" Moreover, the narrative's concern with space is clear. Specifically, the concern is for the preservation of a South Pacific sensibility (the Chinese term is *weidao*, or flavor) in the face of homogenizing social, cultural, and economic forces represented here by brands such as Jeep and the NBA or modern technologies such as the elevated mass transit system recently erected in Taipei. In contrast to these forces, the exactness (uniqueness) of specific addresses and precise botanical nomenclature are marshaled.

Liang-yi Yen discusses *The Ancient Capital* from a "Thirdspace" perspective (the term is Edward Soja's) as a lament for the destruction of spaces of the Merely Local to make way for Placeless spaces (these terms are Ackbar Abbas'). The Merely Local, epitomized in the narrative by colonial era structures and especially by trees and other vegetation, refers to space which is infused with the history of its construction and even more importantly its use; whereas, Placeless spaces are those of multi-lane highways and the ubiquitous glass and steel skyscrapers of transnational capital.[8] The narrative quotes Frank Lloyd Wright, "the architect of the Imperial Hotel [Tokyo]," as saying "The city, the foundation of banks and whores, skyscrapers growing like unkempt grass."[9] The trauma induced in the heroine by the fast-paced alterations to the urban landscape is met with memories of Merely Local spaces of her youth.

These spaces preserved in the heroine's memories include the amusement park her parents took her to as a small child, the coastline at Tamkang she repeatedly visited with A, the apartment A rented and which the heroine could use from time to time for romantic assignations, and so on. These memories of Merely Local spaces are recalled and deployed as bulwarks against the devastating alienation induced by the erection of Placeless spaces on the ruins of Merely Local spaces: like the fourteen large coconut trees, counted and mourned individually, lost to a slab of concrete erected as tribute to the fantasies induced by the NBA as part of the transnational capitalist penetration into local markets.

The structure of the second-person narrative draws the audience into this struggle; it is personal not just for the heroine (and the narrator who is so closely identified with her) but for every "you" out there who is the narrative's target audience. The narrative, then, is not merely an account of one woman wrestling with the issues of global encroachment on local spaces and the resulting sensations of drifting and rootlessness; rather, it becomes, in the process of narrating, a collective bid for resistance to the anonymous and homogenizing forces of globalization.

Describing the narrative as inculcating a sense of rootlessness recalls our earlier discussions of native soil (*xiangtu*) fiction and David Wang's description of it as a rootless literature. Certainly, in its concern with questions of home, homecoming, the value of memory and so on, *The Ancient Capital*, I would argue is equally involved in native soil themes despite the fact that this term is usually reserved for classifications of rural not urban literature. Many of the same issues that were discussed in Chapter Five—the emotional and psychological toll incurred when pristine memories are confronted with present reality, the possibility of discovering utopian space for human life, and the power and meaning of home—are also raised in *The Ancient Capital*. Since the urban space, almost by definition, is bound to modern networks and flows, the responses to these typically native soil questions cannot follow the same patterns we saw in terms of Shen Congwen's writing or that of the Roots movement. This is especially true of a city like Taipei which is enmeshed in regional networks of other cities including Tokyo, Seoul, Hong Kong, Singapore, Kuala Lumpur, and more recently Shanghai; at a slightly further distance with the likes of Mumbai or Sydney; and globally with New York, Paris, London, Vancouver, Los Angeles, and so on. These networks facilitate all sorts of interactions, not only commodity or finance exchanges but also information, fashion trends, cultural or intellectual innovations and the like. An effective response to the loss of a sense of home, for example, in the face of these ever-expanding networks and flows, as Yen's work demonstrates, is the conscious pursuit of conservation. Conservation, in turn, to be successful requires collective action and active organization of community sentiment. The heroine in *The Ancient Capital* is able, as we see in the quotation above, to recognize the destruction wrought in the name of modernization and to advocate for preservation. But her fundamental problem is that she has no community with which she can collectively work for that preservation. I will return to this point again below.

The glaring irony, of course, is that the heroine feels most at home when she is abroad, either abroad in fact, as in her trip to Kyoto which makes up a large portion of the narrative, or in her fantasies (as in the line quoted again here, "from time to time, . . . you have found it necessary to fantasize that a certain part of this city, a certain stretch of road, a certain street scene was a city you had been to or even one you have not visited yet"), or in the extensions of globalized capital such as the Doutor chain cafes—"your secret garden, your own tiny concession"—in both Kyoto and Taipei.[10]

Kyoto Now and Then: An Index of Absence

Kawabata Yasunari's late novel *The Ancient Capital* plays an important role in Zhu's novel; indeed, the latter takes the former's name as its own. Additionally, Kawabata's text is quoted, in translation, on several occasions in that section of the narrative in which the heroine visits Kyoto. Before I discuss the issues of parody and intertextuality that this aspect of the narrative raises, I would first like to address Kawabata's novel individually. Critics of Zhu's novel frequently describe Kawabata's novel, without ever pursuing the matter, as "important" or "canonical" or some other similar adjective. It is certainly true that for a parody such as we find in Zhu's appropriation of *The Ancient Capital*, the cited text must be recognizable to the narrative's audience, and so we must presume a greater or lesser level of familiarity with Kawabata's novel. Certainly, as the first Asian writer to be awarded the Nobel Prize for Literature since Rabindranath Tagore (1913), it is not unreasonable to think that anything authored by Kawabata would enjoy a certain popularity among Asian readers. Additionally, the Nobel committee cited *The Ancient Capital* by name when awarding that prize to Kawabata in 1968. However, the forces influencing the committee's decision are always murky, and it has been suggested that *The Ancient Capital* was included merely to fill out the requisite three works for the prize to be awarded.[11] Be that as it may, for a work of such importance, one would expect a certain level of scholarship devoted to its analysis; yet I have been hard pressed to find any study in English which treats *The Ancient Capital* in whole or in part in any substantive manner.[12] Rather than a canonical text, it seems to me that *The Ancient Capital* is an ignored and forgotten novel in Kawabata's *oeuvre* which tends to come off the worse in comparisons with other Kawabata novels such as *Snow Country* (Yukiguni). As I will discuss in more detail below, since I see Zhu's appropriation of this text as an index of absence, I think this aspect of Kawabata's novel as forgotten fits in well with this sort of reading.

Kawabata's *The Ancient Capital* tells the story of Chieko, a foundling raised by a kimono designer and merchant and his wife from the day they found her abandoned as a baby on their doorstep. The novel follows Chieko in her seventeenth year as she begins the passage from childhood to womanhood. Like Shen Congwen's *Border Town*, the narrative rhythms of *The Ancient Capital* are governed by the annual festivals which punctuate the seasons for Kyoto's populace. Unexpectedly, Chieko discovers that she has an identical twin, Naeko, who had not been abandoned instead being raised by their biological parents in the mountains outside Kyoto. As a result, typical questions of identity, romance, aspirations, or one's place in society that usually accompany adolescence are compounded for Chieko with the impossible dilemmas of why her parents chose to abandon her but keep her sister, the economic and class gulf which has grown between herself and her sister since Chieko now is a member of the merchant class while Naeko works raising cedar trees for their wood, to whom does Chieko owe allegiance, her foster parents who raised her or her biological parents who gave birth to her, and so on. The novel ends at the end of the year when Chieko sends Naeko a gift of a kimono but decides to have no more contact with her. As with many of Kawabata's texts, the entry into adulthood is treated as a loss and diminishment. Childhood innocence is fleeting and in this narrative its absence is mirrored and doubled with the enforced separation of Chieko from her second self, Naeko.

In addition to the intertextual resonances cultivated with Kawabata's *The Ancient Capital*, Zhu's text also quotes from such westerners as I. V. Foscarini, D. H. Lawrence, Robert Frost, as well as more extensively from Chinese texts like *Taiwan tongshi* (A General History of Taiwan) by Lian Heng and, towards the end of the narrative, obsessively from Tao Qian's "Peach Blossom Spring." While most critics acknowledge this aspect of the narrative, as with the second-person narrative discussed above, few delve into these intertextual relationships, and, at least to my way of thinking, the analysis of the intertextual relationships established by such wide ranging quotation that exists remains inadequate. Rosemary Haddon, for example, treats Kawabata's text merely as a model story (of the reunion of sisters) which remains unfulfilled in the later narrative. Equally reductive is her treatment of *Preface to A General History of Taiwan*, which seems to be taken, unproblematically, as a true record of Taiwan's past.[13] Likewise, Jen-yi Hsu refuses to interrogate the ramifications of intertextuality; rather, she understands it as a sign of hybridity, and Zhu's use of Kawabata's text becomes for her a straightforward reflection of the legacy of Japanese colonialism in Taiwan.[14] Most satisfying is Lingchei Letty Chen's analysis employing the rubric of pastiche: "for Zhu, pastiche invokes not so much historical nostalgia as textual hybridity, yielding space for a kind of negotiation specific to Taiwan's unique postcolonial condition."[15] For Chen this space of negotiation opens onto a field, oscillating between authenticity and hybridity, reflecting the process of decolonization (from both Japanese and Nationalist imperialist practices). In this reading, Kawabata's Kyoto signifies authenticity, "a utopian space where the presence of history is felt everywhere."[16] Still, as we saw in Chapter Five, utopia is possible only insofar as history is excluded from its space. As we will see in the discussion below, the history, such as it is, which seems to signify so powerfully for Zhu's heroine, is largely consumed and discarded, like the paper cup for her Doutor coffee, and as a result has no possibility of affecting her in a Benjaminian manner.

Indeed, Kyoto both in the quotations from Kawabata and in the heroine's experience of it is presented largely as such a "utopian space." For example, there is the first quotation from Kawabata:

> Hideo turned his steps toward the bridge at Shijo where he had first met "Chieko's Naeko" or "Naeko's Chieko," but it was hot under the noonday sun. Leaning against the rail at the end of the bridge, he closed his eyes. He listened, not

for the echoes of the crowds or the trains, but for the almost imperceptible sound of the flow of the river.[17]

The important thing in this quotation is the river itself, which orients the built space of the city. The bridge is both a passage over the river and an opening allowing access to "the almost imperceptible sound of the flow of the river." That unceasing murmur, like the river itself as well as other natural images in Kawabata's novel, signifies both the ancientness of the city and its eternal quality. This aspect of the city and Kawabata's novel certainly is what attracts the heroine. In her roaming of Kyoto, Zhu's heroine wanders between the various shrines and sites which host the several festivals so important in marking both the circularity and the passage of time in Kawabata's novel. The sequence and traditions of these festivals, handed down since time immemorial, are what mark the story of Chieko, her maturation and blossoming sexuality (always a threatening force in Kawabata's fiction),[18] as sharing continuity with the city and the larger Japanese culture. Yet, far from cultivating a sense of timeless utopia, already in Kawabata's novel, there is an air of elegy for the disappearance of that city and that culture, which we can glimpse even in the quotation above when the noises of the crowd and trains almost completely overpower the sound of the river flowing past.

Zhu's narrative incorporates and expands this elegiac mood into a full blown contradiction. In fact the line immediately following the quotation cited above reads, "Unlike Hideo, you stood upon the Shijo bridge in the winter wind, where the electronic screen hanging on the nearby high-rise clearly read 4°C, looking down upon pairs of lovers insensible to the cold, as if they would never leave."[19] Similarly, after another quotation from Kawabata which describes Shinichi (a potential love interest) walking along the streets of Kyoto with Chieko, "You decided to reverse the path that Shinichi and Chieko took, turning left at Saigyōan and Kikukei Pavilion and cutting in front of Higashiō Temple to enter Murayama Park."[20] While Zhu's narrative clearly seems to invoke Kawabata's text as the *locus classicus* of a utopian space, it nevertheless immediately highlights the heroine's difference ("unlike Hideo") and contradiction (walking the same path in reverse) of the utopian blueprint.

The architectural and spatial metaphor of a blue print is especially apropos since these citations seem intended to chart the heroine's progress across the city of Kyoto and mark the intersections with Kawabata's characters and the ways they variously interact with that space. As a result, as Chen notes, the narrative's appropriation of Kawabata's text is not based on thematic resonances. Instead, Chen argues that the quotations create a "suggestive power of absence."[21] And of course, the absence invoked by such a spatialized appropriation of Kawabata's text is the storyline of the narrative, specifically the storyline of Chieko and Naeko's reunion. The obvious parody of Kawabata's text in *The Ancient Capital* is naturally the reunion of the heroine and her childhood friend A; their meeting, however, fails to occur. Thus the absence invoked by the narrative's quotations from Kawabata is redoubled. Furthermore, I would like to argue that this absence is tripled because the heroine, rather than focusing on the impending meeting with A, muses over her memories of an earlier visit to the very same sites in Kyoto with her daughter, and, indeed, because of her daughter's absence on this trip comes to regret her decision to come to Kyoto to meet A in the first place.

The daughter plays a crucial role, again, in and through her absence.[22] The recognition of her daughter's absence and the sense of loss or diminution which results from it is met with the heroine's memories of her previous trip to Kyoto in her daughter's company. Close attention to these memories, however, reveal that they revolve around cafes, shops, tourist attractions and the like where they were able to consume "Japanese culture" in tourist/capitalist fashion:

> You clutched your wallet tightly and quickened your pace to appear as if you were a woman just off work hurrying home to make dinner. You walked straight to the Takeda market and bought two pairs of brand name socks that were out of fashion; the weather was colder than usual and there was a kerosene heater warming the shop which was filled with the smell of Bonito soup. The owners' granddaughter had grown, squeezed behind the cash register, she watched TV as she did her homework. Of course, this reminded you of your daughter.
>
> The rear half of Nishiki Market was already deserted, so you had to cross Yanagibaba-dōri to get to Shijō-dōri where there were many places to eat. Yet you chose to eat at the Doutor Café, usually reserved for breakfast, across the street.
>
> You ordered a cup of the café du jour and a kōgen hotdog sandwich; since all the seats by the window were taken, you had to sit at one of the large round tables in the middle of the café. The heater combined with cigarette smoke made your heart race; however, it could have been because you thought you would see your daughter's back hunched over her homework.
>
> You had to bring her homework when you came in the middle of her school term. There was no space in the hotel, so you usually came to the large round tables here to do homework; you helped her with math until third grade when it became too hard for you. That you two spoke a different language did not draw any notice from the other people at the round table, or I should say, didn't elicit any alteration to their facial expressions; they had practiced, implacable faces that did not change no matter what strange things they saw. Because there were too many people in too little space, crowded commuter trains, crowded department stores, crowded cafes, frequent encroachment on personal space, they had no choice but to learn to have expressionless faces, putting on their faces the same as coats and hats when they leave home; how could they survive otherwise?
>
> But you really like this sort of you-mind-your-business-I'll-mind-mine situation; you figured there must be a good number of mental cases among them, but it didn't concern you, you were adept at gauging the dress of a middle aged Oji-san, the two young girls in Chanel with serious nicotine habits, the good looking yuppie who could be Takeshi Kaneshiro's brother . . . ; you slurped your hot coffee, and for no reason quietly said "Tadaima." I'm home.[23]

It certainly is the memory of her daughter which draws her to the Placeless space of the chain café. The process of helping her daughter complete homework helps to domesticate the Placeless space. At the same time, though, the anonymous and indeed insulated quality of the café is perhaps an even stronger draw for the heroine. The processed sandwich, the coffee—if there is a global commodity par excellence, surely it is coffee—the mutual ignorance of and indifference to her fellow consumers, indeed the ability to pass as "a woman just off work hurrying home to make dinner;" it is these things which lead her to say, "Tadaima." We see in the heroine's attraction to this aspect of the international tourist destination Kyoto nearly the complete abrogation of Kawabata's Kyoto.

Language is another important aspect to which we should pay close attention. Globalized Japanese culture, through manga, film, television, pop music, is ubiquitous in Taiwan, and so, the use of basic Japanese terms such as Oji-san or tadaima is more or less analogous to Americans saying "hola" or "enchanté" or "hasta la vista." It does not indicate a deeper connection with the language or culture. At the same time, the fact that Japanese uses Chinese characters in its written form, and this is nearly always true of proper names, means that the heroine can navigate through the city, read signs, and even largely understand descriptions of tourist attractions, such as various Shinto shrines, without the mediation of "translation." The text makes this explicit later when discussing the colonial era guidebook: "the Chinese characters/kanji told you . . . ."[24] Thus, in visual form, "the yuppie who could be Takeshi Kaneshiro's brother" is indistinguishable from "the yuppie who could be Jin Chengwu's brother." Likewise, it is this graphic isomorphism which enables the heroine to employ the Japanese colonial map upon her return to Taipei.

There are definite limits to this sort of transferability, however. For example, the heroine's trek through Murayama Park recalls another incident involving her daughter:

> Unlike your daughter, the first time you came to Murayama Park, you were surprised that they had openly adopted the name of your Yuanshan. Your daughter, however, after a kindergarten field trip to Yuanshan River Park, came home and asked you why on earth would we give it a Japanese name. You were taken off guard and couldn't answer, but you husband teased her for forgetting her heritage.[25]

Yuanshan and Murayama are written with the same characters, but they lead to the question "which came first? which is named after the other?" Indeed, the likely answer that the Japanese colonists named the Taiwanese mountain after the one in Kyoto is willfully reversed by the heroine's husband, whom we learn elsewhere in the narrative is a political supporter of Taiwanese independence.

Even more important than these issues of primacy and origin is the fact that such seemingly effortless transference between the two languages is only true of their written forms. The heroine cannot (or at least does not) interact with the local denizens of Kyoto except in moments of commerce: buying socks or coffee, checking in to the hotel, and so on. She is a tourist, and a timid one at that, belying her own sense of having returned home, which, it bears reiteration, is expressed in the consumable utterance of phrasebook Japanese, tadaima.

It is precisely this lack of human contact which is the defining feature of the Placeless. In Benjaminian terms, it has no aura, and as a result can be mass produced for global consumption irrespective of local tastes. And it is in this sense that the quotations from Kawabata can be seen as an index of absence, to re-phrase Chen. Those citations from that other *Ancient Capital* do not invoke the tale of reunion and homecoming, and by not raising those issues the narrative reveals the absence not only of the heroine's sister figure, A, but also of her daughter. The memories raised to fill that absence, as in the Doutor café, remind the heroine only of her home in that Placeless space. Instead of referring to Ka-wabata's story, the citations from his text point to the names of Kyoto landmarks, names which slip back and forth between Chinese and Japanese, seeming thus to allow a connection, but again returning in the end, at least in the heroine's expe-rience of them, to Placeless tourist attractions.

Cutting her trip to Kyoto short, the heroine returns to Taipei where she con-tinues to pass as a Japanese woman, and continues to act as a tourist. Both of these behaviors continue to isolate her from human contact. At first, adopting the perspective of an outsider seems to allow a new vantage and understanding of her "home": "You had never before seen the land where you have lived and grown for more than thirty years from this angle."[26] However, gradually the constant assault of the experience of the ascendancy of the Placeless causes psychic distress in the heroine because she knows the same space as both Place-less and Merely Local. It is the dissonance between these two kinds of expe-rience superimposed upon the same space that leads in the end to disorientation and wailing, "Where is this? . . . You howl!"[27] The potential for active preserva-tion efforts to stave off the madness of alienation, as I have argued above, is never realized for or by Zhu's heroine because, as tourism is her mode of tra-versing the city, she remains incapable of creating or joining a community which could carry out effective conservation.

Spatialization of History

We have already seen how the narrative deploys various citations of Kawabata to map the heroine's perambulation around the city of Kyoto. These citations, seemingly random and with little if any thematic significance to Kawabata's text, become an index of absence, stripping away any presumed parallels between the two stories—comparisons of Chieko and Naeko with the heroine, and A or her daughter—or, indeed, any meaningful attachment to the locales of Kyoto. In-stead, we are left with the graphic inscriptions of place names and a tourist-level consumption of historical sites as well as global capitalist spaces of the Placeless. Meanwhile, the heroine brings these practices back with her when she returns to Taipei. But here, because she retains memories that infuse these spaces with personal meaning, she is less able to retreat to the antiseptic consumer space and must confront the superimposition of global flows on the Merely Local spaces of her youth without the support which could be provided by collective organiza-tion. In the end this leads to her breakdown.

If we put these observations into terms which we have been using through-out this study, namely, those of the Benjaminian historical constellation, I be-lieve we will be rewarded. The multiple and repeated citations to Kawabata's text, in addition to the various others I have already mentioned, explicitly constitute the construction of such a constellation. However, since as we have seen, the various points which constitute the constellation point not to stories/narratives but to decontextualized spaces, the constellation cannot be historical, in a Benjaminian sense, but at most a sort of abstract cultural constellation. For instance there is this description of New Park, since renamed 2.28 Park:

> You turned towards Hyo-machi, off to the South in New Park you could see the Governor-General Kodama and Chief Civil Engineer Gotō Memorial Museum; the guidebook devoted a large amount of space to describe this building, which was an exemplary work from an outstanding period. It had been something like a hundred years since you had been to the park, and only now did you learn that the flower clock, which had been replaced with a planting of trees at the erection of the 2.28 memorial, had originally been a bronze statue of Governor-General Kodama and that the bronze figure of Chennault had replaced one of Gotō Shinpei that had been erected with donations from Gu Xianrong and Li Chunsheng.
>
> The area around the 2.28 memorial upset your memories of New Park; Good Lord, who had been offended by those olive trees! You searched in vain for them, finally leaving the grove to find that beautiful Spanish house. Only now did you learn that the beautiful Spanish house had been a broadcasting station built sixty years ago; back when you all had used to daydream among the fallen leaves of the sweet gum thicket, it had been offices for Central Broadcasting, and now it was offices for the Parks and Streetlight Maintenance section of the Municipal Works Bureau.
>
> The thicket of sweet gum was still there, but you suspected it had been cut back, otherwise how could those few trees ever have hidden you and your friends and supported the silly conversations and futile dreams of you girls. You all had looked up at a clean, blue sky which provided the forced yellow spots of Autumn on those temperate climate leaves; after looking up for a while, you didn't know where you were and could weave dreams of going somewhere in the future, somewhere at the ends of the earth, abandoning ancestral graves and family to roam across the ocean to far flung lands, how could dreams like this be limited only to those whose fathers had come to Taiwan in '49![28]

The various historical facts unearthed in this experiment by the heroine merely reinforce the erasures perpetrated on history—even those erasures committed in the service of memorializing other histories. Of course, the politics behind erecting a memorial to the 2.28 Incident, which also view "those whose fathers had come to Taiwan in '49" with suspicion, are the immediate cause for the heroine's anxiety and sense of homelessness. But even when the narrative attempts to counteract this by infusing this location with the sort of memory replete with personal meaning, rather than filling the space of the park with the kind of power we would expect from a Benjaminian constellation, it ends up pointing away and outside to "the ends of the earth" and "far flung lands."

The disorientation we see here leads the narrative to discard citations from Kawabata and instead cite Tao Qian's "Peach Blossom Spring," in a sense attempting to revise the constellation it is creating. The new, Japanese inspired, eyes the heroine uses to look anew on her "home" lead the narrator to portray her in the same light as the fisherman in Tao Qian's tale. Although the quotations from "Peach Blossom Spring" differ from the citations of Kawabata's text in that they seem purposeful, "strategically interventionist" in Niranjana's words, they nevertheless remain incapable of instilling a Benjaminian connection to the past which would prove liberating to the heroine. As we have already discussed in Chapter Five, Peach Blossom Spring is a utopian space disconnected from the passing of time, and thus disconnected from history.

In an implicit recognition of the ahistoricity of the utopian space, the citations from "Peach Blossom Spring" amount to a stuttering. That is, the narrative repeatedly quotes the beginning of Tao Qian's text, each time managing to progress a little bit further, but only by the very end of the text recounting the fisherman's first entrance into the utopian space. As with the citations from Kawabata, these quotations from "Peach Blossom Spring" also become an index of absence. This may seem counterintuitive, since a utopian space is so clearly what the heroine has been searching for, but the multiple false starts in the citation of this text builds up a sense of exactly how forced the appropriation of this text is in the narrative. That is, Tao Qian's fisherman stumbles upon Peach Blossom Spring—and of course can never find his way back again once he leaves— whereas, the heroine (and the narrator?) is so clearly actively searching for a perfect space where she can be at home. As if this were not enough, the final lines actually quoted are "they asked what age it was, and they had never heard of the Han Dynasty much less the Wei or Jin Dynasties . . ."[29] which only reinforces how cut off and provincial they are (the analogy would point to a similar closed-mindedness of the Taiwanese).

The novella opens with the question—notably with ellipses instead of a question mark—which heads this chapter, "Could it be that none of your memories count . . ."[30] I think the answer to this question can only be a resounding "Yes!" The attempts to create a historical constellation through access to cultural resources, not only Chinese but also Japanese, American, and European, prove hollow since all that is created are detailed yet decontextualized spaces which provide feeble bulwarks to protect the individual psyche against the onslaught of globalization and the Placeless spaces of capitalism. Collective conservation movements also remain elusive as paths of resistance to Zhu's heroine for two mutually reinforcing reasons. First, the localist politics with which she might otherwise identify given her close connection to many of the spaces described in the narrative, mistrusts and excludes her based on the mainlander label she has inherited from her parents. Second, her own wanderlust and affinity for tourism reveals her own (unintentional) submersion in the flows of modern life, especially consumerism. If she is incapable of putting on an expressionless face "the same as coats and hats when [she] leaves home" that she so admires in her fellow patrons at the Doutor Café, then madness is the only other possible reaction to what Benjamin called the shock of modern experience.

I might have better written that last sentence this way: If you are incapable of putting on an expressionless face "the same as coats and hats when [you] leave home" that you so admire in your fellow patrons at the Doutor Café, then madness is the only other possible reaction to what Benjamin called the shock of modern experience. I end where I began, with the second person narrative struc-

ture, which reaches out and includes each of its audience in an inclusive embrace. We are all implicated in your madness and your social isolation. Even if
you have fallen into desperation and madness, the narrative which constitutes
your story reaches out to us. And it is up to us to enter into that community and
mobilize conservation efforts for the sake of (self) preservation.

In a way quite different from *Song of Everlasting Sorrow*, and yet achieving
a remarkably similar effect, *The Ancient Capital* too reveals the past in ruins.
The demolition of space not only makes room for the erection of global Placeless structures but also devastates memories of pasts so closely linked to those
spaces. Those memories, incomplete and fractured as they are, linger even
though the spaces they are connected to have already vanished. While the heroine herself remains mired in capitalist modes of consumption which leaves her
unshielded from the modern shock of experiencing the destruction of spaces
which hold treasured places in her memories, her narrative reveals the destruction not only of those spaces but also of the histories those spaces touched and
formed and therefore also the danger of persisting in such consumptive habits.
Moreover, the second person narrative insists on making the heroine's story our
story. It creates the community that the heroine cannot find for herself. And it
demands a form of collective action that is not premised on nationalism or
another modern discourse of group identity, but rather is premised on the colla-
boration of self-selected individuals who join forces without submitting themselves to erasure in the name of a "higher" good. That is it rejects the politics of
identity and insists instead on the mutual interests of all the residents of Taiwan,
no matter one's heritage or politics.

Conclusion

In this space I have concerned myself with the ways narrative reveals and obscures a variety of pasts and traditions as a means of creating and understanding history. I have argued, in line with Walter Benjamin, that history, as such, is and can only ever be a reconstruction after the fact of the destruction of the past out of which it is made. It follows that the materials for such reconstruction are necessarily fragmented and incomplete shards of various pasts which are sifted, sorted, and arranged to enable people to understand what has gone before. This sort of abstract formulation, as a general description of the processes involved in the formation of history, remains value-neutral. That is to say, if we are persuaded by Benjamin's conception of history, these essentials of history making, namely that the basic unit is a past in ruins, remain the same regardless of any particular orientation of the historian. As I discussed in the introduction, with the advent of modernity, Chinese modernizers, who like Chen Duxiu often engaged in discourses of revolution, stressed rupture with the past and tradition and turned towards the future as the site of history's culmination and fulfillment. In the process, the fragmentary nature of the past is often lost in a series of causes and effects which lead through the present ultimately to history's zenith in the future. Benjamin, writing in an era of another modernizing discourse, Fascism, counters this turn to the future with a radical, and for him redemptive, vision of the ruination of the past as the understanding that history enables. In the process of this full, for Benjamin, rendering of the past in history, pasts—broken, battered, and above all, incomplete as they are—are transformed and given second lives which are able to powerfully affect the present with their presence.

In practice, neither of these potential historical modes, full orientation towards and expectation of fulfillment from the future on the one hand or the past on the other, is generally found in pure form. One of the lessons I hope to have demonstrated in this study is that for any given text's engagement with history a very wide variety of hopes for the future, of understandings of the present, and of engagement with the past are possible. And each of these is then mixed with the others in different amounts to produce a historical effect in that text.

147

It is in this context that I have argued for an understanding of the phantasmal and vanishing nature of the past. Pasts, as they are invoked and arranged into what Benjamin called historical constellations, are imbued with an afterlife from which they can haunt the present. These pasts return fractured and in the process of being forgotten and erased. Despite this relative weakness, these pasts are not inert. They act on the present, with the present, against the present, or through the present. In some cases, such as "Mending Heaven" and "Shi Xiu" discussed in Chapter Two, they assert their own agenda irrespective of the present goals which led to their invocation in the first place. Likewise in other cases, as in "Wandering the Garden, Waking from Dream" discussed in Chapter Six, they reach through and overwhelm the present in their haunting insistence to be remembered. On the other hand, pasts, as in "The Song of Liang Fu" also discussed in Chapter Six, can, in transformed form, reach into the future as well. Finally, texts such as *Song of Everlasting Sorrow* or *The Ancient Capital* reveal the utter ruination of the past to their audiences, if not their characters, and include those audiences in a kind of collective experience of the past. This collective experience, in its emphasis on the destruction visited on the past, creates community based in a shared comprehension of and responsibility for the fragmentation of the past and a recognition that it is vanishing away. As a result, this collective experience of phantasmal pasts which refuse to be wholly forgotten also thereby obstructs the sublimational processes of future-oriented histories, which serve to create unified subjectivities in the collective body.

Here, I have focused on two analogous techniques of incorporating the past into narratives and exploring the historical effects created therein. The first is the retelling of previous stories, which I have called parody. These parodies can also be divided into two types: retelling the same story with modern supplements, such as "Mending Heaven" and "Shi Xiu" discussed in Chapter Two, and telling a new story but one which noticeably borrows its narrative structure from a predecessor text, such as "The Homecoming" and "Dad Dad Dad" discussed in Chapter Three. The second technique is a more abstract process, indeed often including the parodying of old stories, of redeployment of certain traditions or aspects of traditions in modern narratives. Whether it be the adoption of a lyrical mode and utopian aspirations, as in the narratives discussed in Chapter Five, or the citation—either through direct quotation or allusion—of classic texts such as *Peony Pavilion*, *Romance of the Three Kingdoms*, Du Fu's poetry, Kawabata Yasunari's *The Ancient Capital*, "Peach Blossom Spring," and Bo Juyi's "Song of Everlasting Sorrow" the modern narratives I discuss in Part Two likewise engage this process of confronting previous texts in their modern updates.

The literary practice of reusing previous literature is, I have argued, analogous to Benjamin's historical work of establishing rapport between eras. The difference principally is that the resonances created in these narratives are between texts rather than eras, per se. As a result, I have also been interested in noting the variations in temporal senses that these modern narratives create through their use of previous literature. As with Benjamin's description of the materials available for historical work, there is no guarantee that any reuse of a previous text in modern narrative will necessarily lead to its reanimation or allow it to powerfully affect the modern narrative. The clearest example of this in the studies above is certainly Zhu Tianxin's *The Ancient Capital*, discussed in Chapter Eight. This is why I have argued that, in the case of *The Ancient Capital*, the citation of Kawabata's novel as well as "Peach Blossom Spring," among others, points always to empty categories and so needs to be understood as an index of absence. On the other hand, for Madame Qian in "Wandering the Garden, Waking from Dream," the citations from *Peony Pavilion* not only revive her memories to such an extent that they affect her both physically and emotionally but also revive, in a sense, a transformed Du Liniang in Madame Qian herself.

Consequently, one of the first conclusions to be drawn from this study is that despite typical assertions that the iconoclastic overthrow of tradition is the defining characteristic of Twentieth Century Chinese literature, links to tradition in a broader sense and more specifically to traditional literature have continued to play an important role in Chinese literature across the modern period. Classical literary histories of modern China locate the establishment of such an iconoclastic modern Chinese literature with the May Fourth Movement.[1] More recently, other histories have tried to show that the crucial shift away from traditional modes of thought and narrative occurred even earlier: in the late Qing moment.[2] While I am indebted to the groundbreaking intellectual work of these studies, to the extent that I follow in their footsteps, I hope to have shown in this space that no fundamental break with tradition, indicated by the links between classical texts and modern texts, was ever truly completed in modern Chinese history. This is not to deny the real (and striking) formal and thematic differences between the narratives of the late Qing New Fiction or the May Fourth periods and those of the previous century, for example Shen Fu's *Fusheng liuji* (Six Records of a Floating Life). Nevertheless, despite the revolutionary claims of those like Chen Duxiu, tradition has never been a totalized entity available to be pruned away and discarded; rather, it is an imaginary, amorphous, fragmented and shifting construct always already posited as an "other" against which—and in some cases in alignment with—to define contemporary modernity. Even when tradition as such met the most severe repression with the success of the Communist movement at mid-Twentieth Century, when state-controlled media, education, cultural production, and so on, strongly curtailed access to material manifestations of tradition, the specter of such a repressed past remained to haunt Chinese society.

The individual chapters in this study, are intended to show the varieties of traditional literary resources modern narratives access as well as the range of temporal and historical effects created in the use of those resources. As with Benjamin's historical work, I have been selective in the choice of texts I have examined, and as a result have created a kind of constellation of my own. I believe that the various nodes of this constellation have been arranged in such a way as to allow communication back and forth, so that, for example, the parodic techniques analyzed in Part One inform and illuminate their use in the narratives discussed in Part Two. Likewise the exploration of the citational approach of the narratives in Part Two help us see that parody, as I have used it here, is not merely the retelling of old stories for contemporary purposes, but is also closely linked with larger issues of cultural continuity amidst historical rupture.

At the center of this constellation I have placed a brief exercise in standard modes of literary history, foregrounding development based in a certain understanding of cause and effect. On first consideration, this may seem out of place in a study which is so clearly sympathetic to Benjamin's embrace of the past in his particular approach to history. On the contrary, to begin, as we have said before, the pure form of either a future-oriented or a past-oriented history is rare, if it exists at all. Furthermore, the (too) brief discussion of the great historical rupture for the Chinese at mid-Twentieth Century helps, I feel, ground the discussion in the central divide of before and after in modern Chinese history. Like the Roots authors discussed in Chapter Five, I locate this moment of great, but incomplete, historical rupture across which cultural continuity is sought and asserted in the establishment of the Communist state on Mainland China. As with any break, the result is multiple and fragmented pieces of what was (never) whole before. Thus, I see Chapter Four as the hub across which the other nodes in the constellation I have arranged are able to establish bonds and affinity.

As a result, a second conclusion I believe can be drawn from this study is that, despite—or perhaps because of—the selectivity I have indulged in my choice of texts to examine, these are not idiosyncratic or isolated examples. Certainly the fact that these texts span the Twentieth Century is an indication of the continued pertinence of parodic and citatational modes in Chinese narrative. Likewise the range of authors, from canonical May Fourth writers like Lu Xun to Shanghai modernists like Shi Zhecun to Communist mass writers like Zhao Shuli to post-colonial Taiwanese writers like Zhu Tianxin, indicates that these modes can be deployed not only across historical moments but also by authors with vastly divergent backgrounds for an array of purposes.

Indeed, when we become attune to these narrative modes, we begin to find them in all sorts of writings. Take Lu Xun as an example. Even if critics have had difficulty placing the stories in *Old Tales Retold* in Lu Xun's larger body of writings, as I discussed briefly in Chapter Three, the parodic mode is crucial to Lu's canonical "The True Story of Ah Q." Likewise, the parody of the classical language in the first section of Lu's equally canonical "Madman's Diary," augments the severe castigation of traditional Chinese society to be found in that story. Furthermore, the parodic mode, as I have used it, can be found in many other examples from modern Chinese narrative. And, here, I do not simply mean the stories I did not specifically discuss in Lu Xun's *Old Tales Retold*, Shi Zhecun's *The General's Head*, Bai Xianyong's *Taipei People*, and Zhu Tianxin's collection *The Ancient Capital*, though these certainly can also be considered from the vantage of parody. In addition to these, for example, Mao Dun, another canonical May Fourth writer, also updated an episode from *Water Margin* in his "Baozitou Lin Chong" (Lin Chong the Leopard Head). More recently, Yu Hua's "Gudian aiqing" (Classical Love) parodies traditional scholar-beauty romances not to mention the ways the "Hooligan" novels of Wang Shuo quote and parody official Communist sloganeering language as well as committee-driven decision making and centrally directed social life. Likewise, the citational strategies of

Zhu Tianwen's *Huangren shouji* (Notes of a Desolate Man) in which the works of Levi-Strauss and Foucault, among others, are prominently discussed also work to establish constellations of resonance between these various texts. The title of this novel, moreover, has to be taken as an allusion to Lu Xun's "Kuang-ren riji" (Madman's Diary) and as such the latter can be seen to serve as a parodic source for Zhu's novel. To be sure, much of what is routinely classified as historical fiction could, in my opinion, be usefully considered from the viewpoint of parody.

Finally, we can see that the traumas induced by modernity continue to be topics that most if not all of these narratives confront. I start with a consideration of the adoption of Freudian psychology among other Western discourses for the express purpose of instigating modernity in Chinese culture. From *Red Sorghum*'s narrator to the heroine of *The Ancient Capital*, from Yin Xueyan to Huang Zhixian/Glasses Ma, the characters discussed in these texts in one way or another attempt to cope with the ever-expanding modern modes of life, especially capitalism. It is perhaps ironic that *The Ancient Capital*, like "Mending Heaven" or "Shi Xiu," appeals fruitlessly to global discourses to help cope with the destruction evident as a result of Taipei's modernization. This provides a vantage from which to critique the modernization movement of the early Twentieth Century in China because of the debilitating and destructive forces it has loosed on Chinese culture. The search for and ultimately finding of continuity, of personal connections both cultural and social, remains a fundamental task these narratives set for themselves.

Notes

Chapter 1: Introduction

1. Chen Duxiu, "Wenxue Geming Lun," *Xin qingnian* 2, no. 6 (1917). An etext is available from http://www.pku.edu.cn/lib&mus/archives/mren/chen/chdx11.htm (accessed December 3, 2007).

2. Chen Duxiu, "Wenxue Geming Lun." For a discussion of Chen's iconoclasm and radical rhetoric, see Theodore Huters, *Bringing the World Home: Appropriating the West in Late Qing and Early Republican China* (Honolulu: University of Hawai'i Press, 2005).

3. Ban Wang, *Illuminations from the Past: Trauma, Memory, and History in Modern China* (Stanford: Stanford University Press, 2004), 33.

4. The magazine was actually founded in 1915 with the name *Qingnian zazhi* (Youth Journal) but was renamed *Xin qingnian* the next year after a brief pause in publication as Chen Duxiu relocated to Beijing from Shanghai.

5. Shu-mei Shih, *The Lure of the Modern: Writing Modernism in Semicolonial China, 1917-1937* (Berkeley: University of California Press, 2001), 54.

6. For an excellent summary of this debate and the cultural-political uses to which it was put by May Fourth thinkers, see Shih, *The Lure of the Modern*, 49-72. See also Lydia He Liu, *Translingual Practice: Literature, National Culture, and Translated Modernity—China, 1900-1937* (Stanford: Stanford University Press, 1995), 87-99.

7. See Yü-sheng Lin, *The Crisis of Chinese Consciousness: Radical Antitraditionalism in the May Fourth Era* (Madison: University of Wisconsin Press, 1979).

8. Theodore Huters, *Bringing the World Home:Appropriating the West in Late Qing and Early Republican China* (Honolulu: University of Hawai'I Press, 2005), 10.

9. Lydia Liu notes that *chuantong* is a "return graphic loan," or a classical Chinese word that in the modern period was used by the Japanese to translate a

European term, in this case *tradition*, and then reintroduced into Chinese. Liu, *Translingual Practice*, Appendix D.

10. Raymond Williams, *Keywords: A Vocabulary of Culture and Society*, Rev. ed. (New York: Oxford University Press, 1985), 319.

11. Williams, too, notes this phenomenon in *Keywords*. For the Chinese context, see (among others) Leo Ou-fan Lee, *Shanghai Modern: The Flowering of a New Urban Culture in China, 1930-1945* (Cambridge: Harvard University Press, 1999) and Shih, *The Lure of the Modern*.

12. Wang, *Illuminations from the Past*, 26.

13. See Wang, *Illuminations from the Past*, 25-32. See also the essays collected in Milena Doleželová-Velingerová, Oldrich Král, and Graham Martin Sanders, eds., *The Appropriation of Cultural Capital: China's May Fourth Project* (Cambridge: Harvard University Asia Center: Distributed by Harvard University Press, 2001).

14. Elissa Marder, *Dead Time: Temporal Disorders in the Wake of Modernity (Baudelaire and Flaubert)* (Stanford: Stanford University Press, 2001), 122-30. One of the basic premises of Matei Calinescu's important study of modernism is the distinction between economic modernity—of progress and the capitalist vision of ever-expanding production—and aesthetic modernity—psychological development of the self within a temporal *durée*—a distinction that Marder implicitly supports in her study. No doubt, in the West this distinction is and has been an important analytical tool; in semicolonial China, in socialist China, and in postsocialist China, however, the political and national drives for modernization have left little conceptual space for an aesthetic modernity. See Matei Calinescu, *Five Faces of Modernity: Modernism, Avant-Garde, Decadence, Kitsch, Postmodernism* (Durham: Duke University Press, 1987).

15. Wang, *Illuminations from the Past*, 5.

16. I have drawn inspiration for this consideration from Marilyn Ivy's discussion of these ideas in the Japanese context. Japan is analogous to China because it faced (and continues to face) Western monopolization of modernizing discourses. However, Japan, unlike China, has been able to pass as a modernized first-world nation (in fact the first and possibly the only non-white nation to "fit in") since at least the turn of the twentieth century. See Marilyn Ivy, *Discourses of the Vanishing: Modernity, Phantasm, Japan* (Chicago: University of Chicago Press, 1995).

17. I have used the translation from Yang Hsien-yi and Gladys Yang in Lu Xun, "Preface to the First Collection of Short Stories, 'Call to Arms,'" in *Selected Stories of Lu Hsun* (Beijing: Foreign Language Press, 1972), 1. For Lu Xun's original text, see "Zixu" in *Lu Xun quan ji*, vol. 1 (Beijing: Renmin wenxue chubanshe, 2005), 437.

18. This translation is in the introduction, called "Abreaction through Artistic Mediation: An Introduction to Lu Xun's Aesthetic Praxis," to Kaldis' forthcoming book on Lu's prose poems *Yecao*. In this piece, Kaldis explores the psychological ramifications of repressed memories for Lu Xun's artistic production. Many thanks to Kaldis for making his thoughts available to me prior to their publication.

19. Kaldis, "Abreaction through Artistic Mediation," np.

20. Tejaswini Niranjana, *Siting Translation: History, Post-Structuralism, and the Colonial Context* (Berkeley: University of California Press, 1992), 173. See also Walter Benjamin, "The Task of the Translator," and "Theses on the Philosophy of History," both in Hannah Arendt ed., *Illuminations* (New York: Schocken Books, 1969), 69-82, 253-64.

21. Niranjana, *Siting Translation*, 162.

22. Benjamin, "Theses on the Philosophy of History," 261.

23. Benjamin, "Theses on the Philosophy of History," 257-58.

24. Ching Kwan Lee and Guobin Yang, "Introduction: Memory, Power, and Culture," in Ching Kwan Lee and Guobin Yang eds., *Re-envisioning the Chinese Revolution: The Politics and Poetics of Collective Memories in Reform China* (Washington D.C.: Woodrow Wilson Center Press, 2007), 10-11.

25. There are two major editions of this novel, one published in Beijing: Mo Yan, *Honggaoliang jiazu* (Beijing: Jiefangjun wenyi chubanshe, 1987); the other in Taipei: Mo Yan, *Honggaoliang jiazu* (Taipei:Hongfan shudian, 1988). Howard Goldblatt, in his translation of the novel, says that Mo Yan himself preferred the Taipei edition because it preserved certain aspects edited out of the Beijing edition. All references to *Honggaoliang jiazu* will, therefore, be to the Taipei edition. All translations are my own, though for reference see Goldblatt's translation: Mo Yan, *Red Sorghum: A Novel of China*, trans. Howard Goldblatt (New York: Viking, 1993).

26. See, for example, David Der-wei Wang, "Imaginary Nostalgia: Shen Congwen, Song Zelai, Mo Yan, and Li Yongping," in Ellen Widmer and David Der-wei Wang eds., *From May Fourth to June Fourth: Fiction and Film in Twentieth Century China* (Cambridge: Harvard University Press, 1993), 107-32, Ying-hsiung Chou, "Romance of the Red Sorghum Family," *Modern Chinese Literature* 5, no. 1 (1989): 33-42, and Gui Wei, "Lishi bianjie de zuihou wancan: Cong Honggaoliang dao Tanxiangxing," *Journal of Zhejiang Business Technology Institute* 1, no. 3 (2002): 54-56.

27. See, for example, Tonglin Lu, "Red Sorghum: Limits of Transgression," in Kang Liu and Xiaobing Tang eds., *Politics, Ideology, and Literary Discourse in Modern China : Theorectical Interventions and Cultural Critique* (Durham: Duke University Press, 1993), 188-208, Guan Yuhong and Li Li, "Ganjue shijiezhong de lixing sikao: Huigu Mo Yan de 'Honggaoliang xilie,'" *Journal of Langfang Teachers College* 19, no. 1 (2003):31-3, and Tan Xuechun, "Chongdu Honggaoliang: Zhanzheng xiuci huayu de linglei shuxie," *Journal of Qinghai Normal University* 95, no. 4 (2002): 100-104.

28. Degeneration of the race is first brought up on page 2 and is largely the subject of the last section (Chapter 5, Section 10) of the novel. What comes between these ends of the novel is evidence that the race truly has degenerated from its former glory.

29. Mo, *Honggaoliang jiazu*, 493.

30. Mo, *Honggaoliang jiazu*, 496.

31. Mo, *Honggaoliang jiazu*, 2-3.

32. Tonglin Lu has highlighted the illusoriness of this originary pre-communist past, and I have argued elsewhere that the narrator's personal quest is likewise illusory. See Lu, "Red Sorghum," and my "Memory or Fantasy? *Honggaoliang*'s Narrator," *Modern Chinese Literature and Culture* 18, no. 2 (Fall 2006): 131-62.

33. Mo, *Honggaoliang jiazu*, 91.

34. Both Tonglin Lu and Zhu Ling have commented on Grandma's role in the novel as a cipher ostensibly representing female strength but all the while undermining that message. See Lu, "Red Sorghum," and Zhu Ling, "A Brave New World? On the Construction of 'Masculinity' and 'Femininity' in the Red Sorghum Family," in Tonglin Lu ed., *Gender and Sexuality in Twentieth-Century Chinese Literature and Society* (Albany: State University of New York Press, 1993), 121-34.

35. Genette calls this pseudo-diegetic narrative. Gérard Genette, *Narrative Discourse: An Essay in Method*, trans. Jane E Lewin (Ithaca, N.Y.: Cornell University Press, 1980), 237.

36. Genette, *Narrative Discourse*, 35.

37. Luohan's surname is Liu but he is almost exclusively called Luohan Daye in the novel. Luohan is the Chinese rendering of the Buddhist term Arhat, or one who is enlightened; so his name translates as Master Arhat.

38. Mo, *Honggaoliang jiazu*, 1.

39. This is the paragraph from pages 2 and 3 of the novel, which I quoted above.

40. Genette, *Narrative Discourse*, 255-57.

41. Mo, *Honggaoliang jiazu*, 5.

42. A closer analysis of the various durations of the different segments of this section, although beyond the scope of this study, would be quite illuminating because manipulating the temporal rhythms back and forth across time is arguably another method the narrator employs in his creation of a historical constellation.

43. See my "Memory or Fantasy?"

44. Ivy, *Discourses of the Vanishing*, 22.

45. David Wang, *The Monster That Is History: History, Violence, and Fictional Writing in Twentieth-Century China* (Berkeley: University of California Press, 2004), 266-67.

Chapter 2: Tradition Redux

1. Margaret A. Rose, *Parody//Meta-Fiction: An Analysis of Parody as a Critical Mirror to the Writing and Reception of Fiction* (London: Croom Helm, 1979), 18, Linda Hutcheon, *A Theory of Parody: The Teachings of Twentieth-Century Art Forms* (New York: Methuen, 1985), 32, and Margaret A. Rose, *Parody: Ancient, Modern, and Post-Modern* (Cambridge: Cambridge University Press, 1993), 6-19.

2. Gay Sibley, "Satura from Quintilian to Joe Bob Briggs: A New Look at an Old Word," in Brian A. Connery and Kirk Combe eds., *Theorizing Satire: Essays in Literary Criticism* (New York: St. Martin's Press, 1995), 58.

3. Hutcheon, *A Theory of Parody*, 53.

4. See Simon Dentith's definition which attempts to take all these modes as well as reader reception into consideration and as a result is so broad as to be almost meaningless. Simon Dentith, *Parody* (New York: Routledge, 2000), 1-21.

5. Andreas Böhn, "Parody and Quotation: A Case Study of E.T.A Hoffman's *Kater Murr*," in Beate Müller ed., *Parody: Dimensions and Perspectives* (Amsterdam: Rodopi, 1997), 48.

6. Böhn, "Parody and Quotation," 52.

7. Fredric V Bogel, "The Difference Satire Makes: Reading Swift's Poems," in *Theorizing Satire*, 45.

8. Jacques Derrida, "Structure, Sign and Play in the Discourse of the Human Sciences," in Hazard Adams and Leroy Searle eds., *Critical Theory since 1965* (Tallahassee: Florida State University Press, 1986), 91. The resonance between *supplement*'s dual meaning and parody's dual action is, I think, not accidental.

9. Jacques Derrida, "Différance," in Adams and Searle eds., *Critical Theory since 1965*, 122.

10. Derrida, "Différance," 130.

11. Rose, *Parody*, 25.

12. See Qin Xianci, "Lu Xun Nianbiao," in Yang Ze ed., *Lu Xun Xiaoshuoji*, (Taipei: Hongfan shudian, 1994), 489.

13. As just one example, Leo Lee discusses the collection in his biographical and introductory section (called "Genesis of a Writer"), before moving on to the meatier matter of analyzing the bulk of Lu Xun's creative output (this section is called "Creative Writings") in his study of Lu Xun. Leo Ou-fan Lee, *Voices from the Iron House: A Study of Lu Xun* (Bloomington: Indiana University Press, 1987), 32-7.

14. Respective examples include Wu Ying and Li Sangwu; see their studies in Meng Guanglai and Han Rixin eds., *Gushi Xinbian Yanjiu Ziliao* (Jinan: Shandong wenyi chubanshe, 1984), 191-207, 208-19.

15. See, for example, Marston Anderson, "Lu Xun's Facetious Muse: The Creative Imperative in Modern Chinese Fiction," in Ellen Widmer and David Der-wei Wang eds., *From May Fourth to June Fourth: Fiction and Film in Twentieth Century China* (Cambridge: Harvard University Press, 1993), 249-68 and Liu Yukai, "'Youhua' de dingwei: Lu Xun *Gushi Xinbian* yishu xinlun," *Social Science Front* 4 (1998): 148-57.

16. Lu Xun, "*Gushi xinbian* xuyan," in *Lu Xun quanji*, vol. 2 (Beijing: Renmin wenxue chubanshe, 2005), 353.

17. Anderson, "Lu Xun's Facetious Muse," 260.

18. Lu Xun, "Lishui," in *Lu Xun quanji*, vol. 2, 386.

19. See Lu, "*Gushi xinbian* xuyan."

20. See Andrew Plaks' thorough tracing of the Nü Wa myth in Andrew H. Plaks, *Archetype and Allegory in the Dream of the Red Chamber* (Princeton, N.J.: Princeton University Press, 1976), 27-42. Also see Liu An, *Huainanzi: 21*

Juan, (Beijing: Beijing yanshan chubanshe, 1995), 154, and Ying Shao, *Xinxu Tongjian; Fengsu Tongyi Tongjian*, (Shanghai: Shanghai guji chubanshe, 1987), 83.

21. Lu Xun, "Butian," in *Lu Xun quanji*, vol. 2, 357. Translations, unless otherwise noted are my own, but compare Lu Xun, *Old Tales Retold*, trans. Yang Xianyi and Gladys Yang, (Beijing: Waiwen chubanshe, 2000).

22. Lu, "Butian," 361-62.

23. Lu, "Butian," 362.

24. Lu, "Butian," 358. In Roman letters in the original.

25. The juxtaposition and opposition of *baihua* with *wenyan* is a standard May Fourth shorthand for the continued pernicious influence of traditional society on modernization drives. See my discussion of this issue in the previous chapter. For a discussion of the role of *baihua* in modern fiction, see Leo Ou-fan Lee's essay "Incomplete Modernity: Rethinking the May Fourth Intellectual Project" and Stephen Owen's essay "The End of the Past: Rewriting Chinese Literary History in the Early Republic" both in Milena Doleželová-Velingerová, Oldrich Král, and Graham Martin Sanders, eds., *The Appropriation of Cultural Capital: China's May Fourth Project* (Cambridge: Harvard University Asia Center: Distributed by Harvard University Press, 2001), 31-65, 167-92. Also see Milena Doleželová-Velingerová, "The Origins of Modern Chinese Literature" in Merle Goldman, ed., *Modern Chinese Literature in the May Fourth Era* (Cambridge: Harvard University Press, 1977), 17-35.

26. Lu, "Butian," 357-58.

27. Anderson, "Lu Xun's Facetious Muse," 261.

28. *Short Story Monthly* 22, no. 2 (1931). See entries for February 10 and October 25, 1931 in Huang Dezhi and Xiao Xia, "Shi Zhecun nianbiao," *Journal of Huaiyin Teacher's College* 25, no. 1 (2003): 28.

29. See Shi Zhecun, "Yinyan," in *Shinian Chuangzuo Ji* (Shanghai: Huadong shifan daxue chubanshe, 1996).

30. Shu-mei Shih, *The Lure of the Modern: Writing Modernism in Semicolonial China, 1917-1937* (Berkeley: University of California Press, 2001), 241-53 and Leo Ou-fan Lee, *Shanghai Modern: The Flowering of a New Urban Culture in China, 1930-1945* (Cambridge, Mass.: Harvard University Press, 1999), 130-37.

31. Shu-mei Shih's examination of Shi's fiction in her *The Lure of the Modern* is a notable exception to this statement.

32. Shih, *The Lure of the Modern*, 231-75.

33. Here I differ from Shih, who states that the stories in *The General's Head* reflect "a remote past of no immediate consequence to the present." Shih, *The Lure of the Modern*, 366.

34. Shih, *The Lure of the Modern*, 229.

35. In "Mending Heaven" Lu Xun had also limited the perspective to Nü Wa herself, except for the final section after her death. This access to the characters' interiority enables the supplement of Freudian psychology to the stories.

36. Andrew Jones, "The Violence of the Text: Reading Yu Hua and Shi Zhicun," *positions: east asia cultures critiques* 2, no. 3 (1994): 579.

37. Shi Zhecun, "Shi Xiu," in Leo Ou-fan Lee ed., *Shanghai de hubuwu: xinganjuepai xiaoshuo xuan* (Taibei Shi: Yunchen wenhua shiye gufen youxian gongsi, 2001), 93.

38. Shi, "Shi Xiu," 66

39. Jones, "The Violence of the Text," 577.

40. Shi, "Shi Xiu," 68-69, emphasis added

41. Maureen O'Harra, "Constructing Emancipatory Realities," in Walter Truett Anderson ed., *The Fontana Post-Modernism Reader* (London: Fontana Press, 1995), 148.

42. Julia Kristeva, "Women's Time," in *Critical Theory since 1965*, 477.

43. Shi, "Shi Xiu," 85.

44. Shi, "Shi Xiu," 96.

45. Jones, "The Violence of the Text," 580. The last statement in this passage leads to the extremely interesting, though ultimately unanswerable, question: why did Shi Zhecun choose to parody this episode from *Water Margin* and not the much more famous episode of Wu Song which follows more or less the same story of adultery and revenge?

46. See my brief discussion in the previous chapter as well as Wang Xiaoming, "Yifen Zazhi He Yige "Shetuan"—Chongping Wusi Wenxue Chuantong," in Wang Xiaoming ed., *Piping Kongjian De Kaichuang: Ershi Shiji Zhongguo Wenxue Yanjiu* (Shanghai: Dongfang chuban zhongxin, 1998) and Huters, *Bringing the World Home*, chapter 8.

47. Jones, "The Violence of the Text," 594.

48. Shi, "Shi Xiu," 86, 87.

49. Shi, "Shi Xiu," 92.

50. Shi, "Shi Xiu," 92-93.

51. Shi, "Shi Xiu," 93.

52. Shi, "Shi Xiu," 93.

53. Shi, "Shi Xiu," 90.

54. Shi, "Shi Xiu," 100.

55. Shi, "Shi Xiu," 101.

56. Jones, "The Violence of the Text," 589.

57. Shi, "Shi Xiu," 90, 79.

58. Hélène Cixous, "The Laugh of the Medusa," in *Critical Theory since 1965*, 319.

59. See the discussion of fetishism in Elissa Marder, *Dead Time: Temporal Disorders in the Wake of Modernity (Baudelaire and Flaubert)* (Stanford: Stanford University Press, 2001), 45-47, 116-22.

Chapter 3: Return to the Primitive

1. I discuss this essay in greater detail in Chapter 5, "The Lyrical and the Local."

2. Han Shaogong, "Guiqulai," in *Guiqulai* (Beijing: Zuojia chubanshe, 1996), 112-13.

3. Han, "Guiqulai," 113.

4. Anneleen Masschelein, "A Homeless Concept: Shapes of the Uncanny in Twentieth-Century Theory and Culture," *Image [&] Narrative: Online Magazine of the Visual Narrative* 5 (2003) http://www.imageandnarrative.be/uncanny/anneleenmasschelein.htm (accessed February 28, 2008).

5. Han, "Guiqulai," 122.

6. Han, "Guiqulai," 122.

7. Joseph S. M. Lau, "Visitation of the Past in Han Shaogong's Post-1985 Fiction," in Ellen Widmer and David Der-wei Wang eds., *From May Fourth to June Fourth: Fiction and Film in Twentieth-Century China* (Cambridge, MA: Harvard University Press, 1993), 27.

8. Lau, "Visitation of the Past," 28.

9. Chuang Tzu, *Basic Writings*, tr. Burton Watson (New York: Columbia University Press, 1964), 45. I have converted the Romanization of this passage to standard pinyin.

10. Interestingly, Jeanne Tai, in her translation of this story, does not translate the section concerning the blueish steam, instead skipping directly to the scar. See Han Shaogong, "The Homecoming," in Jeanne Tai ed. and tr., *Spring Bamboo: A Collection of Contemporary Chinese Short Stories* (New York: Random House, 1989), 34.

11. Peter Brooks, *Reading for the Plot: Design and Intention in Narrative* (Cambridge, MA: Harvard University Press, 1984), 99.

12. Homi K. Bhabha, *The Location of Culture* (London: Routledge, 1994), 9.

13. Han, "Guiqulai," 127.

14. Han's own rustification took place in western Hunan Province, and the physical settings for his stories are said to be modeled on this locale. See Lau, "Visitation of the Past," and Rong Cai, *The Subject in Crisis in Contemporary Chinese Literature* (Honolulu: University of Hawai'l Press, 2004), 60-62.

15. Rey Chow, *Primitive Passions: Visuality, Sexuality, Ethnography, and Contemporary Chinese Cinema* (New York: Columbia University Press, 1995), 35-43.

16. Chow, *Primitive Passions*, 38.

17. Chow, *Primitive Passions*, 22.

18. See my discussion of the formation of this tradition in Chapter 4, "Interlude: The Maoist (Anti)Tradition and the Nationalist (Neo)Tradition."

19. Chow, *Primitive Passions*, 173-202.

20. Han, "Guiqulai," 117.

21. Lau, "Visitation of the Past in Han Shaogong's Post-1985 Fiction," 30.

22. Han Shaogong, "Ba ba ba," in *Zhongguo xungen xiaoshuo xuan* (Hong Kong: Joint Publishing, 1993), 136.

23. Han, "Ba ba ba," 136.

24. The following discussion refers to Lu Xun, "Ah Q zhengzhuan," in Lu Xun quanji, vol. 1 (Beijing: Renmin wenxue chubanshe, 2005), 512-59. See also the translation in Lu Hsun, *Selected Stories*, Hsien-i Yang and Gladys Yang tr., Reissue Edition (New York: W W Norton & Co, 2003), 65-112.

25. Lu, "Ah Q zhengzhuan," 512-15.

26. For a discussion of Lu Xun's concern with the issue of national character, see Lydia H Liu, *Translingual Practice: Literature, National Culture, and Translated Modernity—China, 1900-1937* (Stanford: Stanford University Press, 1995).

27. Lu, "Ah Q zhengzhuan," 552.

28. Han, "Ba ba ba," 137.

29. Rong Cai, *The Subject in Crisis in Contemporary Chinese Literature*, 62.

30. Cai, *The Subject in Crisis in Contemporary Chinese Literature*, 71-72.

31. Han, "Ba ba ba," 145-46.

32. Han, "Ba ba ba," 147-48.

33. Han, "Ba ba ba," 165.

34. The narrator in Mo Yan's *Red Sorghum* series is interestingly also concerned with the "degeneration of the race;" however, he seeks a return to his primitive roots to remedy this decline. See my "Memory or Fantasy? *Hongaoliang*'s Narrator," *Modern Chinese Literature and Culture* 18.2 (Fall 2006): 131-162.

35. Han, "Ba ba ba," 136.

36. Han, "Ba ba ba," 137.

37. Han, "Ba ba ba," 166-67.

38. Han, "Ba ba ba," 178.

39. Han, "Ba ba ba," 140.

40. Han, "Ba ba ba," 152.

41. See Chow, *Primitive Passions*, 173-202.

42. I discuss these practices in greater detail in the next chapter "Interlude: The Maoist (Anti)Tradition and the Nationalist (Neo)Tradition."

43. This phrase is, of course, Jürgen Habermas'.

Chapter 4: Interlude

1. Li Haofei delves in depth into this question; see Li Haofei, "Jielun: 1979 nian yiqian de jiandan zhuangkuang," *Contemporary Writers Review* 5 (1994), 30-43.

2. Mao Zedong, "Zai Yanan wenyi zuotanhuishang de jianghua," in *Mao Zedong zhuzuo xuandu* (Beijing: Renmin·chubanshe, 1986), 523-56. The *Talks* were first published in the October 19, 1943 issue of *Jiefang ribao* (Liberation Daily). A revised version of the *Talks* was first published in *Mao Zedong xuanji* (Selected Works of Mao Zedong) (Beijing: Renmin chubanshe, 1952). Translations abound; a simple internet search should reveal several of varying quality. For a translation of the earlier version and comparison with the later version, see Bonnie S. McDougall, *Mao Zedong's "Talks at the Yan'an Conference on Literature and Art": A Translation of the 1943 Text with Commentary* (Ann Arbor: Center for Chinese Studies the University of Michigan, 1980). For a translation of the later text, see Mao Zedong, "Talks at the Yan'an Forum on Literature and Art," in Kirk A. Denton ed., *Modern Chinese Literary Thought: Writings on Literature, 1893-1945*, (Stanford: Stanford University Press, 1996), 458-84.

3. Mao Zedong, "Zai Yanan wenyi zuotanhuishang de jianghua," 541.

4. David Holm, "Folk Art as Propaganda: The *Yangge* Movement in Yan'an," in Bonnie S. McDougall ed., *Popular Chinese Literature and Performing Arts in the People's Republic of China, 1949-1979* (Berkeley and Los Angeles: University of California Press, 1984), 3-35.

5. The rectification campaign, actually began earlier that year and focused on the communist bureaucracy. But with the May conference on art and literature, the campaign was officially extended to cultural workers.

6. The fourth and fifth sections of *Modern Chinese Literary Thought*, in fact, are devoted to these two debates. See Denton ed., *Modern Chinese Literary Thought*.

7. See translations of Qu's "Wenyi de ziyou he wenxuejia de bu ziyou" (Freedom for Literature but Not the Writer) and "Dazhong wenyi de wenti" (The Question of Popular Literature and Art) in Denton ed., *Modern Chinese Literary Thought*, 376-82, 418-27. Discussions of Qu's role in these debates can be found in Paul G Pickowicz, "Qu Qiubai's Critique of the May Fourth Generation: Early Chinese Marxist Literary Criticism," in Merle Goldman ed., *Modern Chinese Literature in the May Fourth Era* (Cambridge: Harvard University Press, 1977), 351-84 and Theodore Huters, "The Difficult Guest: May Fourth Revisits," *Chinese Literature: Essays, Articles, Reviews* 6, no. 1-2 (1984): 125-49.

8. Huters, "The Difficult Guest," 147.

9. Mao Zedong, "Zhongguo gongchandang zai minzu zhanzhengzhong de diwei," in *Mao Zedong zhuzuo xuandu*, vol. 1, (Beijing: Renmin chubanshe: Xinhua shudian faxing, 1986), 288. See also the translation of relevant passages in Denton ed., *Modern Chinese Literary Thought*, 428-30.

10. Mao Zedong, "Xin minzhu zhuyi lun," in *Mao Zedong zhuzuo xuandu*, vol. 1, (Beijing: Renmin chubanshe: Xinhua shudian faxing, 1986), 398-9. See also the translation of this section in Denton ed., *Modern Chinese Literary Thought*, 430-2.

11. Mao, "Xin minzhu zhuyi lun," 398.

12. In the West Cyril Birch was one of the first critics to make this connection; see Cyril Birch, "Chinese Communist Literature: The Persistence of Traditional Forms," *The China Quarterly* 13 (1963): 74-91 and Cyril Birch, "Change and Continuity in Chinese Fiction," in Merle Goldman ed., *Modern Chinese Literature in the May Fourth Era* (Cambridge: Harvard University Press, 1977), 385-404. See also Robert E. Hegel, "Making the Past Serve the Present in Fiction and Drama: From the Yan'an Forum to the Cultural Revolution," in Bonnie S. McDougall ed., *Popular Chinese Literature and Performing Arts in the People's Republic of China, 1949-1979*, 197-223.

13. Most of my information on Zhao Shuli's life has come from the brief biography and various reminiscences collected in Huang Xiuji ed., *Zhao Shuli yanjiu ziliao*, (Taiyuan: Beiyue wenyi chubanshe: Shanxi sheng xinhua shudian faxing, 1985), 3-89.

14. Incidentally, Zhao Shuli's father also seems to have served such a role in his village. See Wang Chun, "Zhao Shuli zeyang chengwei zuojiade," in Huang Xiuji ed., *Zhao Shuli yanjiu ziliao*, 11-13.

15. Zhao Shuli, "Xiao Erhei jiehun," in Zhongguo xiandai wenxueguan ed., *Zhao Shuli daibiao zuo* (Beijing: Huaxia chubanshe, 1999), 23.

16. Zhao Shuli, "Ye suan jingyan," in Huang Xiuji ed., *Zhao Shuli yanjiu ziliao*, 98.

17. Huang Ke'an, "Dazhonghua xushi celüe yu keshuoxing de wenben: Xueshujie guanyu Zhao Shuli xiaoshuo chuangzuo de yizhong jiedu," *Gansu Theory Research* 3 (2004): 108.

18. Huang, "Dazhonghua xushi celüe yu keshuoxing de wenben." For a discussion of native soil fiction see Chapter Five, "Lyrical Links: Shen Congwen, Roots, and Temporality in the Lyrical Tradition."

19. This statement is not unlike Fan Jiajin's observation that political involvement, at least in the case of Zhao Shuli, led to creative flowering. See Fan Jiajin, "Zai pannizhe duiwuzhong xunzhao rensheng jiazhi de shixian jiyu: Lun Zhao Shuli de zhengzhi canyu he wenxue xuanze," *Journal of Zhejiang Normal University* 5, no. 28 (2003): 7-11.

20. Literally the text here reads "are you dressed like a person or not?"

21. Zhao, "Xiao Erhei jiehun," 27.

22. Zhao Shuli, "Li Youcai banhua," in Zhongguo xiandai wenxueguan ed., *Zhao Shuli daibiao zuo*, 30.

23. Birch, "Chinese Communist Literature," 77.

24. Cui Zhihui, "Hualong dianjing shuiru jiaorong: Tan 'Li Youcai banhua' zhong de 'banhua,'" *Journal of Urumchi Education Academy* 3 (2002): 35-37.

25. This translation is Jack Belden's. I have used it because, despite its looseness, this translation really does capture the verse's flavor. Jack Belden, *China Shakes the World*, 1st ed. (New York: Harper, 1949), 87.

26. Zhao, "Li Youcai banhua," 32.

27. McDougall, *Mao Zedong's "Talks at the Yan'an Conference on Literature and Art"*

28. Huang Ke'an makes a similar observation. See Huang, "Dazhonghua xushi celüe yu keshuoxing de wenben."

29. See David Holm's discussion of *Yangge* in Holm, "Folk Art as Propaganda." See Also Helen Rees' description of how the Communists made traditional music "scientific" by enforcing even temperament and even the importation of Western instruments to play traditional tunes in Helen Rees, *Echoes of History: Naxi Music in Modern China* (Oxford: Oxford University Press, 2000).

30. Zhao Shuli, "Li Youcai banhua," 63.

31. Zhao Shuli, "Li Youcai banhua," 69.

32. See Huang ed., *Zhao Shuli yanjiu ziliao*, 7-8, 41-70. The remembrance of Zhao's son, Zhao Guangjian (50-6), is especially moving.

33. See McDougall, *Mao Zedong's "Talks at the Yan'an Conference on Literature and Art,"* 38-40.

34. McDougall, *Mao Zedong's "Talks at the Yan'an Conference on Literature and Art,"* 76, 99 n. 186.

35. While D E Pollard argues that the contrast between socialist realism and the two revolutionaries constitutes a distinction without a difference since socialist realism already encompassed a combination of revolutionary realism with

revolutionary romanticism, it seems that the latter formulation is meant as much to discourage the naturalistic tendencies of realism as to conceive of a truly new theoretical approach. See D E Pollard, "The Short Story in the Cultural Revolution," *The China Quarterly* 73 (1978): 99-121 and Richard King, "A Fiction Revealing Collusion: Allegory and Evasion in the Mid-1970s," *Modern Chinese Literature* 10, no. 1-2 (1998): 71-90. For a more detailed comparison see Su Wei, "The School and the Hospital: On the Logics of Socialist Realism," Charles Laughlin trans., in Pang-yuan Chi and David Der-wei Wang eds., *Chinese Literature in the Second Half of a Modern Century: A Critical Survey* (Bloomington: Indiana University Press, 2000), 65-75.

36. See Pollard, "The Short Story in the Cultural Revolution," 100-103.

37. For the seminal account of dialogism against which I am contrasting monologism, see M. M. Bakhtin, *The Dialogic Imagination: Four Essays*, Michael Holquist ed., Caryl Emerson and Michael Holquist trans. (Austin: University of Texas Press, 1981).

38. King, "A Fiction Revealing Collusion," 77-78.

39. According to Bonnie McDougall, the English language *Chinese Literature* was the only cultural magazine published between 1966 and 1972. Furthermore, she states that during this period only Lu Xun, Hao Ran, and Mao himself escaped censure; see McDougall, *Mao Zedong's "Talks at the Yan'an Conference on Literature and Art,"* 39-40. See also King, "A Fiction Revealing Collusion," 72 n. 74

40. *Zhaoxia* (Shanghai: Shanghai renmin chubanshe, 1973), 319.

41. King, "A Fiction Revealing Collusion," 73-75.

42. Hegel, "Making the Past Serve the Present in Fiction and Drama," 205

43. Michael Egan argues that Hao Ran's Cultural Revolution novel *Jinguang dadao* (The Golden Road, vol. 1 1972, vol. 2 1974) "[switches] filiations" from traditional narrative style to one of political bent midway through the novel. In a longer work such as Hao Ran's novel such doubling is possible, but I will argue that the short stories I examine here do not have space for a similar technique and so jettison the traditional style in favor of the indispensable political content. See Michael Egan, "A Notable Sermon: The Subtext of Hao Ran's Fiction," in McDougall ed., *Popular Chinese Literature and Performing Arts in the People's Republic of China, 1949-1979*, 238-40.

44. Bell Yung, "Model Opera as Model: From *Shajiabang* to *Sagabong*," in McDougall ed., *Popular Chinese Literature and Performing Arts in the People's Republic of China, 1949-1979*, 145-48.

45. Yao Wenyuan, quoted in Gu Yuanqing, "'San tuchu' de gouzao guocheng jiqi lilun tezheng," *Journal of Ezhou University* 9, no. 1 (2002): 28.

46. See Richard King, "Revisionism and Transformation in the Cultural Revolution Novel," *Modern Chinese Literature* 7, no. 1 (1993): 105-29.

47. Quoted in Gu Yuanqing, "'San tuchu' de gouzao guocheng jiqi lilun tezheng."

48. Gu Yuanqing, "'San tuchu' de gouzao guocheng jiqi lilun tezheng."

49. For more on Duan as well as *Zhaoxia* and its association with the Gang of Four see King, "A Fiction Revealing Collusion."

50. *Zhaoxia*, iv.

51. A translation is available as "Not Just One of the Audience," *Chinese Literature* 9 (September 1973): 51-64.

52. Duan Ruixia, "Tebie guanzhong," in *Zhaoxia*, 3.

53. Duan, "Tebie guanzhong," 8-9.

54. Other turnabout characters in the anthology are even more clearly heroic, for example, the captain in "Anjiao" (Hidden Reef) and the young marksman in "Tan zhaodian" (Bull's-Eye).

55. There are no quotations from Mao in "Tebie guanzhong," but in other stories quotations of Mao are printed in bold type and reliably encapsulate the theme of that story.

56. Indeed, for this reason, Fangming Chen sees the retrocession of Taiwan to China in 1945 not as decolonization after fifty years of Japanese rule but as a renewal of colonialist policies. See Fangming Chen, "Postmodern or Postcolonial? An Inquiry into Postwar Taiwanese Literary History," in David Der-wei Wang and Carlos Rojas eds., *Writing Taiwan: A New Literary History* (Durham: Duke University Press, 2007), 26-50.

57. For Japanese colonial practices, see Leo T. S. Ching, *Becoming "Japanese": Colonial Taiwan and the Politics of Identity Formation* (Berkeley: University of California Press, 2001).

58. For more on wartime mobilization efforts, see Charles A. Laughlin, "The Battlefield of Cultural Production: Chinese Literary Mobilization during the War Years," *Journal of Modern Chinese Literature in Chinese* 2, no. 1 (July 1998): 83-103.

59. See David Der-wei Wang, *The Monster That Is History: History, Violence, and Fictional Writing in Twentieth-Century China* (Berkeley and Los Angeles: University of California Press, 2004), 156-8 and Sung-sheng Yvonne Chang, *Literary Culture in Taiwan: Martial Law to Market Law* (New York: Columbia University Press, 2004), 45-89.

60. Wang, *The Monster That Is History*, 170-71.

61. Jiang Gui, *Xuanfeng*, reprint edition (Taipei: Jiuge chubanshe, 2005), 43.

62. Jiang, *Xuanfeng*, 9.

63. David Wang makes the same observation. See Wang, *The Monster That Is History*, 194-5.

64. Wang, *The Monster That Is History*, 196.

65. Wang, *The Monster That Is History*, 183-223.

66. Jiang, *Xuanfeng*, 10.

67. Chang, *Literary Culture in Taiwan*, 73-89.

68. Chang, *Literary Culture in Taiwan*, 90-121.

69. Chang, *Literary Culture in Taiwan*, 91.

70. Bai Xianyong, *Taibei ren*, new edition, (Taipei: Erya chubanshe youxian gongsi, 1983), 53.

71. Bai, *Taibei ren*, 59-60.

72. Walter Benjamin, "Theses on the Philosophy of History," in Hannah Arendt ed., *Illuminations* (New York: Schocken Books, 1969), 261.

73. See Chang, *Literary Culture in Taiwan*, 122-38; Sung-sheng Yvonne Chang, "Representing Taiwan: Shifting Geopolitical Frameworks," Fangming Chen, "Postmodern or Postcolonial," and Xiaobing Tang, "On the Concept of Taiwanese Literature," all inWang and Rojas eds., *Writing Taiwan*, 17-89.

74. See Chaohua Wang ed., *One China, Many Paths*, (London: Verso, 2003), 1-159, and Dai Jinhua, "Redemption and Consumption: Depicting Culture in the 1990s," trans. Edward Gunn, *positions: east asia cultures critiques* 4, no. 1 (1996): 124-43.

Chapter 5: Lyrical Links

1. See Jaroslav Průšek, *The Lyrical and the Epic: Studies of Modern Chinese Literature*, Leo Ou-fan Lee ed. (Bloomington: Indiana University Press, 1980).

2. Marston Anderson, *The Limits of Realism: Chinese Fiction in the Revolutionary Period* (Berkeley: University of California Press, 1990), 1-26. The quote is from p. 8.

3. David Der-wei Wang, *Fictional Realism in Twentieth-Century China: Mao Dun, Lao She, Shen Congwen* (New York: Columbia University Press, 1992), ch. 6, especially 203-10.

4. Lu Xun, "Guxiang," in *Lu Xun Quanji* (Beijing: Renmin wenxue chubanshe, 1981), 476-86. A translation of this story is available in Joseph S. M. Lau, C. T. Hsia and Leo Ou-Fan Lee eds., *Modern Chinese Stories and Novellas: 1919-1949* (New York: Columbia University Press, 1981), 11-6.

5. Lu, "Guxiang," 477.

6. Lu, "Guxiang," 481.

7. Lu, "Guxiang," 485.

8. According to Kinkley, Shen had accompanied Ding Ling back to Hunan to take her infant son to her mother sometime after her husband, Hu Yepin, had been executed. However they did not go as far as Shen's home. See Jeffrey C. Kinkley, *The Odyssey of Shen Congwen* (Stanford, Calif.: Stanford University Press, 1987), 203.

9. Shen Congwen, "Biancheng," in Zhang Zhaohe ed., *Shen Congwen quan ji*, vol. 8, (Taiyuan Shi: Beiyue wenyi chubanshe, 2002), 66-67.

10. Shen first left his hometown, Fenghuang, in 1917, but remained in Western Hunan as a soldier until 1922.

11. Notwithstanding academic disputes over whether Qu Yuan actually authored all of the poems in the *Chuci*, because of the popular belief that Qu Yuan wrote them as well as the importance of the dragon boat races to *Biancheng*, I have attributed authorship to Qu Yuan here.

12. This translation is my own. The text to *Taohuayuan ji* can be found in Tao Qian and Xie Lingyun, *Tao Yuanming quan ji: fu Xie Lingyun ji*, ed. Cao Minggang (Shanghai: Shanghai guji chubanshe: Xinhua shudian Shanghai faxingsuo faxing, 1998), 33-4. Translation and commentary are available in A. R. Davis and T'ao Ch'ien, *T'ao Yüan-ming, His Works and their Meaning*, vol. 1, (Cambridge: Cambridge University Press, 1983), 195-201.

13. Shen, *Biancheng*, 73.

14. See note 16 below.

15. Shen, *Biancheng*, 105.

16. These two routes to marriage represent, respectively, a Han custom and a Miao (Hmong) custom. West Hunan was and is, of course, an ethnically diverse region; potential and real ethnic tensions, though, are mostly irrelevant to the story of *Biancheng*. Thus, Cuicui's grandfather, in insisting on a free marriage for his granddaughter, can act as a critic of Chinese culture from the edges, but by leaving the ethnic origin of the marriage customs unspecified, the ethnic-other source of this criticism is side-stepped. For more on multi-racial interaction in Western Hunan including differences in marriage customs, see Donald S. Sutton, "Myth Making on an Ethnic Frontier: The Cult of the Heavenly Kings of West Hunan, 1715-1996," *Modern China* 26, no. 4 (2000).

17. For a description of the rise of May Fourth authoritarianism, see Wang Xiaoming, "Yifen Zazhi He Yige 'Shetuan'—Chongping Wusi Wenxue Chuantong," in Wang Xiaoming ed., *Piping Kongjian De Kaichuang: Ershi Shiji Zhongguo Wenxue Yanjiu* (Shanghai: Dongfang chuban zhongxin, 1998), 192-7. Wang convincingly argues that, despite claims to be concerned solely with art and culture, the driving force behind the May Fourth Movement and the New Culture Movement was a sense of urgency over the decline of the nation. The need to reform society and government was felt to be so compelling that anything not believed to be of immediate aid in that cause was passionately denounced.

18. This, indeed, is a common analysis applied to traditional literature, perhaps especially *Hongloumeng*, because of the Chinese yin-yang cosmology. For example, see Andrew H. Plaks, *Archetype and Allegory in the Dream of the Red Chamber* (Princeton: Princeton University Press, 1976), Andrew H. Plaks ed., *Chinese Narrative: Critical and Theoretical Essays* (Princeton, N.J.: Princeton University Press, 1977), and Wai-yee Li, *Enchantment and Disenchantment: Love and Illusion in Chinese Literature* (Princeton, N.J.: Princeton University Press, 1993).

19. See Kinkley, *The Odyssey of Shen Congwen*, 228-35 and Qin Xianci "Shen Congwen nianbiao," in Peng Xiaoyan ed., *Shen Congwen xiaoshuoxuan*, vol. 2 (Taipei: Hongfan shudian, 1995), 475-89.

20. Shen Congwen, *Xiangxing sanji*, in Zhang Zhaohe ed., *Shen Congwen quan ji*, vol. 11, (Taiyuan Shi: Beiyue wenyi chubanshe, 2002), 297.

21. Shen, *Xiangxing sanji*, 278, emphasis added.

22. Shen, *Xiangxing sanji*, 279.

23. This is probably why Kinkley sees *Xiangxing sanji* as a transition between realism and naturalism. See Kinkley, *The Odyssey of Shen Congwen*, 232-35.

24. David Der-wei Wang, "Imaginary Nostalgia: Shen Congwen, Song Ze-lai, Mo Yan, and Li Yongping," in Ellen Widmer and David Der-wei Wang eds., *From May Fourth to June Fourth: Fiction and Film in Twentieth Century China* (Cambridge: Harvard University Press, 1993), 116.

25. See my discussion of translation in the Introduction.

26. Wang, "Imaginary Nostalgia," 117.

27. See Kinkley, *The Odyssey of Shen Congwen*, 266.

28. Han Shaogong, "Wenxue de 'gen,'" in *Wanmei de jiading: Sanwen ji* (Beijing: Zuojia chubanshe, 1996), 1

29. Han, "Wenxue de 'gen,'" 2. This argument is, in fact, a recapitulation of a traditional Chinese mode of analysis comparing root to stem (*ben* and *mo*).

30. Han, "Wenxue de 'gen,'" 5.

31. Han, "Wenxue de 'gen,'" 5.

32. Wang Zengqi, "Xu," in Li Tuo ed., *Zhongguo xungen xiaoshuoxuan*, (Hong Kong: Joint Publishing, 1993), 1.

33. Wang, "Xu," 2.

34. See note 17 above. Although Wang does not explicitly link the authoritarianism of the reformers with the Communist Party, the well known links between the two groups as well as similar intellectual backgrounds makes the connection implicit.

35. Li Tuo, "Haiwai Zhongguo zuojia taolunhui jiyao," *Jintian* 2 (1990): 96.

36. Li Tuo, "Haiwai Zhongguo zuojia taolunhui jiyao," 97.

37. Elsewhere Li Tuo has argued for just such styles of writing as resistance to "Mao style" (*Mao wenti*). See Li Tuo, "Resisting Writing," in Kang Liu and Xiaobing Tang eds., *Politics, Ideology, and Literary Discourse in Modern China: Theoretical Interventions and Cultural Critique* (Durham, N.C.: Duke University Press, 1993).

38. Jia Pingwa, "Shangzhou chutan," in Li Tuo ed., *Zhongguo xungen xiaoshuoxuan* (Hong Kong: Joint Publishing, 1993), 21-22.

39. See my discussion of Communist writing in the previous chapter.

40. There may also be a slight allusion to "Peach Blossom Spring" in the use of *tao* (peach) in the place name.

41. See my discussion of parody in Chapter 2. Also see the discussion of Han Shaogong in Chapter 3.

42. Jia, "Shangzhou chutan," 32. The dystopian transformation of Peach Blossom Spring in the reference to wilted peach blossoms almost goes without saying.

43. Jia, "Shangzhou chutan," 23.

44. Li Hangyu, "Zuihou yige yulaoer," in Li ed., *Zhongguo xungen xiaoshuoxuan*, 59-60.

45. Li, "Zuihou yige yulaor," 62.

46. This inversely resembles Joseph Levenson's classic argument that Communism made a museum piece of Confucianism and thereby neutralized it as a force in contemporary society.

47. One of the best discussions of this displacement in the Chinese context can be found in Shu-mei Shih, *The Lure of the Modern: Writing Modernism in Semicolonial China, 1917-1937* (Berkeley: University of California Press, 2001).

Chapter 6: Tradition in Exile

1. The title *gong*, is a term of respect with which Commissioner Lei addresses Pu Gong, a retired high-ranking military man, and his friend Zhong Gong. It may translate to something like Master or Your Excellency, but to avoid awkward constructions in English, I have not translated the title.

2. Bai Xianyong, *Taibei ren*, new edition, (Taipei: Erya chubanshe youxian gongsi, 1983), 192-93.

3. Joseph Lau notes that "Nearly all of [Bai's] best stories are cast against the background of winter, autumn, or evenings. Spring, if it appears at all, is seen as . . . as violent as it is beautiful; summer is identified with madness and depravity." In this case, the story is set against both winter and evening. See Joseph S. M Lau, "'Crowded Hours' Revisited: The Evocation of the Past in *Taipei jen*," *The Journal of Asian Studies*, 35, no. 1 (November 1975): 38.

4. Compare Burton Watson's translation: "Brocade River, hues of spring spread over heaven and earth; / Jade Rampart, drifting clouds transform it, now as long ago." Du Fu, *The Selected Poems of Du Fu*, tr. Burton Watson (New York: Columbia University Press, 2002), 106. While my translation cannot compete with Watson's, I want to emphasize the temporal displacement of the second line.

5. Lau, "'Crowded Hours' Revisited," 38.

6. Pu Gong mentions at one point in the story that Wang Mengyang insisted that his remains be reburied, in full dress military uniform, in the mainland once it is retaken.

7. It is an interesting fact that many of China's literary heroes were more or less failures in their non-literary, and especially political, lives; Confucius, Sima Qian, Su Shi, Wu Jingzi, and Shen Fu come to mind.

8. See the discussion of Communist cultural practices in Chapter Five, "Interlude: The Maoist (Anti)Tradition and the Nationalist (Neo)Tradition."

9. See *Sanguo yanyi*, chapter 36, and "Zhuge Liang zhuan," in *Sanguo zhi*. The complete text of "Liang fu yin" can be found in Huang Jie ed., *Han Wei yuefu fengjian* (Hong Kong: Shangyi yinshuguan, 1961), 51-52.

10. This story can be found in Sun Yanlin et al eds., *Yanzi chunqiu yizhu*, juan 2, section 24 (Jinan: Qi Lu shushe, 1991), 112-16.

11. Bai, *Taibei ren*, 182.

12. Bai, *Taibei ren*, 183.

13. Bai, *Taibei ren*, 184.

14. Bai, *Taibei ren*, 272.

15. Lau, "'Crowded Hours' Revisited," 42.

16. Bai, *Taibei ren*, 266-67.

17. Lau notes the similarity not only between the two colonels' appearances but also their family names, Zheng and Cheng. See Lau, "'Crowded Hours' Revisited," 39.

18. Bai, *Taibei ren*, 285.

19. See Chapter Seven, "Back to the Future: Cliché and Temporality in Wang Anyi's *Song of Everlasting Sorrow*," for a fuller discussion of the story of Emperor Xuanzong and Yang Yuhuan's love.

20. Bai, *Taibei ren*, 280.

21. Lau, "'Crowded Hours' Revisited," 40, 46-47.

22. I have used Cyril Birch's translation. Tang Xianzu, *The Peony Pavilion (Mudan Ting)*, trans. Cyril Birch (Bloomington: Indiana University Press, 1980), 46-47. These lines are quoted on Bai, *Taibei ren*, 282.

23. Bai, *Taibei ren*, 286.

24. Tang, *The Peony Pavilion*, 47. these lines are quoted on Bai, *Taibei ren*, 286-87.

25. Bai, *Taibei ren*, 287.

26. Lau, "'Crowded Hours' Revisited," 45.

Chapter 7: Back to the Future

1. For discussions on the social and cultural ramifications of the June Fourth incident in Tiananmen Square and Deng's southern trip see the "Introduction" as well as the interviews with Wang Hui, Zhu Xueqin, Chen Pingyuan, and Qin Hui in Part I of Chaohua Wang ed., *One China, Many Paths*, (London: Verso, 2003), 1-159.

2. Dai Jinhua, "Redemption and Consumption: Depicting Culture in the 1990s," trans. Edward Gunn, *positions: east asia cultures critiques* 4.1 (1996): 133.

3. For example, see Jingyuan Zhang, "Breaking Open: Chinese Women's Writing in the Late 1980s and 1990s," in Pang-yuan Chi and David Der-wei Wang eds., *Chinese Literature in the Second Half of a Modern Century: A Critical Survey*, (Bloomington: Indiana University Press, 2000), 161-79.

4. Walter Benjamin, *Charles Baudelaire: A Lyric Poet in the Era of High Capitalism*, trans. Harry Zohn (London: NLB, 1973), 152.

5. Elissa Marder, *Dead Time: Temporal Disorders in the Wake of Modernity (Baudelaire and Flaubert)* (Stanford: Stanford University Press, 2001), 78.

6. Benjamin, *Charles Baudelaire*, 154.

7. Benjamin, *Charles Baudelaire*, 134.

8. Marder, *Dead Time*, 83. See also Benjamin, *Charles Baudelaire*, 44-6.

9. Wang Anyi, *Changhenge: Changpian xiaoshuo juan*, (Beijing: Zuojia chubanshe, 1996), 20.

10. Wang, *Changhenge*, 20-21.

11. Wang, *Changhenge*, 21.

12. Marder, *Dead Time*, 79.

13. Walter Benjamin, "Theses on the Philosophy of History," in Hanna Arendt ed., *Illuminations*, Harry Zohn tr. (New York: Shocken Books, 1968), 255.

14. Benjamin, "Theses on the Philosophy of History," 263.

15. Wang, *Changhenge*, 24.

16. Wang, *Changhenge*, 37.

17. Wang, *Changhenge*, 37-38.

18. Walter Benjamin, "The Work of Art in the Age of Mechanical Reproduction," in *Illuminations*, 217-51.

19. Benjamin, "The Work of Art in the Age of Mechanical Reproduction," 234.

20. As an omen of the disastrous effects their love would have for the nation, Yang was originally intended to be the wife of the emperor's son, Prince Shou, but was taken for the emperor himself when he saw how beautiful she was. This fact is omitted in Bo Juyi's poem, but mentioned in the accompanying prose piece. See Chen Hong, "Changhenge zhuan," in Hu Lun-ch'ing ed., *Chuanqi xiaoshuo xuan* (Taibei: Zhengzhong shuju, 1991), 102-12.

21. Stephen Owen, *The End of the Chinese "Middle Ages": Essays in Mid-Tang Literary Culture* (Stanford, Calif.: Stanford University Press, 1996), especially ch. 7 "Romance;" Ping Yao, "Women, Femininity, and Love in the Writings of Bo Juyi (772-846)," (Ph.D. diss., University of Illinois at Urbana-Champaign, 1997).

22. Bo Juyi, "Changhenge," in Hengtangtuishi, et al. eds., *Tangshi sanbaishou / Songci sanbai shou / Yuanqu sanbaishou* (Beijing: Zhongguo xiju chubanshe, 2000), 55, ll. 119-20.

23. Wai-yee Li, *Enchantment and Disenchantment: Love and Illusion in Chinese Literature* (Princeton, N.J.: Princeton University Press, 1993), 77-81; Stephen Owen, "Salvaging Poetry: The 'Poetic' in the Qing," in Theodore Huters, et al. eds., *Culture & State in Chinese History: Conventions, Accommodations, and Critiques* (Stanford: Stanford University Press, 1997), 116-25.

24. Jacques Derrida, "Structure, Sign and Play in the Discourse of the Human Sciences," in Hazard Adams and Leroy Searle eds., *Critical Theory Since 1965*, Alan Bass tr. (Tallahassee: Florida State University Press, 1986), 83-94.

25. Wang, *Changhenge*, 65-66.

26. Winners were selected, in part, by average people placing red or white carnations in the basket designated for each contestant: "Wang Qiyao was not Empress [i.e. first place] of the Miss Shanghai Pageant, but she was Empress of carnations. Her wedding dress [the last round of competition] was of the most simple and ordinary kind; it made way for flashier dresses. But the other contestants were [merely] performing in wedding dresses, were modeling wedding dresses, only she was a bride" (Wang, *Changhenge*, 63). It is this (self)recognition by her fellow Shanghainese that propels Wang Qiyao to third place. The irony is that Wang Qiyao never wears a wedding dress at her own wedding: her embodiment of a true bride is itself a negative image revealing absence in her own life.

27. My thanks to Professor Lothar von Falkenhausen for reminding me of this fact.

28. Wan Yan, "Jiegou de 'diangu': Wang Anyi changpian xiaoshuo Changhenge xinlun," *Shenzhen daxue xuebao* 15, no. 3 (August 1998): 50-54.

29. The deconstruction of the allusion, in Wan Yan's title, is therefore not only in her analysis of the relationship between the two texts but also embodied

in Wang Anyi's very revision of the Yang Guifei story. See Wan, "Jiegou de 'diangu.'"

30. To be exactly regular, references would need to occur every 77 pages of the 384 page Beijing edition. Instead they come on pages 52, 130, 183, and 282. As the novel is itself divided into three Books (*bu*), these references can also be parsed as one for Book 1, two for Book 2, and one again for Book 3.

31. Wang, *Changhenge*, 52.

32. Wang Anyi has spoken to both of these issues (i.e. ignoring difference between the sexes and sexual prudery) in two interviews with Laifong Leung and Wang Zheng: Laifong Leung, *Morning Sun: Interviews with Chinese Writers of the Lost Generation* (Armonk, N.Y.: M.E. Sharpe, 1994), 177-87; Wang Zheng, "Three Interviews: Wang Anyi, Zhu Lin, Dai Qing," *Modern Chinese Literature* 4, no. 1-2 (1988): 99-148. For a fuller discussion of feminism and femininity in the Chinese context, see Shu-mei Shih, "Towards an Ethics of Transnational Encounter, or 'When' does a 'Chinese' Woman Become a 'Feminist'?" *differences: A Journal of Feminist Cultural Studies* 13, no. 2 (Summer 2002): 90-126.

33. Xudong Zhang, "Shanghai Nostalgia: Postrevolutionary Allegories in Wang Anyi's Literary Production in the 1990s," *positions: east asia cultures critiques* 8, no. 2 (2000): 386. Zhang packs his notes with interesting statistics about Shanghai's industrialization, but fails to note the drastic changes to Shanghai's cultural life enabled thereby.

34. Wang, *Changhenge*, 3.

35. Wang, *Changhenge*, 40.

36. Benjamin, "Theses on the Philosophy of History," 261.

37. In addition to these, at the beginning of the chapter titled "Going to America," the text reads "the twenty-three years [she had spent] raising Weiwei were gone all of a sudden" (Wang, *Changhenge*, 317). Since we know that Weiwei was born in 1961, we can calculate that this chapter is set in 1984.

38. Wang, *Changhenge*, 155.

39. Specifically, it is the iterability of these people, activities, and locations which is made possible by this minor temporality. This iterability, in turn, contributes to the novel's allegorical objectives. I discuss iterability in more detail in the next section concerned with nostalgia.

40. This alignment was, of course, never one hundred percent, and conflicts led to several minor "rectifications" and ultimately to the 1989 student demonstrations in Tiananmen Square. See Jing Wang, *High Culture Fever: Politics, Aesthetics, and Ideology in Deng's China* (Berkeley: University of California Press, 1996) and Chaohua Wang, "Introduction: Minds of the Nineties," in *One China, Many Paths*, 9-45.

41. Wang, *Changhenge*, 274-75.

42. Wang, *Changhenge*, 190-91.

43. See my discussion of Maoist writing in Chapter Four.

44. David Der-wei Wang, "Haipai zuojia youjian chuanren," *Dushu* 6 (1996): 37-43.

45. Zhang, "Shanghai Nostalgia."

46. Zhang, "Shanghai Nostalgia," 354.

47. Zhang, "Shanghai Nostalgia," 358.

48. Ban Wang, "Love at Last Sight: Nostalgia, Commodity, and Temporality in Wang Anyi's Song of Unending Sorrow," *positions: east asia cultures critiques* 10, no. 3 (2002): 671.

49. Wang, "Love at Last Sight," 686.

50. Wang, "Haipai zuojia youjian chuanren," 43.

51. Li Feng, "Shilun *Changhenge* de fuzhi shoufa," *Wenzhou shifan xueyuan xuebao* 23, no. 2 (April 2002): 61-64.

52. Wang, *Changhenge*, 233.

53. Wang, *Changhenge*, 234.

54. Wang, *Changhenge*, 27-28.

55. Wang, *Changhenge*, 384.

56. Shu-mei Shih, "Marxist Humanism in Ruins: Negative Nostalgia and Contemporary Chinese Literature," paper presented at *Translating Universals: Theory Moves Across Asia* (UCLA: 2004). There is a remarkable convergence, it seems to me, between this notion of negative nostalgia and Marder's discussion of "A une passante" when she calls the flash, "the mechanical reproduction of a look that is repeated without ever having actually occurred," Marder, *Dead Time*, 84.

57. Shuqin Cui, "Stanley Kwan's 'Center Stage': The (Im)possible Engagement between Feminism and Postmodernism," *Cinema Journal* 39, no. 4 (2000): 60-80

58. For a discussion of the afterlife of Ruan Lingyu's film work and suicide see Cui, "Stanley Kwan's 'Center Stage.'"

59. My thanks to the graduate seminar taught by Shu-mei Shih at UCLA in the winter term of 2005 where many of the following issues were first raised and discussed.

60. Wang, *Changhenge*, 337.

61. Shih makes a fascinating comparison of the Lao Kela episode to a ghost story from *Liaozhai zhiyi* (Liaozhai's Tales of the Strange). See Shih,"Marxist Humanism in Ruins."

Chapter 8: Globalized Traditions

1. The novella was first published in a short-story collection also named *The Ancient Capital*: Zhu Tianxin, *Gudu* (Taipei: Maitian chuban gufen youxian gongsi, 1997). I have used the reprint edition: Zhu Tianxin, *Gudu* (Taipei: INK, 2002). All references will be to this second edition.

2. The one exception to this is Ying-hsiung Chou, but he relegates his comments to the notes of his article. See Ying-hsiung Chou, "Between Temporal and Spatial Transformations: An Ancient Capital City at the End of Time," *Tamkang Review* 31, no. 2 (2000): 51-70.

3. See Tang Xiaobing, "*Gudu*, Feixu, Taohuayuanwai," in *Gudu* (Taipei: INK, 2002) and Lingchei Letty Chen, "Mapping Identity in a Postcolonial City: Intertextuality and Cultural Hybridity in Zhu Tianxin's *Ancient Capital*," in Da-

vid Der-wei Wang and Carlos Rojas eds., *Writing Taiwan: A New Literary History* (Durham: Duke University Press, 2007), 301-23.

4. Zhu, *Gudu*, 179-80.

5. Jaroslav Průšek, *The Lyrical and the Epic: Studies of Modern Chinese Literature*, ed. Leo Ou-fan Lee (Bloomington: Indiana University Press, 1980).

6. This is what Chou calls the "phatic effect" of the text. Chou, "Between Temporal and Spatial Transformations," 68, n. 10.

7. Zhu, *Gudu*, 228.

8. Liang-yi Yen, "Heterotopias of Memory: The Cultural Politics of Historic Preservation in Taipei" (dissertation, University of California, Los Angeles, 2003), 106-14.

9. Zhu, *Gudu*, 201.

10. Zhu, *Gudu*, 179, 232.

11. Donald Keene, *Five Modern Japanese Novelists* (New York: Columbia University Press, 2003), 24-26.

12. In fact, in a personal conversation with one scholar of Japanese literature, I was asked, "Isn't that that insipid book about twins?"

13. Rosemary Haddon, "Being/Not Being at Home in the Writing of Zhu Tianxin," in John Makeham and A-chin Hsiau eds., *Cultural, Ethnic, and Political Nationalism in Contemporary Taiwan: Bentuhua* (New York: Palgrave Macmillan, 2005), 112-14.

14. Jen-yi Hsu, "Ghosts in the City: Mourning and Melancholia in Zhu Tianxin's *The Old Capital*," *Comparative Literature Studies* 41, no. 4 (2004): 555-60.

15. Chen, "Mapping Identity in a Postcolonial City," 305.

16. Chen, "Mapping Identity in a Postcolonial City," 314.

17. Yasunari Kawabata, *The Old Capital*, trans. J Martin Holman (Emeryville, CA: Shoemaker & Hoard, 2006; reprint of 1987 text), 113. The quotation is found on p. 180 of Zhu's text.

18. Roy Starrs, *Soundings in Time: The Fictive Art of Kawabata Yasunari* (Richmond, Surrey: Japan Library, 1998).

19. Zhu, *Gudu*, 180.

20. Zhu, *Gudu*, 185.

21. Chen, "Mapping Identity in a Postcolonial City," 314.

22. Indeed, although characters such as A and the heroine's daughter are described in such detail that they seem fully present, with the exception of a few service personnel—shop clerks, waitresses, taxi drivers—the only character truly present in the narrative is the heroine herself. All the other characters are mediated by the narrator's rendition of "your" memories.

23. Zhu, *Gudu*, 192-93.

24. Zhu, *Gudu*, 232.

25. Zhu, *Gudu*, 185.

26. Zhu, *Gudu*, 223.

27. Zhu, *Gudu*, 246.

28. Zhu, *Gudu*, 225.

29. Zhu, *Gudu*, 246.

30. Zhu, *Gudu*, 160.

Conclusion

1. Here I am thinking of works such as T. C. Hsia, *A History of Modern Chinese Fiction, 1917-1957* (New Haven: Yale University Press, 1961), Leo Ou-fan Lee, *The Romantic Generation of Modern Chinese Writers* (Cambridge: Harvard University Press, 1973), and Yü-sheng Lin, *The Crisis of Chinese Consciousness: Radical Antitraditionalism in the May Fourth Era* (Madison: University of Wisconsin Press, 1979).

2. Here I am thinking of works such as David Der-wei Wang, *Fin-de-Ciècle Splendor: Repressed Modernities of Late Qing Fiction, 1849-1911* (Stanford, CA: Stanford University Press, 1997), Yuan Jin, *Zhongguo xiaoshuo de jindai biange* (Beijing: Zhongguo shehui kexue chubanshe, 1992), and Chen Pingyuan, *Zhongguo xiaoshuo xushi moshi de zhuanbian* (Shanghai: Shanghai renmin chubanshe, 1988).

Glossary

Texts, Terms, and Character Names

"Ah Q zhengzhuan"	阿 Q 正傳	"The True Story of Ah Q"
"Ailisi gongyu"	愛麗絲公寓	"Alice Apartments"
"Anjiao"	暗礁	"Hidden Reef"
An Lushan	安祿山	rebellion leader, lived 703-757
"Bababa"	爸爸爸	"Bababa"
baihua	白話	modern vernacular Chinese
baogao	報告	report
Baosi	褒姒	Chinese femme fatale, lived Zhou Dynasty
baotie	報帖	re-orial
benmo	本末	root and stem
Biancheng	邊城	*Border Town*
bihua xiuyue	閉花羞月	outshine flowers and the moon
Bingzai	丙崽	character in "Dad Dad Dad"
bintie	稟帖	memorial
"Butian"	補天	"Mending Heaven"
buyi	不義	disrespectful
"Buzhoushan"	不周山	"Broken Mount"
cansheng	殘生	residual life

Cao Cao	曹操	Ruler of Wei during the Three Kingdoms period, lived 155-220
Cao Zhi	曹植	Cao Cao's son and poet, lived 192-232
Chadong	茶峒	setting for *Border Town*
Chai Fukui	柴福奎	character in "The Last Fisherman"
Changshengdian	長生殿	*Palace of Everlasting Life*
Changhenge	長恨歌	*Song of Everlasting Sorrow*
chaonong	嘲弄	sarcasm
Cheng Canmou	程參謀	Colonel Cheng, character in "Wandering the Garden, Waking from Dream"
Cheng Xiansheng	程先生	Mr. Cheng, character in *Song of Everlasting Sorrow*
chongjing	憧憬	long for
chuchu dongren	楚楚動人	enticing
Chuci	楚辭	*Songs of Chu*
chuochuo yueying	綽綽月影	overflowing moonlight
Cuicui	翠翠	character in *Border Town*
dabushanglai	答不上來	speechless
"Dazhong wenyi de wenti"	大眾文藝的問題	"The Question of Popular Literature and Art"
dai	呆	dull, stupid
daizi guizhong	待字閨中	unbetrothed
daizuo	呆坐	to sit staring into space
dianxing	典型	typical, cliché
dongxi wenhua lunzhan	東西文化論戰	Eastern/Western culture debate
Dou Furen	竇夫人	Madame Dou, character in "Wandering the Garden, Waking from Dream"
douge shuafang	逗個耍方	to jest
Fang Peilan	方培蘭	charcter in *The Whirlwind*
Fang Xiangqian	方詳千	charcter in *The Whirlwind*

fanshen	翻身	a reversal of situation
"Fengqiao yebo"	楓橋夜泊	"Mooring for the Night by Maple Bridge"
feiyue	飛躍	advancing by leaps and bounds
Fengsu tongyi	風俗通義	*Penetrating Customs*
fukan	副刊	literary supplement
fuqin xiang	父親想	father thought
fuqin xiangqi	父親想起	father recalled
futian shaidu	伏天曬毒	air out clothes
ganrou	趕肉	to pursue meat
"Gezi"	鴿子	"Pigeons"
Gudu	古都	*The Ancient Capital*
"Guan youyu"	觀游魚	"Gazing on Swimming Fish"
gui	鬼	ghost, devil, strange
gui	歸	to return (home)
"Guige"	閨閣	"The Inner Chamber"
"Guiqulai"	歸去來	"The Homecoming"
"Guofeng"	國風	"Airs of the States"
Gushi xinbian	故事新編	*Old Tales Retold*
"Guxiang"	故鄉	"My Old Home"
haoxiang	好像	as if
Henhai	恨海	*The Sea of Regret*
Honggaoliang jiazu	紅高粱家族	*Red Sorghum Clan*
Honglou meng	紅樓夢	*Dream of the Red Chamber*
huafen	話份	status
Huainanzi	淮南子	*The Huainanzi*
Huang Zhixian	黃治先	character in "The Homecoming"
Huangren shouji	荒人手記	*Notes of a Desolate Man*
"Hunli"	婚禮	"Weddings"
huoxu	或許	perhaps
Jiang Biyue	蔣碧月	character in "Wandering the Garden, Waking from Dream"
Jiangjun di tou	將軍底頭	*The General's Head*
Jin taowu zhuan	今檮杌傳	*A Tale of Modern Monsters*

Jinguang dadao	金光大道	*The Golden Road*
Jinpingmei	金瓶梅	*The Plum in the Golden Vase*
Jinwang	金旺	character in "Little Blacky Gets Married"
jiuping zhuang xinjiu	舊瓶裝新酒	to pour new wine into an old bottle
kan	看	to see
Kang Mingxun	康明遜	character in *Song of Everlasting Sorrow*
Koto	古都	*The Ancient Capital*
kuaiban	快板	rhymes
"Kuangren riji"	狂人日記	"Madman's Diary"
"Lanmingxun"	覽冥訓	"Peering into the Obscure"
"Laoban"	老伴	"Old Friend"
Lao Kela	老克臘	Old Color, character in *Song of Everlasting Sorrow*
Li Changchun	李長春	Eternal Spring Li, character in "Not Just One of the Audience"
"Li Youcai banhua"	李有才板話	"Rhymes of Li Youcai"
Li zhuren	李主任	character in *Song of Everlasting Sorrow*
"Lishui"	理水	"Curbing the Flood"
"Liang fu yin"	梁父吟	"The Song of Liang Fu"
Lin Ying	林纓	character in "Not Just One of the Audience"
"Liuyan"	流言	"Gossip"
Luo shen	洛神	*Goddess of the Luo River*
Ma Yanjing	馬眼鏡	Glasses Ma, character in "The Homecoming"
Mao wenti	毛文體	Mao style
"Meiyu zhixi"	梅雨之夕	"One Rainy Evening"
menglong	朦朧	misty (poetry)
"Modao"	魔道	"Devil's Way"
Nahan	吶喊	*Call to Arms*
"*Nahan* zixu"	吶喊自序	"Preface to *Call to Arms*"
Nichang yuyi	霓裳羽衣	*Coats of Feathers, Rainbow Skirts*
nongjiuhui	農救會	agricultural association

"Nongtang/Longtang"	弄堂	"The Alleys"
Nü Wa	女媧	character in "Mending Heaven"
Nuosong	儺送	character in *Border Town*
Nuoyou	儺右	character in *Border Town*
Panghuang	彷徨	*Hesitation*
peiyang	培養	nurturing
posuo dengguang	婆娑燈光	dancing lamplight
Pu gong	樸公	character in "The Song of Liang Fu"
Qian Furen	錢夫人	Madame Qian, character in "Wander"ing the Garden, Waking from Dream"
qianrengao	千人糕	thousand person cake
qing	情	*eros*, love
Qingnian zazhi	青年雜志	*Youth Journal*
quanpan xihua	全盤西化	complete Westernization
queshuo	卻說	as we were saying . . .
Ruan Lingyu	阮玲玉	Chinese movie star, lived 1910-1935
Rulin waishi	儒林外史	*The Scholars*
Runtu	閏土	character in "My Old Home"
san tuchu	三突出	three prominences
Shangyuandeng	上元燈	*Festival Lantern*
"Shangzhou chutan"	商州初探	"First Visit to Shangzhou"
shenying yingying	身影裊裊	voluptuous
shi	視	to see
"Shi Xiu"	石秀	"Shi Xiu"
Shiji	史記	*Records of the Grand Historian*
Shijing	詩經	*Book of Odes*
Shuihuzhuan	水滸傳	*Water Margin*
"Shouke"	熟客	"Regular Guests"
sihu	似乎	seems
siren xiang	死人相	corpse, figure of a dead person
Su Qi	蘇琪	character in "Not Just One of the Audience"

Taiwan tongshi	臺灣通史	*A General History of Taiwan*
Taizhen	太真	Ultimate Truth
"Tan zhaodian"	彈著點	"Bull's-Eye"
Tang Xuanzong	唐玄宗	Tang Dynasty emperor, r. 712-756
"Taochong"	桃沖	"Peach Wash"
Taohuayuan ji	桃花源記	*Peach Blossom Spring*
"Tebie guanzhong"	特別觀眾	"Not Just One of the Audience"
tian bu you de	天不祐德	But Heaven does not support the virtuous
tian shi you de	天實祐德	Forsooth, Heaven supports the virtuous
Tianbao	天保	character in *Border Town*
Wang Qiyao	王琦瑤	character in *Song of Everlasting Sorrow*
Wan'rde jiushi xintiao	玩兒的就是心跳	*Playing for Thrills*
wazai	蛙崽	baby
weidao	味道	taste
"Weilu zaihua"	圍爐在話	"Chatting around the Stove"
Weiwei	薇薇	Wang Qiyao's dughter, character in *Song of Everlasting Sorrow*
"Wenxue de 'gen'"	文學的" 根"	"The 'Roots' of Literature"
"Wenxue gailiang chuyi"	文學改良芻議	"A Modest Proposal for the Reform of Literature"
"Wenxue geminglun"	文學革命論	"On Literary Revolution"
"Wenyi de ziyou he wenxuejia de bu ziyou"	文藝的自由和文學家的不自由	"Freedom for Literature but Not the Writer"
wenyi gongzuozhe	文藝工作者	workers in literature and art
wo	我	I
wohou gongxing tiantao, zhan yu jiao	我后躬行天討，戰與郊	My lord personally saw to his righteous suppression and [they] battled in the wilderness
wu	吾	I
"Wuhui"	舞會	"Dances"
Xiandai	現代	*Les Contemporains*
xiangtu	鄉土	native soil

Xiangxing sanji	湘行散記	*Random Sketches on a Trip to Hunan*
xianzhi	縣志	gazetteer
"Xiangziyan"	箱子岩	"Box Cliff"
"Xiao Baicai"	小白菜	"Little Cabbage"
"Xiao Erhei jiehun"	小二黑結婚	"Little Blacky Gets Married"
Xiao Qin	小芹	Little Celery
Xiaocui	小翠	character in *Random Sketches on a Trip to Hunan*
Xiaoxian	效先	character in "The Song of Liang Fu"
"Xin minzhu zhuyi lun"	新民主主義論	"On New Democracy"
Xin Qingnian	新青年	*New Youth*
xinghuo liaoyuan	星火燎原	setting the prairie ablaze
Xingwang	興旺	character in "Little Blacky Gets Married"
xinli	心理	heart/mind or psychology
Xin Nüxing	新女性	*New Woman*
Xishi	西施	Chinese femme fatale, lived c. 500 BCE-??
Xiyou ji	西遊記	*Journey to the West*
Xuanfeng	旋風	*The Whirlwind*
xungen	尋根	searching for roots
Yan Hengyuan	閻恒元	character in "Rhymes of Li Youcai"
Yan Jiaxiang	閻家祥	character in "Rhymes of Li Youcai"
Yang Guifei	楊貴妃	Imperial Consort Yang
Yang Guozhong	楊國忠	Yang Guifei's cousin and Prime Minister
Yang Zirong	楊子榮	character in *Taking Tiger Mountain by Strategy*
yangban xi	樣板戲	model theater
yaoxiang miman	藥香彌漫	fragrance fills the air
yi	義	brotherhood
yinmou wenyi	陰謀文藝	conspiratorial literature
youhua	油滑	facetiousness
"Yongyuan de Yin Xueyan"	永遠的尹雪艷	"The Eternal Yin Xueyan"
"Yugezi"	漁歌子	"Fishing Song"

Yukiguni	雪國	*Snow Country*
"Zai Bali da xiyuan"	在巴黎大戲院	"In the Paris Theater"
"Zai Yanan wenyi zuotan-huishang de jianghua"	在延安文藝座談會上的講話	"Talks at the Yan'an Forum on Literature and Art"
Zhang Dihua	張棣華	character in *Sea of Regret*
Zhang Yonghong	張永紅	character in *Song of Everlasting Sorrow*
zhanghuiti xiaoshuo	章回體小說	traditional chapter novel form
Zhaoxia	朝霞	*Morning Clouds*
Zheng Yanqing	鄭彥青	character in "Wandering the Garden, Waking from Dream"
zhiqing	知青	"sent-down" youth
Zhiqu weihushan	智取威虎山	*Taking Tiger Mountain by Strategy*
zhong	種	race/seed
zhong de tuihua	種的退化	degeneration of the race/seed
"Zhouzhong yeqi"	舟中夜起	"Waking in the Night on the Boat"
"Zhuli guan"	竹裡館	"In the Bamboo Grove"
zhuanbian renwu	轉變人物	turnaround character
Zhuge Liang	諸葛亮	Minister of Shu during the Three Kingdom's period, lived 181-234
"Zuihou yige yulaor"	最後一個漁佬兒	"The Last Fisheman"

Authors

Bai Xianyong	白先勇	b. 1937
Bo Juyi	白居易	772-846
Chen Duxiu	陳獨秀	1879-1942
Dai Wangshu	戴望舒	1905-1950
Ding Ling	丁玲	1904-1986
Du Fu	杜甫	712-770
Duan Ruixia	段瑞夏	??
Guo Moruo	郭沫若	1892-1978
Han Shaogong	韓少功	b. 1953
Hao Ran	浩然	1932-2008

Hong Sheng	洪昇	1645-1704
Hu Feng	胡風	1902-1985
Hu Shi	胡適	1891-1962
Hu Yepin	胡也頻	1902-1931
Jia Pingwa	賈平凹	b. 1952
Jiang Gui	姜貴	1908-1981
Jiang Qing	江青	1914-1991
Kawabata Yasunari	川端康成	1899-1972
Lao She	老舍	1899-1966
Li Hangyu	李杭育	b. 1957
Lian Heng	連橫	1878-1936
Liu Na'ou	劉吶鷗	1900-1939
Lu Xun	魯迅	1881-1936
Mao Dun	茅盾	1896-1981
Mao Zedong	毛澤東	1893-1976
Mo Yan	莫言	b. 1955
Mu Shiying	穆時英	1912-1940
Qian Zhongshu	錢鍾書	1910-1998
Qu Qiubai	瞿秋白	1899-1935
Qu Yuan	屈原	ca. 340-278 BCE
Shen Congwen	沈從文	1902-1988
Shi Zhecun	施蟄存	1905-2003
Su Shi	蘇軾	1037-1101
Takeshi Kaneshiro/Jin Chengwu	金城武	b. 1973
Tao Qian	陶潛	365-427
Tao Yuanming	陶淵明	367-427
Wang Anyi	王安憶	b. 1954
Wang Shuo	王朔	b. 1958
Wang Wei	王維	701-761
Wang Zengqi	汪曾祺	b. 1920
Wu Jianren	吳趼人	1866-1910
Xiao Jun	蕭軍	1907-1988
Zhang Ailing	張愛玲	1920-1995
Zhang Ji	張繼	Tang d.
Zhang Zhihe	張志和	Tang d.
Zhao Shuli	趙樹理	1906-1970
Zhou Yang	周陽	1908-1989

Zhu Tianwen (Chu T'ien-wen)	朱天文	b. 1956
Zhu Tianxin (Chu T'ien-hsin)	朱天心	b. 1958

Bibliography

Adams, Hazard, and Leroy Searle eds. *Critical Theory since 1965*. Tallahassee: Florida State University Press, 1986.

Anderson, Marston. "Lu Xun's Facetious Muse: The Creative Imperative in Modern Chinese Fiction." Pp. 249-68 in *From May Fourth to June Fourth: Fiction and Film in Twentieth-Century China*, edited by Ellen Widmer and David Te-wei Wang. Cambridge, Mass.: Harvard University Press, 1993.

————. *The Limits of Realism: Chinese Fiction in the Revolutionary Period*. Berkeley: University of California Press, 1990.

Bai Xianyong 白先勇. *Taibei ren* 臺北人 [Taipei people]. New edition. Taipei: Erya chubanshe youxian gongsi, 1983.

Bakhtin, M. M. *The Dialogic Imagination: Four Essays*. Translated by Caryl Emerson and Michael Holquist. Edited by Michael Holquist. Austin: University of Texas Press, 1981.

Belden, Jack. *China Shakes the World*. 1st ed. New York: Harper, 1949.

Benjamin, Walter. *Charles Baudelaire: A Lyric Poet in the Era of High Capitalism*. Translated by Harry Zohn. London: NLB, 1973.

————. *Illuminations*. Translated by Harry Zohn. Edited by Hannah Arendt. New York: Schocken Books, 1969.

Bhabha, Homi K. *The Location of Culture*. London ; New York: Routledge, 1994.

Birch, Cyril. "Change and Continuity in Chinese Fiction." Pp. 385-404 in *Modern Chinese Literature in the May Fourth Era*, edited by Merle Goldman. Cambridge: Harvard University Press, 1977.

————. "Chinese Communist Literature: The Persistence of Traditional Forms." *The China Quarterly* 13 (1963): 74-91.

Bo Juyi白居易. "Changhenge 長恨歌 [Song of everlasting sorrow]." Pp. 52-55 in *Tangshi sanbaishou* 唐詩三百首 [300 Tang poems] / *Songci sanbaishou* 宋詞三百首 [300 Song lyrics] / *Yuanqu sanbaishou* 元曲三百首 [300 Yuan arias], edited by Hengtangtuishi, Shangqiangcunmin, Ren Na and Lu Qian. Beijing: Zhongguo xiju chubanshe, 2000.

Bogel, Fredric V. "The Difference Satire Makes: Reading Swift's Poems." Pp. 43-53 in *Theorizing Satire: Essays in Literary Criticism*, edited by Brian A. Connery and Kirk Combe. New York: St. Martin's Press, 1995.

Böhn, Andreas. "Parody and Quotation: A Case Study of E.T.A Hoffman's *Kater Murr*." Pp. 47-66 in *Parody: Dimensions and Perspectives*, edited by Beate Müller, ii, 313. Amsterdam: Rodopi, 1997.

Calinescu, Matei. *Five Faces of Modernity: Modernism, Avant-Garde, Decadence, Kitsch, Postmodernism*. Durham: Duke University Press, 1987.

Chang, Sung-sheng Yvonne. Representing Taiwan: Shifting Geopolitical Frameworks." Pp. 17-25 in *Writing Taiwan: A New Literary History*, edited by David Der-wei Wang and Carlos Rojas. Durham: Duke University Press, 2007.

———. *Literary Culture in Taiwan: Martial Law to Market Law*. New York: Columbia University Press, 2004.

———. *Modernism and the Nativist Resistance: Contemporary Chinese Fiction from Taiwan*. Durham: Duke University Press, 1993.

Chen Duxiu 陳獨秀. "Wenxue geming lun 文學革命論 [On literary revolution]." *Xin qingnian* 2, no. 6 (1917).

Chen, Fangming. "Postmodern or Postcolonial? An Inquiry into Postwar Taiwanese Literary History." Pp. 26-50 in *Writing Taiwan: A New Literary History*, edited by David Der-wei Wang and Carlos Rojas. Durham: Duke University Press, 2007.

Chen Hong 陳鴻. "Changhenge zhuan 長恨歌傳 [The tale of song of everlasting sorrow]." P. 102-12 in *Chuanqi xiaoshuo xuan* 傳奇小說選 [Selected chuanqi tales], edited by Hu Lun-ch'ing. Taipei: Zhengzhong shuju, 1991.

Chen, Lingchei Letty. "Mapping Identity in a Postcolonial City: Intertextuality and Cultural Hybridity in Zhu Tianxin's *Ancient Capital*." Pp. 301-23 in *Writing Taiwan: A New Literary History*, edited by David Der-wei Wang and Carlos Rojas. Durham: Duke University Press, 2007.

Chen Pingyuan 陳平原, *Zhongguo xiaoshuo xushi moshi de zhuanbian* 《中國小說敘事模式的轉變 [The Change in the Chinese Fictional Narrative Mode]. Shanghai: Shanghai renmin chubanshe, 1988.

Ching, Leo T. S. *Becoming "Japanese": Colonial Taiwan and the Politics of Identity Formation*. Berkeley: University of California Press, 2001.

Chou, Ying-hsiung. "Between Temporal and Spatial Transformations: An Ancient Capital City at the End of Time." *Tamkang Review* 31, no. 2 (2000): 51-70.

———. "Romance of the Red Sorghum Family." *Modern Chinese Literature* 5, no. 1 (1989): 33-42.

Chow, Rey. *Primitive Passions: Visuality, Sexuality, Ethnography, and Contemporary Chinese Cinema*. New York: Columbia University Press, 1995.

Cixous, Hélène. "The Laugh of the Medusa." Pp. 309-20 in *Critical Theory since 1965*, edited by Hazard Adams and Leroy Searle. Tallahassee: Florida State University Press, 1986.

Cui, Shuqin. "Stanley Kwan's 'Center Stage': The (Im)Possible Engagement between Feminism and Postmodernism." *Cinema Journal* 39, no. 4 (2000):

60-80.

Cui Zhihui 崔志輝. "Hualong dianjing shuiru jiaorong: Tan 'Li Youcai banhua' zhong de 'banhua'畫龍點睛水乳交融—談「李有才板話」中的 '板話' [Finishing touches and mixing: On the 'rhymes in 'The rhymes of Li Youcai']." *Journal of Urumchi Education Academy* 3 (2002): 35-37.

Davis, A. R., and T'ao Ch'ien. *T'ao Yüan-Ming, His Works and Their Meaning*. 2 vols. Cambridge: Cambridge University Press, 1983.

Dentith, Simon. *Parody*. London ; New York: Routledge, 2000.

Denton, Kirk A., ed. *Modern Chinese Literary Thought: Writings on Literature, 1893-1945*. Stanford: Stanford University Press, 1996.

Derrida, Jacques. "Différance." Pp. 120-36 in *Critical Theory since 1965*, edited by Hazard Adams and Leroy Searle. Tallahassee: Florida State University Press, 1986.

———. "Structure, Sign and Play in the Discourse of the Human Sciences." Pp. 83-94 in *Critical Theory since 1965*, edited by Hazard Adams and Leroy Searle. Tallahassee: Florida State University Press, 1986.

Doleželová-Velingerová, Milena, Oldrich Král, and Graham Martin Sanders, eds. *The Appropriation of Cultural Capital: China's May Fourth Project*. Cambridge: Harvard University Asia Center: Distributed by Harvard University Press, 2001.

Egan, Michael. "A Notable Sermon: The Subtext of Hao Ran's Fiction." Pp. 224-43 in *Popular Chinese Literature and Performing Arts in the People's Republic of China, 1949-1979*, edited by Bonnie S. McDougall. Berkeley: University of California Press, 1984.

Genette, Gérard. *Narrative Discourse: An Essay in Method*. Translated by Jane E Lewin. Ithaca, N.Y.: Cornell University Press, 1980.

Goldman, Merle, ed. *Modern Chinese Literature in the May Fourth Era*. Cambridge: Harvard University Press, 1977.

Gu Yuanqing 古遠清. "'San tuchu' de gouzao guocheng jiqi lilun tezheng '三突出' 的構造過程及其理論特徵 [The process of constructing 'the three prominences' and characteristics of its theory]." *Journal of Ezhou University* 9, no. 1 (2002): 28-31.

Guan Yuhong 關玉紅, and Li Li 李麗. "Ganjue shijiezhong de lixing sikao: Huigu Mo Yan de 'Honggaoliang xilie'感覺世界中的理性思考--回顧莫言的 '紅高粱系列' [Rational thought in a sensual world: Reviewing Mo Yan's 'Red Sorghum series']." *Journal of Langfang Teachers College* 19, no. 1 (2003): 31-33.

Gui Wei 桂蔚. "Lishi bianjie de zuihou wancan: Cong Honggaoliang dao Tanxiangxing 歷史邊界的最後晚餐—從《紅高粱》到《檀香刑》[Last supper on the margins of history: From *Red Sorghum* to *Incense Punishment*." *Journal of Zhejiang Business Technology Institute* 1, no. 3 (2002): 54-56.

Haddon, Rosemary. "Being/Not Being at Home in the Writing of Zhu Tianxin." Pp. 103-23 in *Cultural, Ethnic, and Political Nationalism in Contemporary Taiwan: Bentuhua*, edited by John Makeham and A-chin Hsiau. New York: Palgrave Macmillan, 2005.

Han Shaogong 韓少功. "Guiqulai 歸去來 [The homecoming]." Pp. 112-27 in *Guiqulai* 歸去來 [The homecoming]. Beijing, Zuojia chubanshe, 1996.

———. "Wenxue de 'gen' 文學的 '根' [The 'roots' of literature]." Pp. 1-8 in *Wanmei de jiading: Sanwen ji* 完美的假定：散文集 [A hypothetical definition of perfection: Essays]. Beijing: Zuojia chubanshe, 1996.

———. "Bababa 爸爸爸 [Dad dad dad]." Pp. 136-78 in *Zhongguo xungen xiaoshuoxuan* 中國尋根小說選 [Selected Chinese roots stories], edited by Li Tuo. Honk Kong: Joint Publishing, 1993.

Hegel, Robert E. "Making the Past Serve the Present in Fiction and Drama: From the Yan'an Forum to the Cultural Revolution." Pp. 197-223 in *Popular Chinese Literature and Performing Arts in the People's Republic of China, 1949-1979*, edited by Bonnie S. McDougall. Berkeley: University of California Press, 1984.

Holm, David. "Folk Art as Propaganda: The Yangge Movement in Yan'an." Pp. 3-35 in *Popular Chinese Literature and Performing Arts in the People's Republic of China, 1949-1979*, edited by Bonnie S. McDougall. Berkeley: University of California Press, 1984.

Hsu, Jen-yi. "Ghosts in the City: Mourning and Melancholia in Zhu Tianxin's *The Old Capital*." *Comparative Literature Studies* 41, no. 4 (2004): 546-64.

Huang Dezhi 黃德志, and Xiao Xia 肖霞. "Shi Zhecun nianbiao 施蟄存年表 [Chronology of Shi Zhecun]." *Journal of Huaiyin Teacher's College* 25, no. 1 (2003): 25-47.

Huang Ke'an黃科安.. "Dazhonghua xushi celüe yu keshuoxing de wenben: Xueshujie guanyu Zhao Shuli xiaoshuo chuangzuo de yizhong jiedu 大眾化敘事策略與可說性的文本—學術界關於趙樹理小說創作的一種解讀 [Mass style and the text: Academic reading of Zhao Shuli's fictional creation]." *Gansu Theory Research* 3 (2004): 106-09.

Huang Xiuji 黃修己, ed. *Zhao Shuli yanjiu ziliao* 趙樹理研究資料 [Research materials on Zhao Shuli]. Taiyuan, Shanxi, China: Beiyue wenyi chubanshe: 1985.

Hutcheon, Linda. *A Theory of Parody: The Teachings of Twentieth-Century Art Forms*. New York: Methuen, 1985.

Huters, Theodore. *Bringing the World Home: Appropriating the West in Late Qing and Early Republican China*. Honolulu: University of Hawai'i Press, 2005.

———. "The Difficult Guest: May Fourth Revisits." *Chinese Literature: Essays, Articles, Reviews* 6, no. 1-2 (1984): 125-49.

Ivy, Marilyn. *Discourses of the Vanishing: Modernity, Phantasm, Japan*. Chicago: University of Chicago Press, 1995.

Jia Pingwa 賈平凹. "Shangzhou chutan 商州初探 [First trip to Shangzhou]." Pp. 7-47 in *Zhongguo xungen xiaoshuoxuan* 中國尋根小說選 [Selected Chinese roots stories], edited by Li Tuo. Hong Kong: Joint Publishing, 1993.

Jiang Gui 姜貴. *Xuanfeng* 旋風 [The Whirlwind]. Reprint edition. Taipei: Jiuge chubanshe youxian gongsi, 2005.

Jones, Andrew. "The Violence of the Text: Reading Yu Hua and Shi Zhicun."

positions: east asia cultures critiques 2, no. 3 (1994): 570-602.

Kawabata, Yasunari. *The Old Capital.* Translated by J Martin Holman. Emeryville, CA: Shoemaker & Hoard, 2006.

Keene, Donald. *Five Modern Japanese Novelists.* New York: Columbia University Press, 2003.

King, Richard. "A Fiction Revealing Collusion: Allegory and Evasion in the Mid-1970s." *Modern Chinese Literature* 10, no. 1-2 (1998): 71-90.

———. "Revisionism and Transformation in the Cultural Revolution Novel." *Modern Chinese Literature* 7, no. 1 (1993): 105-29.

Kinkley, Jeffrey C. *The Odyssey of Shen Congwen.* Stanford: Stanford University Press, 1987.

Kristeva, Julia. "Women's Time." Pp. 570-602 in *Critical Theory since 1965,* edited by Hazard Adams and Leroy Searle. Tallahassee: Florida State University Press, 1986.

Lee, Ching Kwan and Guobin Yang, eds. *Re-envisioning the Chinese Revolution: The Politics and Poetics of Collective Memories in Reform China.* Washington: Woodrow Wilson Center Press, 2007.

Lee, Leo Ou-fan. *Shanghai Modern: The Flowering of a New Urban Culture in China, 1930-1945.* Cambridge: Harvard University Press, 1999.

———. *Voices from the Iron House : A Study of Lu Xun.* Bloomington: Indiana University Press, 1987.

Leung, Laifong. *Morning Sun: Interviews with Chinese Writers of the Lost Generation.* Armonk, N.Y.: M.E. Sharpe, 1994.

Li Feng 李楓. "Shilun Changhenge de fuzhi shoufa 試論《長恨歌》的複製手法 [Duplication in *Song of Everlasting Sorrow*]." *Journal of Wenzhou Normal College* 23.2 (2002

Li Hangyu 李杭育. "Zuihou yige yulaoer 最後一個漁佬兒 [The last fisherman]." Pp. 48-64 in *Zhongguo xungen xiaoshuoxuan*中國尋根小說選 [Selected Chinese roots stories], edited by Li Tuo. Hong Kong: Joint Publishing, 1993.

Li Haofei 李浩非. "Jielun: 1979 nian yiqian de jiandan zhuangkuang 結論：1979 年以前的簡單狀況 [Conclusion: The basic situation prior to 1979]." *Contemporary Writers Review* 5 (1994): 30-43.

Li Tuo 李陀, ed. *Zhongguo xungen xiaoshuoxuan*中國尋根小說選 [Selected Chinese roots stories]. Hong Kong: Joint Publishing, 1993.

———. "Resisting Writing." Pp. 273-77 in *Politics, Ideology, and Literary Discourse in Modern China: Theoretical Interventions and Cultural Critique,* edited by Kang Liu and Xiaobing Tang. Durham: Duke University Press, 1993.

———. "Haiwai Zhongguo zuojia taolunhui jiyao 海外中國作家討論會紀要 [Important notes from the overseas Chinese writers conference]." *Jintian,* no. 2 (1990): 94-103.

Li, Wai-yee. *Enchantment and Disenchantment: Love and Illusion in Chinese Literature.* Princeton: Princeton University Press, 1993.

Liu An 劉安. *Huainanzi* 淮南子. Beijing: Beijing yanshan chubanshe, 1995.

Liu, Kang, and Xiaobing Tang, eds. *Politics, Ideology, and Literary Discourse in Modern China: Theoretical Interventions and Cultural Critique*. Durham, N.C.: Duke University Press, 1993.

Liu, Lydia He. *Translingual Practice: Literature, National Culture, and Translated Modernity—China, 1900-1937*. Stanford: Stanford University Press, 1995.

Liu Xiang 劉向, and Ying Shao 應邵. *Xinxu tongjian; Fengsu Tongyi tongjian* 新序通檢；風俗通義通檢 [The annotated Fengsu Tongyi]. Shanghai: Shanghai guji chubanshe, 1987.

Liu Yukai 劉玉凱. ""Youhua" de dingwei: Lu Xun *Gushi Xinbian* yishu xinlun '油滑' 的定位－魯迅《故事新編》藝術新論 [The definition of 'facetiousness': New thoughts on the art of Lu Xun's *Old Tales Retold*]." *Social Science Front* 4 (1998): 148-57.

Lu, Tonglin. "Red Sorghum: Limits of Transgression." Pp. 188-208 in *Politics, Ideology, and Literary Discourse in Modern China: Theorectical Interventions and Cultural Critique*, edited by Kang Liu and Xiaobing Tang. Durham: Duke University Press, 1993.

Lu Xun魯迅. "Butian 補天 [Mending heaven]." Pp. in *Lu Xun quanji* 魯迅全集 [The complete Lu Xun], vol. 2. Beijing: Renmin wenxue chubanshe, 2005.

———. "Gushi Xinbian Xuyan 故事新編序言 [Preface to *Old Tales Retold*]." Pp. in *Lu Xun quanji* 魯迅全集 [The complete Lu Xun], vol. 2. Beijing: Renmin wenxue chubanshe, 2005.

———. "Guxiang 故鄉 [My old home]." Pp. in *Lu Xun quanji* 魯迅全集 [The complete Lu Xun], vol. 2. Beijing: Renmin wenxue chubanshe, 2005.

———. *Old Tales Retold*. Translated by Yang Xianyi and Gladys Yang. Beijing: Waiwen chubanshe, 2000.

———. *Selected Stories of Lu Hsun*. Translated by Hsien-i Yang and Gladys Yang. Facsimile ed. San Francisco: China Books & Periodicals, 1994.

Mao Zedong 毛澤東. "Xin minzhu zhuyi lun 新民主主義論 [On new democracy]." Pp. 348-400 in *Mao Zedong zhuzuo xuandu* 毛澤東著作選讀 [Mao Zedong reader]. Beijing: Renmin chubanshe: Xinhua shudian faxing, 1986.

———. "Zai Yanan wenyi zuotanhuishang de jianghua 在延安文藝座談會上的講話 [Talks at the Yan'an forum on art and literature]." Pp. 523-56 in *Mao Zedong zhuzuo xuandu* 毛澤東著作選讀 [Mao Zedong reader]. Beijing: Renmin chubanshe: Xinhua shudian faxing, 1986.

———. "Zhongguo gongchandang zai minzu zhanzhengzhong de diwei 中國共產黨在民族戰爭中的地位 [The position of the Chinese Communist Party in the national war]." Pp. 271-89 in *Mao Zedong zhuzuo xuandu* 毛澤東著作選讀 [Mao Zedong reader]. Beijing: Renmin chubanshe: Xinhua shudian faxing, 1986.

Marder, Elissa. *Dead Time: Temporal Disorders in the Wake of Modernity (Baudelaire and Flaubert)*. Stanford: Stanford University Press, 2001.

McDougall, Bonnie S. *Mao Zedong's "Talks at the Yan'an Conference on Literature and Art": A Translation of the 1943 Text with Commentary*. Ann Arbor: Center for Chinese Studies the University of Michigan, 1980.

———, ed. *Popular Chinese Literature and Performing Arts in the People's Republic of China, 1949-1979*. Berkeley: University of California Press, 1984.

Meng Guanglai 孟廣來, and Han Rixin 韓日新, eds. *Gushi xinbian yanjiu ziliao* 《故事新編》研究資料 [Research materials on *Old Tales Retold*]. Jinan: Shandong wenyi chubanshe, 1984.

Mo Yan 莫言. *Honggaoliang Jiazu* 紅高粱家族 [Red sorghum]. Beijing: Jiefangjun wenyi chubanshe, 1987.

———. *Honggaoliang Jiazu* 紅高粱家族 [Red sorghum]. Taibei Shi: Hongfan shudian, 1988.

———. *Red Sorghum: A Novel of China*. Translated by Howard Goldblatt. New York: Viking, 1993.

Müller, Beate, ed. *Parody: Dimensions and Perspectives*. Amsterdam: Rodopi, 1997.

Niranjana, Tejaswini. *Siting Translation: History, Post-Structuralism, and the Colonial Context*. Berkeley: University of California Press, 1992.

Owen, Stephen. "Salvaging Poetry: The 'Poetic' in the Qing." Pp. 105-25 in *Culture & State in Chinese History: Conventions, Accommodations, and Critiques*, edited by Theodore Huters, R. Bin Wong and Pauline Yu. Stanford: Stanford University Press, 1997.

———. *The End of the Chinese 'Middle Ages': Essays in Mid-Tang Literary Culture*. Stanford: Stanford University Press, 1996.

Pickowicz, Paul G. "Qu Qiubai's Critique of the May Fourth Generation: Early Chinese Marxist Literary Criticism." Pp. 351-84 in *Modern Chinese Literature in the May Fourth Era*, edited by Merle Goldman. Cambridge: Harvard University Press, 1977.

Plaks, Andrew H. *Archetype and Allegory in the Dream of the Red Chamber*. Princeton: Princeton University Press, 1976.

Pollard, D. E. "The Short Story in the Cultural Revolution." *The China Quarterly* 73 (1978): 99-121.

Průšek, Jaroslav. *The Lyrical and the Epic: Studies of Modern Chinese Literature*. Edited by Leo Ou-fan Lee. Bloomington: Indiana University Press, 1980.

Qin Xianci 秦賢次. "Lu Xun nianbiao 魯迅年表 [Chronology of Lu Xun]." Pp. 475-89 in *Lu Xun xiaoshuoji* 魯迅小說集 [Collected fiction of Lu Xun], edited by Yang Ze. Taipei: Hongfan shudian, 1994.

———. "Shen Congwen nianbiao 沈從文年表 [Chronology of Shen Congwen]." Pp. 795-842 in *Shen Congwen xiaoshuoxuan* 沈從文小說選 [Selected fiction of Shen Congwen], edited by Peng Xiaoyan. Taipei: Hongfan shudian, 1995.

Rees, Helen. *Echoes of History: Naxi Music in Modern China*. Oxford; New York: Oxford University Press, 2000.

Rose, Margaret A. *Parody: Ancient, Modern, and Post-Modern*. Cambridge: Cambridge University Press, 1993.

———. *Parody//Meta-Fiction: An Analysis of Parody as a Critical Mirror to the Writing and Reception of Fiction.* London: Croom Helm, 1979.

Shen Congwen 沈從文. "Biancheng 邊城 [Border town]." Pp. 55-192 in *Shen Congwen quanji* 沈從文全集 [The complete Shen Congwen], vol. 8, edited by Zhang Zhaohe. Taiyuan, Shanxi, China: Beiyue wenyi chubanshe, 2002.

———. "Xiangxing Sanji 湘行散記 [Random sketches on a trip to western Hunan]." Pp. 221-324 in *Shen Congwen quanji* 沈從文全集 [The complete Shen Congwen], vol. 8, edited by Zhang Zhaohe. Taiyuan, Shanxi, China: Beiyue wenyi chubanshe, 2002.

Shi Zhecun 施蟄存. "Shi Xiu 石秀." Pp. 61-102 in *Shanghai de hubuwu: xinganjuepai xiaoshuo xuan*上海的狐步舞：新感覺派小說選 [Shanghai foxtrot: Selected New Sensationist stories], edited by Leo Ou-fan Lee. Taipei: Yunchen wenhua shiye gufen youxian gongsi, 2001.

———. *Shinian Chuangzuoji* 十年創作集 [Collected works for ten years]. Shanghai: Huadong shifan daxue chubanshe: 1996.

Shih, Shu-mei. "Marxist Humanism in Ruins: Negative Nostalgia and Contemporary Chinese Literature." Paper presented at Translating Universals: Theory Moves Across Asia, UCLA, May 24 2004.

———. "Towards an Ethics of Transnational Encounter or 'When' Does a 'Chinese' Woman Become a 'Feminist'?" *differences: A Journal of Feminist Cultural Studies* 13, no. 2 (2002): 90-126.

———. *The Lure of the Modern: Writing Modernism in Semicolonial China, 1917-1937.* Berkeley: University of California Press, 2001.

Sibley, Gay. "Satura from Quintilian to Joe Bob Briggs: A New Look at an Old Word." Pp. 57-72 in *Theorizing Satire: Essays in Literary Criticism*, edited by Brian A. Connery and Kirk Combe. New York: St. Martin's Press, 1995.

Starrs, Roy. *Soundings in Time: The Fictive Art of Kawabata Yasunari.* Richmond, Surrey: Japan Library, 1998.

Stuckey, G. Andrew. "Memory or Fantasy? *Hongaoliang*'s Narrator." *Modern Chinese Literature and Culture* 18, no. 2 (2006): 131-62.

Su Wei. "The School and the Hospital: On the Logics of Socialist Realism." Pp. 65-75 in *Chinese Literature in the Second Half of a Modern Century: A Critical Survey*, translated by Charles Laughlin, edited by Pang-yuan Chi and David Der-wei Wang. Bloomington: Indiana University Press, 2000.

Sutton, Donald S. "Myth Making on an Ethnic Frontier: The Cult of the Heavenly Kings of West Hunan, 1715-1996." *Modern China* 26.4 (2000): 448-500.

Tan Xuechun 譚學純. "Chongdu Honggaoliang: Zhanzheng xiuci huayu de linglei shuxie 重讀《紅高粱》：戰爭修辭話語的另類書寫 [Rereading *Red Sorghum*: An alternative writing of war discourse]." *Journal of Qinghai Normal University* 95, no. 4 (2002): 100-04.

Tang Xiaobing 唐小兵. "On the Concept of Taiwan Literature." Pp. 51-89 in *Writing Taiwan: A New Literary History*, edited by David Der-wei Wang and Carlos Rojas. Durham: Duke University Press, 2007.

———. "*Gudu*, Feixu, Taohuayuanwai 《古都》、廢墟、桃花源外 [*The Ancient Capital*, ruins, outside peach blossom spring]." Pp. 247-60 in *Gudu*古

都 [The ancient capital]. Taipei: INK, 2002.

Tao Qian 陶潛, and Xie Lingyun 謝靈運. *Tao Yuanming quanji: Fu Xie Lingyun ji*陶淵明全集：附謝靈運集 [The complete Tao Yuanming and collected works of Xie Lingyun]. Edited by Cao Minggang. Shanghai: Shanghai guji chubanshe, 1998.

Wan Yan 萬燕. "Jiegou de 'diangu': Wang Anyi changpian xiaoshuo Changhenge xinlun 結構的 '典古' 一王安憶長篇小說《長恨歌》新論 [A deconstructed 'allusion': New thoughts on Wang Anyi's novel *Song of Everlasting Sorrow*]." *Journal of Shenzhen University* 15, no. 3 (1998): 50-54.

Wang Anyi 王安憶. *Changhenge: Changpian xiaoshuo juan* 長恨歌：長篇小說卷 [Song of everlasting sorrow: A novel]. Beijing: Zuojia chubanshe, 1996.

Wang, Ban. *Illuminations from the Past: Trauma, Memory, and History in Modern China*. Stanford: Stanford University Press, 2004.

———. "Love at Last Sight: Nostalgia, Commodity, and Temporality in Wang Anyi's Song of Unending Sorrow." *positions: east asia cultures critiques* 10, no. 3 (2002): 669-94.

Wang, Chaohua. "Introduction: Minds of the Nineties." Pp. 9-45 in *One China, Many Paths*, edited by Chaohua Wang. London: Verso, 2003.

Wang Chun 王春. "Zhao Shuli zeyang chengwei zuojia de 趙樹理怎樣成為作家的 [How Zhao Shuli became a writer]." Pp. 11-3 in *Zhao Shuli yanjiu ziliao* 趙樹理研究資料 [Research materials on Zhao Shuli], edited by Huang Xiuji. Taiyuan, Shanxi, China: Beiyue wenyi chubanshe, 1985.

Wang, David Der-wei 王德威. *The Monster That Is History: History, Violence, and Fictional Writing in Twentieth-Century China*. Berkeley: University of California Press, 2004.

———. "Haipai zuojia youjian chuanren 海派作家又見傳人 [An heir to the Shanghai school appears]." *Dushu* 6 (1996): 37-43.

———. "Imaginary Nostalgia: Shen Congwen, Song Zelai, Mo Yan, and Li Yongping." Pp. 107-32 in *From May Fourth to June Fourth: Fiction and Film in Twentieth Century China*, edited by Ellen Widmer and David Derwei Wang. Cambridge: Harvard University Press, 1993.

———. *Fictional Realism in Twentieth-Century China: Mao Dun, Lao She, Shen Congwen*. New York: Columbia University Press, 1992.

Wang, David Der-wei and Carlos Rojas, eds. *Writing Taiwan: A New Literary History*. Durham: Duke University Press, 2007.

Wang, Jing. *High Culture Fever: Politics, Aesthetics, and Ideology in Deng's China*. Berkeley: University of California Press, 1996.

Wang Xiaoming 王曉明. "Yifen zazhi he yige 'shetuan'—Chongping wusi wenxue chuantong 一份雜誌和一個 '社團' 一重評五四文學傳統 [A magazine and a 'society': Reevaluating the tradition of may fourth literature]." Pp. 192-97 in *Piping Kongjian De Kaichuang: Ershi Shiji Zhongguo Wenxue Yanjiu* 批評空間的開創：二十世紀中國文學研究 [The opening of critical space: Studies on twentieth-century Chinese literature], edited by

Wang Xiaoming. Shanghai: Dongfang chuban zhongxin, 1998.

Wang Zengqi 汪曾祺. "Xu 序 [Preface]." Pp. 1-5 in *Zhongguo xungen xiao-shuoxuan*中國尋根小說選 [Selected Chinese roots stories], edited by Li Tuo. Hong Kong: Joint Publishing, 1993.

Wang Zheng. "Three Interviews: Wang Anyi, Zhu Lin, Dai Qing [PRC Women Writers]." *Modern Chinese Literature* 4, no. 1-2 (1988): 99-148.

Widmer, Ellen, and Te-wei Wang, eds. *From May Fourth to June Fourth: Fiction and Film in Twentieth-Century China.* Cambridge: Harvard University Press, 1993.

Williams, Raymond. *Keywords: A Vocabulary of Culture and Society.* Rev. ed. New York: Oxford University Press, 1985.

Yao, Ping. "Women, Femininity, and Love in the Writings of Bo Juyi (772-846)." dissertation. University of Illinois, Urbana-Champaign, 1997.

Yen, Liang-yi. "Heterotopias of Memory: The Cultural Politics of Historic Preservation in Taipei." dissertation, University of California, Los Angeles, 2003.

Yuan Jin 袁進. *Zhongguo xiaoshuo de jindai biange* 中國小說的近代變革 [The Trajectory of the Development of Chinese Fiction in the Modern Period]. Beijing: Zhongguo shehui kexue chubanshe, 1992.

Yung, Bell. "Model Opera as Model: From Shajiabang to Sagabong." Pp. 144-64 in *Popular Chinese Literature and Performing Arts in the People's Republic of China, 1949-1979*, edited by Bonnie S. McDougall. Berkeley: University of California Press, 1984.

Zhang Aiping 張愛萍. "Yige chongman yexing de ziyou jingling: Mo Yan Honggaoliang jiazuzhong Yu Zhan'ao xingxiang fenxi一個充滿野性的自由精靈－莫言《紅高粱》家族中余占鰲形象分析 [A wild and free spirit: An analysis of Yu Zhan'ao from Mo Yan's *Red Sorghum*]." *Journal of West Anhui University* 18, no. 6 (2002): 77-79.

Zhang, Xudong. "Shanghai Nostalgia: Postrevolutionary Allegories in Wang Anyi's Literary Production in the 1990s." *positions: east asia cultures critiques* 8, no. 2 (2000): 349-87.

Zhao Shuli 趙樹理. "Li Youcai banhua 李有才板話 [Rhymes of Li Youcai]." Pp. 30-69 in *Zhao Shuli daibiao zuo* 趙樹理代表作 [Representative works of Zhao Shuli], edited by Xu Jianhua. Beijing: Hua xia chu ban she, 1999.

———. "Xiao Erhei Jiehun 小二黑結婚 [Little Blacky gets married]." Pp. 16-29 in in *Zhao Shuli daibiao zuo* 趙樹理代表作 [Representative works of Zhao Shuli], edited by Xu Jianhua, 16-29. Beijing: Hua xia chu ban she, 1999.

———. "Ye Suan Jingyan 也算經驗 [Also counts as experience]." Pp. 97-9 in *Zhao Shuli yanjiu ziliao* 趙樹理研究資料 [Research materials on Zhao Shuli], edited by Huang Xiuji. Taiyuan, China: Beiyue wenyi chubanshe: 1985.

Zhaoxia 朝霞 [Morning clouds]. Shanghai wenyi congkan, vol. 1. Shanghai: Shanghai renmin chubanshe, 1973.

Zhu, Ling. "A Brave New World? On the Construction of 'Masculinity' and

'Femininity' in The Red Sorghum Family." Pp. 121-34 in *Gender and sexuality in twentieth-century Chinese literature and society*. Edited by Tonglin Lu. Albany: State University of New York Press, 1993.

Zhu Tianxin 朱天心. *Gudu* 古都 [The ancient capital]. Taipei: INK, 2002.

Index

199

About the Author

Andrew Stuckey graduated from the Department of Asian Languages and Cultures at the University of California, Los Angeles in 2005. Since then he has taught Chinese language, modern Chinese literature, and Chinese film at institutions including Kalamazoo College, Ohio State University, and the University of California, Irvine. Currently, he is assistant professor of Chinese in the Department of Asian Languages and Civilizations at the University of Colorado, Boulder.